AF738070

The Myth of Desire

Dialog-on-Freud Series
Series Editor: M. Andrew Holowchak

The Dialog-on-Freud series invites authors to explore the history and practice of analytic therapies through critical analysis of and expatiation on the seminal work of Freud. It seeks books that critically scrutinize the numerous facets of Freud's work over the course of his life, that investigate how or to what extent Freud's thinking causally gave rise to the various sorts of therapies that currently exist, and that examine the relevance of Freud's thinking today for those therapies.

Titles in series:

The Myth of Desire: Sexuality, Love, and the Self by Carlos Domínguez-Morano and translated by Veronica Polo Torok

Repetition, the Compulsion to Repeat, and the Death Drive: An Examination of Freud's Doctrines by M. Andrew Holowchak and Michael Lavin

The Mythology Surrounding Freud and Klein: Implications for Psychoanalysis by Charlotte Schwartz

How Culture Runs the Brain: A Freudian View of Collective Syndromes by Jay Evans Harris

Nabokov's Mimicry of Freud: Art as Science by Teckyoung Kwon

Freud's Theory of Dreams: A Philosophico-Scientific Perspective by Michael T. Michael

The Unconscious without Freud by Rosemarie Sand

How Talking Cures: Revealing Freud's Contributions to All Psychotherapies by Lee Jaffe

The Myth of Desire

Sexuality, Love, and the Self

Carlos Domínguez-Morano
Translated by Veronica Polo Torok

LEXINGTON BOOKS
Lanham • Boulder • New York • London

Published by Lexington Books
An imprint of The Rowman & Littlefield Publishing Group, Inc.
4501 Forbes Boulevard, Suite 200, Lanham, Maryland 20706
www.rowman.com

6 Tinworth Street, London SE11 5AL, United Kingdom

Copyright © 2021 The Rowman & Littlefield Publishing Group, Inc.

All rights reserved. No part of this book may be reproduced in any form or by any electronic or mechanical means, including information storage and retrieval systems, without written permission from the publisher, except by a reviewer who may quote passages in a review.

British Library Cataloguing in Publication Information Available

Library of Congress Cataloging-in-Publication Data Available

ISBN 9781793605764 (cloth)
ISBN 9781793605771 (electronic)

To Mª Carmen and Carlos,
my heart family.

When two beings embrace,
They don’t know what they are doing,
They don’t know what they want,
They don’t know what they are looking for,
They don’t know what they are finding.

—Paul Ricoeur

Contents

Foreword to the English Edition

Choosing a title for this book in its original Spanish version was quite a challenge. I eventually opted for something along the lines of *The Expressions of Desire: Of Affection, Love, and Other Passions*, avoiding the term *sexuality* due to the frequent misunderstandings that can arise from its use. Few concepts have undergone such radical change throughout the 20th century. The various fields of human sciences, particularly the field of psychoanalysis, have revolutionized how sexuality is perceived, implicating it in previously ignored or undervalued psychological and social dimensions. The term *desire*, central to psychoanalytic theory and in particularly Jacques Lacan's work, seemed a more suitable concept from which to embark on this multivaried reality. It is a reality that encompasses dimensions as diverse as heterosexual and homosexual couple relationships, the notion of self-esteem, the bonds of friendship, and the role of sublimation in society.

For the present English edition, doubts about the title arose once again, and arriving at something satisfactory was not any easier this time around (considering the complexities of desire, this is no surprise). Finally, I opted for *The Myth of Desire: Sexuality, Love, and the Self*, maintaining the term *desire* for the reasons outlined above but now also including the term *sexuality* because, despite the potential for misunderstanding, it is true that the pages of this book touch upon this subject frequently. We speak about sexuality from an essentially psychoanalytic and Freudian perspective. Hence, we look at sexuality with an open mind, beyond the biological aspect, moving into the personal, social, aesthetic, political, and religious dimensions. We also see how sexuality ties into our personal reality in the form of narcissism or self-esteem, which explains the words *love* and *self* in the title. All of these terms, *desire*, *sexuality*, *love*, and *self*, point to a reality that extends throughout all of the human dimensions, without any of them residing exclusively in one place.

In order to speak of desire so broadly, we must first attempt to understand what we mean by desire as well as its corresponding obscure and unattainable object (the object of desire is impossible, Lacan reminded us). Thus, each individual will experience a need for love that will shift through one's life. Ironically, only by giving up on the attainment of that end goal, by accepting our condition as "separate beings," will we find our "unstable stability." Then, by accepting our innate separation and difference that prohibits that longed-for fusion, desire will enable a real opening to others, whether similar or different, and within ourselves too as well as the surrounding sociocultural reality, always within a dynamic of incomplete satisfaction that generates restlessness and continual seeking.

The aim of this book is to attempt to approach desire's global dynamic, a task that, while ambitious, also has its limits—constricted by the approximations we must take in describing the way desire moves tirelessly through the different aspects of life. Each one of these dimensions (like the couple, homosexuality, friendship, self-esteem, and sublimation) would require a deepening that we have sacrificed in order to offer an approachable overview of our desiderative life. This is the price we must pay to offer a panorama of that almost infinite landscape that the realm of desire occupies.

It is a deep satisfaction for me to see the work translated into English by a prestigious publisher such as Lexington, allowing this work to reach a much larger readership in essential geographic areas around the world, facilitating access to students and people interested in psychology, psychoanalysis, and the human sciences in general. For this English edition, an attempt has been made to make some concepts more universal and less focused on Spanish culture, although some cultural and linguistic overtones are still likely to be felt. The source material has also been updated, and Spanish sources have been replaced with their English equivalents whenever possible.

I have to thank the meticulous and rigorous translation work carried out by Verónica Polo Torok, without which I would not have realized my dream of being read with pleasure by an English-speaking audience. Any quoted material from non-English sources (for which a published English translation could not be found) has also been translated by her.

Carlos Dominguez Morano
Granada, Spain
March 4, 2020

Part I

DESIRE

Chapter One

Understanding Desire through Science and Myth

THE DRIVES OF FREUDIAN MYTHOLOGY

Throughout time, sexuality has proven to be one of the most significant and defining aspects of human existence and also one of the most enigmatic. The diverse myths, taboos, norms, and rites have always tried to channel sexuality's power and simultaneously decipher its mysteries. In our current society, the scientific and technological advances seem to offer explanations that finally reveal its secrets, allowing us to manage and control it through rational means. But it is precisely through that deepening into its essence that we have learned that it cannot be reduced to rational thought. Rather, sexuality will continue to need to be expressed through mythology and symbols in order to be approached, although perhaps never fully understood. Importantly, Freudian thought showcases the difficulties that arise when exploring this subject and the necessary and illuminating exchange that can happen between the mythical and the scientific.

We know that the positivist, materialist, and mechanist philosophies of the 19th century influenced Freud's work. His first project coincides with the predominant aspirations of the time that reduced psychology to neurology, always attempting to conform to the physical sciences model.[1] From the start, Freud tried to portray psychoanalysis as a branch of that scientific knowledge. In his treatment of dreams, neurosis, or psychotherapy, he established his scientific purpose clearly, thus distancing himself from other types of methodologies related to the mind. For this reason, he always maintained the most emphatic refusal to frame psychoanalysis as its own worldview

1. See Sigmund Freud (1910/1958), "Project for a Scientific Psychology," in *Standard Edition* (London: Hogarth, 1966), 1: 283–397.

(*Weltanschauung*).[2] "Psycho-analysis, in my opinion," he said, "is incapable of creating a *Weltanschauung* of its own. It does not need one; it is part of science and can adhere to the scientific *Weltanschauung*."[3]

Its sole purpose is to "arrive at a consistent view of one portion of reality,"[4] aspiring to be "an impartial instrument, like the infinitesimal calculus, as it were."[5] From there, we can understand his ongoing struggle to mitigate the illusory, mythical, or religious dimensions that shaped his culture. "Our best hope for the future," he tells us, "is that intellect—the scientific spirit, reason—may in process of time establish a dictatorship in the mental life of man."[6]

But, like G. A. Miller expressed so adeptly, Freud reluctantly became a "loyal rebel" to that tradition in which he always believed and tried to fit into. And it was in that very process of theorizing about sexuality where his desire to remain true to the orthodoxy of the scientific world became compromised. We find indications of this in the following elucidating text.

In *Beyond the Pleasure Principle*, he thus confessed, "Science has so little to tell us about the origin of sexuality that we can liken the problem to a darkness into which not so much as a ray of a hypothesis has penetrated."[7] Since science shed such little light on this critical issue, a change in perspective was thus called for in order to go deeper into this neglected subject. If the scientific provision was exhausted, other hypotheses had to be arbitrated from a different domain, even though this called for the renunciation of an ideal as well as journeying on a possibly perilous path. "In quite a different region," he says, "it is true, we *do* meet with such a hypothesis; but it is so fantastic a kind—a myth rather than a scientific explanation—that I should not venture to produce it here, were it not that it fulfills precisely the one condition whose fulfillment we desire. For it traces the origin of an instinct to "a need to restore an earlier state of things."[8] The myth of the split of the human being into two halves, extracted from Plato's *Symposium*, became the method used to gain an understanding of this enigma.

This text is revelatory, but it is not the only place where this connection between sexuality and mythology can be detected. In the whole of *On Metapsychology*, we hear about the drives (either sexual or, later on, destructive) as-

2. Freud (1919), "Lines of Advance in Psycho-Analytic Therapy," in *Standard Edition*, 17: 165.
3. Freud (1933), "New Introductory Lectures on Psycho-Analysis," in *Standard Edition*, 22: 181.
4. Freud (1923), "Two Encyclopaedia Articles," in *Standard Edition*, 18: 252.
5. Freud (1927), "The Future of an Illusion," in *Standard Edition*, 21: 36.
6. Freud (1920), *Beyond the Pleasure Principle*, in *Standard Edition*, 18: 57.
7. Freud (1920), *Beyond the Pleasure Principle*, in *Standard Edition*, 18: 57.
8. Freud (1926), "The Question of Lay Analysis," in *Standard Edition*, 20: 210. In previous pages, he had already affirmed: "The outcome may give an impression of mysticism or of sham profundity; but we can feel quite innocent of having had any such purpose in view. We seek only for the sober results of research or of reflection based on it; and we have no wish to find in those results any quality other than certainty."

sociated with the mythical. Along these lines, it was stated on more than one occasion, "The theory of the instincts is so to say our mythology. Instincts are mythical entities, magnificent in their indefiniteness. In our work we cannot for a moment disregard them, yet we are never sure that we are seeing them clearly."[9] Freud was forced to accept the relationship between sex and myth, which also led him to adopt a fuller understanding of sexuality that would, in one sense require anatomical and physiological knowledge, but in addition "the familiarity with the history of civilization and with mythology."[10]

SCIENCE'S MUTILATION OF SEXUALITY

The theoretical and practical aspects of the *scientific* investigation of sexuality tend to tackle the problem from a biological or purely *behavioral* paradigm (whereby behavior is only that which is observed), while totally ignoring other aspects of the mind (*need*, *desire*, *affection*, and *fantasies* are rejected terms due to their poor reliability). The philosophy that underlies this biological or behavioral concept of sexuality is a dualistic one, which splits the techno-scientific and human factors and conceives the body and the soul as separate, the somatic and the psychic. At its root, we find the Cartesian anthropological dualism.

It was, in fact, Descartes (whose thought was vital in shaping contemporary psychology) that painted a dualistic image of man, composed of two totally different substances, consisting of a material body and a spiritual soul. According to his thinking, each substance existed independently. The body was a machine governed by natural laws and could be explained using physical and mathematical terms; it was subordinate to the principles and laws of mechanics. Animals were "automatons," and man, who with the exception of his rational spirit that related to the body through the pineal gland, found its physiological roots in the principles of physics. From there, a sexual understanding emerged as something essentially biological at the service of reproduction or, at most, as a mechanism understood following certain mechanical laws of learning. Everything that fell outside of the material–chemical model would be a topic for poets, mystics, or philosophers. The scientific investigation of sex would fall only within the domain of *res extensa*.[11]

---

9. Freud (1933), "New Introductory Lectures on Psycho-Analysis," in *Standard Edition*, 22: 171.

10. Freud (1926), "The Question of Lay Analysis," in *Standard Edition*, 20: 210–11. Regarding what Freud saw as the relationship between sexuality and myth, see my work titled *El psicoanálisis freudiano de la religión* (Madrid: Paulinas, 1991). Jung also explored myth and sexuality in depth, although he had a different methodology and a different concept of sex, for example, C. G. Jung, *Symbols of Transformation: Collected Works of C.G. Jung*, vol. 5 (Princeton: Princeton University Press, 2014).

11. It is quite revealing, for example, that in the work that served as the de facto manual for Skinnerian psychology in American and most Spanish universities there were only two pages devoted to human sexuality and that they were mostly dedicated to providing data on the sexual behavior of rats

But the Freudian revolution consisted precisely in transcending the limits of the *res extensa* and going beyond those perceived sexual boundaries. Because of this, Freud was forced to look at the sexual and corporal realms with a wider lens and into the affective psyche, both conscious and unconscious. He considered these explorations worthy of scientific research, even though they created considerable methodological problems.

Freud, therefore, approached the idea of *libido* as a psychic energetic expression of the sexual instinct. Being aware that both with this term and that of sexuality he was betraying the important human dimension of affection, he began to refer to this realm with the term *psychosexuality*, which permitted the inclusion of a deep and complex reality of everything that might fall under the term *Liebe* (love). It is likely that with the use of this term he would have avoided the accusation of pansexualism that would shadow Freudian theory thereafter. However, some of Freud's critics did not welcome the change. Freud discarded the term but remained unsatisfied with the use of a term like sexuality, so firmly ingrained in the minds of people as something merely biological. He then spoke of *life instincts* as a set of forces that aim to generate and maintain a bond between different love objects that surface throughout a person's life. *Eros*, thereafter, became the default term within psychoanalytic circles to refer to this set of vital impulses that function as a catalyst for life, allowing living beings to come together. *Thanatos* would represent an opposing force that aspires to separate, disengage, and abandon, even to the point of annihilation and death.[12]

In scientific circles, it seemed that this way of treating sexuality was "extra-medical," and, in a sense, this was true in that it strayed from the physical, biological, or reproductive functions. But, for Freud, although a retrospective look at his own evolution would oblige us to take a more nuanced view today, this sexuality was expressed from the biologically reproductive type to the perverse behavior of the sadist or the fetishist, to the platonic Eros, or even in the style of the love proclaimed by Paul in the letter to the Corinthians.[13] The clear Cartesian separation between *matter* and *spirit*, or between their respective attributes of *extension* and *thought*, was thus melded into a comprehensive and unifying concept, preventing it from ever being split back into dualistic concepts.

[Fred S. Keller and William N. Schoenfeld, *Principles of Psychology* (New York: Appleton-Century-Croft, Inc., 1950), *Fundamentos de Psicología* (Barcelona: Fontanella, 1975, 266–68)]. All of this after lamenting how difficult the "scientific" study of human sexuality was. The work of B. F. Skinner, after discussing the use of concepts such as necessity or impulse related to sexuality, does not dedicate a chapter to sexuality nor include the concept in the index: Burrus F. Skinner, *Science and Human Behavior* (New York: Macmillan, 1953).

12. Jean Laplanche, *Freud and the Sexual: Essays, 2000–2006* (New York: International Psychoanalytic Books, 2011).

13. Freud suggests that psychoanalysis joins the ranks of Plato and Paul when it offers a broader concept of love: "Group Psychology and the Analysis of the Ego," in *Standard Edition* (London: Hogarth, 1966), 18: 91.

Thus, we see that standard scientific process is insufficient for approaching this new way of understanding sexuality and that we need to look at myth, history, literature, and art in general as places where sexuality could reveal crucial dimensions of its particular subtleties. This, on the other hand, coincides with a movement that, since the development of anthropology, has taken a lead in recovering mythical and symbolic thought as essential dimensions of knowledge.

MYTHOLOGY'S COMPLEMENTARY ROLE

Mythology thus becomes a necessary component of knowledge and a structure for human thought. As Mircea Eliade explained,[14] it is something inherent to culture, to its symbolism, and, therefore, to the individual. So, although it is possible that certain myths can vanish due to historical circumstances, as long as human societies exist, mythology can never fully disappear.

Claude Lévi-Strauss, in his questioning the ethnocentrism of Western man, made it clear that mythological and symbolic thought cannot be looked at as inferior to rational and scientific thought. The "savage mind" of mythology or magic and the "domesticated thinking" of science and technology are ways to gain knowledge, differing in their theoretical and practical results but similar in the paths they take. Both differ less in their nature than in the kinds of phenomena to which they are applied.[15] They offer two types of understanding and action that make use of signs or symbols and that thus provide a different type of validation, the first being of an existential nature and the latter of the scientific sort.[16] Myth and reason not only have a common origin but, through their differences, can contrast and complement each other.

Psychology, born out of an anti-metaphysical sentiment that had to be maintained to achieve certain respect within the scientific community, strongly repudiated any kind of symbolic thought, thereby considerably limiting its development. Today, there are signs of healing, of redressing this early reductive illness and even casting doubt over the scientific philosophy that backed it, and, lastly, respecting the value of the symbolic when investigating basic problems of behavior.

If science gives us objective explanatory knowledge of the external world, the world of myth and symbolism tends to offer subjective participation in the

14. Mircea Eliade, *Images and Symbols: Studies in Religious Symbolism* (Princeton, NJ: Princeton University Press, 1991).

15. See Claude Lévi-Strauss, *The Savage Mind* (Hertfordshire: The Garden City Press Limited, 1966).

16. See Edgar Morin, *La Méthode 3: La Connaissance de la connaissance* (Paris: Seuil, 1986); *Science avec conscience* (Paris: Fayard, 1982).

most intimate aspects of life. This is critical, as we will see, in regard to understanding sexuality. As Eliade taught, the role of mythology is essentially the integration of the individual with the cosmos, guiding its doings and molding its perception. While science explains this through a positivist approach that dictates what can and cannot be empirically established, the mythical lens is evaluative; it deliberates and assesses possible outcomes and calibrates what should and should not be—what makes sense. As Lévi-Strauss says, mythical thought is "at play every time the spirit asks itself about its meaning."[17]

The issue is then not about which methodology is right or wrong but rather acknowledging that the two different approaches are valid in different ways. As Pedro Gómez affirms, rational thought needs its opposite so that it does not through its empirically and logically controlled objectivity do irreparable damage over subjectivity, emotion, the individual, and the communal, without which life would be impossible.[18] This is particularly true of sexuality.

THE COMPLICIT OBSERVER

In reality, Freud had already set the foundations for preventing an exclusively scientific approach to sexuality prior to the verification of its dark origins, as he expressed in a text quoted from *Beyond the Pleasure Principle*. And, if sex cannot be approached as a finalized scientific object, it is essentially because of the observer's inevitable influence or bias over what is being studied. Sexuality implicates the observer like no other sphere. And, truth be told, no other aspect of human activity, from what we can observe, think about, or comment on, is so conditioned by what we have experienced at a conscious and, more importantly, unconscious level.

It was precisely the insight into the inevitable subjective implication of "the observer," that gave rise to the revolutionary, psychoanalytic approach to problems. The case of Anna O., which is etched into the very origins of psychoanalysis, is a memorable example of this.

This girl, who was treated using the "cathartic" method developed by Freud's mentor and friend, Dr. J. Breuer, was visited by her doctor once a day and eventually twice. The girl progressed surprisingly well through "reviving" and "purging" her past traumatic life events. But, after two years, it was Dr. Breuer's wife who poured salt in the wound by expressing discomfort for what rightly seemed to her an excessive interest in this patient. She doubted that such interest was merely due to medical and scientific necessity. This led

17. Claude Lévi-Strauss, *The Jealous Potter* (Chicago: Chicago University Press, 1988).
18. Pedro Gómez García, *Religión popular y mesianismo* (Granada: Universidad de Granada, 1991), 15.

to the demise of Dr. Breuer's well-intentioned treatment of her patient. Anna O. reacted by having a sudden hysterical breakdown that took the form of a simulated birth, which she, of course, blamed her doctor for. Breuer limited his response to calming her and soon after abandoned the case definitively by way of a "second honeymoon" to Venice with his wife.[19]

This phenomenon, which we now call transference, shows us the unavoidable involvement of the sexed subject who observes, casting doubt on the façade of objectivity that scientific mythology aims to portray. From a psychoanalytic perspective, however, it should be noted, as Clavreul has rightly pointed out, that perversion (in its psychopathological sense) consists precisely in denying that subjective implication in sexuality, believing that it can be converted into an external, analyzable, and controllable object.[20]

The psychoanalytic treatment of sexuality caused scandal and confusion in society, but it also highlighted the flaws of theories that claim to achieve an understanding of humans by exclusive scientific–technical means. In short, and as earlier stated, this sprung from erroneous Cartesian dualistic thinking, which, although helpful in paving the way to modern science, also came at a high price, something contemporary "scientific" psychology is well aware of.

IRREDUCIBLE SEXUALITY: INSTINCTUAL DESIRE

Sexuality is not a type of simple organic tension. It should not even be seen as the driver of human behavior. Furthermore, understood in its broadest sense through the concept of *instinctual desire*, is the same open arena where all existential conflicts play out and where we see both *lack of being* and the *appetite for being* as essential expressions of humanity.

In fact, we can no longer view sexuality as a purely biological instinct for the perpetuation of the species but as a force that, starting with the organism, ultimately aspires to satisfy an impossible hope—to be recognized in a pleasurable holistic fusion. Beyond biology, it is therefore determined by the biographical, historical, and cultural aspects. That is why we prefer the term *instinctual desire* (which we will explore in next chapter) to the more traditional and mistaken *sexuality*.

The search for this elusive concept is expressed in numerous ways by various cultural collectives. The encounter between the sexes has been imagined and played out by different sectors of society. Cultural anthropology

19. See Ernest Jones, *The Life and Work of Sigmund Freud*, vol. 2 (New York: Basic Books, 1953), 223–26; Peter Gay, *Freud: A Life of Our Time* (New York: Norton, 2006), chapter 2.

20. See J. Jean Clavreul, "Aspects cliniques des perversions," in Centre d'études Laënec, *Sexualité humaine* (Paris: Aubier-Montaigne, 1970); "Le couple pervers," in *Le désir et la perversion*, ed. J. Clavreul, 93–126 (Paris: Seuil 1967).

has given us much evidence of this.[21] It is as if no community were able to capture and confine the unique and universal nature of this illusive seeking force traversing them. And it would be difficult to pinpoint a type of sexual behavior (like homosexuality) that has not been both reviled or sacralized by one cultural institution or another. While limited by the law, sexuality has demonstrated its ability to express itself through diverse normative situations. Its ambitions cannot be silenced or suppressed.

Caught between the law's constricting role and desire's aspiration toward an impossible object, that of sexuality, we get the conflict between subject/object, desire/reality, and appetite/norm. Therefore, it is a place of self-vindication vis-à-vis authority, a space in which the liberation of the inevitable reification of existence in interpersonality is sought, which objectifies us with age, position, social role, and so on. When faced with everyday limitations and realities, it is also a place for all kinds of fantasizing. Because of this, sexuality is diametrically opposed to any theorization that seeks to turn it into a lucid object, one that is managed and inventoried. Each aspect of sexuality that becomes known is, therefore, an aspect of sexuality that becomes distorted. And precisely, the most recent attack on sexuality's irreducible character, as Foucault bemoaned, lies in attempting to turn it into a scientific discipline, into data alongside other objectified data. It is the *scientia sexualis* hoping to displace the *ars erotica*.[22]

Paul Ricoeur expressed it beautifully when he affirmed that sexuality may be impervious to reflection and immune to human domination. Being *Eros* and not *Logos*, its restitution in the Logos is unfeasible, irreducible to man's "language–tool–institution" trilogy. It belongs to a prelinguistic life, which mobilizes language but at the same time traverses it, tramples it, sublimates it, and pulverizes it into a murmur, a mere invocation. The relationship between intention, tool, and thing is also strange and refuses to be reduced to contractual terms.[23]

THE IMPOSSIBLE SCIENCE OF SEXUALITY

The unconscious nature of instinctual desire places it outside the field of science as it is traditionally understood. It is worth noting that the science of

21. See, for example, Kathleen Gough, Claude Lévi-Strauss, and Melford Spiro, *Polémica sobre el origen y la universalidad de la familia* [Controversy over the origin and universality of the family] (Barcelona: Anagrama, 1976); and G. A. Marshall, "Matrimonio. Análisis comparativo," in *Enciclopedia Universal de las ciencias sociales* (Madrid: Aguilar, 1974), 7: 14.
22. See Michel Foucault, *Histoire de la sexualité* (Paris: Gallimard, 1976–1984).
23. Paul Ricoeur, "Wonder, Eroticism and Enigma," in *Sexuality and the Sacred*, ed. James B. Nelson and Sandra P. Longfellow, 80–84 (Louisville, KY: WJK Press, 1994).

sexuality, what some might call sexology,[24] currently plays an important role. None of what has been conveyed in these pages so far should be used to belittle or discredit what the field has to offer. We should simply remember that "sexology" will limit itself to certain aspects of sex and will not contribute to the most profound and significant emotional dimensions of sexuality.

However, the biological functions that sustain sexual behavior will tell us interesting things about the neurological and chemical processes that play an important role in sexuality. Meanwhile, behavioral and cognitive psychology will continue to provide interesting data about the role of learning in establishing certain patterns of behavior. Social psychology and sociology will illuminate important aspects of sociocultural conditioning. Cultural anthropology will help us understand the enormous diversity of sexual behaviors across cultures. All of these are critical in some way in helping to shed light on this complex reality.

From the pioneering and already classic works of Kraft-Ebing,[25] Havelock,[26] and Olds's research on the cerebral centers of pleasure[27]; to the hormonal studies by John Money[28]; to the sociological research presented by the likes of Alfred Kinsey and Shere Hite[29] or the behavioral research work carried out by William Masters, Virginia Johnson, and Helen Kaplan,[30] we have a collection of data regarding sexuality that allows us to understand and engage in this area of behavior that was unthinkable only fifty years ago. Psychoanalysts, therefore, should never display contempt or willful ignorance toward this research.

It would, however, be very misleading if we came to believe that all this data and information about the mechanisms of sexual activity erase what psychoanalysis has revealed, that, ultimately, the sexuality that lies beyond the biological and the sociocultural realms also takes root in a space outside theory and scientific reason.

---

24. According to George Bastin, *Dictionnaire de la psychologie sexuelle* (Bruxelles: Charles Desart, 1970), it is science that studies man's normal and pathological sexual life looking at both biological and psychosocial identity, s.v. "Sexology."

25. Richard von Kraft-Ebing, *Psychopathia sexualis, eine klinisch-forensische Studie* (Stuttgart: Enke, 1886).

26. Henri Havelock Ellis, *Studies in the Psychology of Sex* (vol. 1–4) (New York: Random House, 1936).

27. M. E. Olds and J. L. Forbes, "The Central Basis of Motivation: Intracranial Self-Stimulation Studies," *Annual Review of Psychology* 32 (1981): 523–74.

28. "Prenatal Influences and Subsequent Sexuality," in Benjamin B. Wolman and John Money, *Handbook of Human Sexuality* (Upper Saddle River, NJ: Prentice Hall, 1980).

29. Alfred C. Kinsey, Wardell Baxter Pomeroy, and Clyde E Martin, *Sexual Behavior in the Human Male* (Philadelphia: Saunders, 1948); Alfred C. Kinsey, Wardell Baxter Pomeroy, and Clyde E. Martin, *Sexual Behavior in the Human Female* (Philadelphia: Saunders, 1953); Shere Hite, *The Hite Report: A National Study on Female Sexuality* (New York: Seven Stories Press, 1976); Shere Hite, *The Hite Report on Male Sexuality* (New York: MacDonald, 1978).

30. William H. Masters and Virginia E. Johnson, *Human Sexual Response* (Boston: Little Brown, 1966); Helen Kaplan, *New Sex Therapy: Active Treatment of Sexual Dysfunctions* (New York: Random House, 1974).

Therefore, the realm of the symbolic in which myth expresses itself should be seen as the ideal place for the interpretation and understanding (rather than explanation) of what sexuality means to us. It will be a type of symbolic understanding, exegesis, or hermeneutics in which we will partake, not by limitation, but the very nature of sexuality.

While the different types of research concerning various aspects of sexual behavior must continue, we must remember that whoever is doing the observation is biased in some way. This is because the observer is also an individual steeped in his own sexual context and experiences, however much he might want to project an image of neutrality.

All information or education within this realm must, therefore, be continually mindful of this potential bias and avoid insinuating that the data is 100 percent objective and neutral. In this regard, it is interesting to note that it was precisely psychoanalysts who, in the 1970s, put up barriers when sexuality was proposed as a subject in French secondary schools. The psychoanalyst revolutionaries and the conservative representatives of French society thus came to be on the same side of the opposition, albeit for different reasons.

Sexuality cannot be taught in the way mathematics or geography is taught simply because, by trying to convert sexuality into a theory alongside other theoretical systems within the education framework, something essential gets lost in translation. The lens by which teachers and education systems understand and teach the subject is fundamentally different from what a mathematics or geography curriculum might be. The presentation of sexuality as a system of essentially biological or social character yet cut off from its deep affective roots, as certain progressive sectors have advocated in academic circles, reveals a problematic mindset and, what is more paradoxical, a defensive reaction toward sexuality's meaning at its deepest levels.

THE MYTHOLOGY OF CONTEMPORARY SEXUALITY

We will have to look inward to the "primitive thinking" that exists within us, despite our attempt to exorcise and sacrifice it to the supposedly superior scientific understanding. Myths understood as symbolic stories that reveal enigmatic human dimensions will find a way to express themselves, calling us to interact with them, these essential expressions of our psychosexual world.

Myths, for example, built around the dream of sexual liberation, aim to dismantle the impositions of sociopolitical interests while simultaneously alleviating the anguish that sexuality itself generates. We find the timeless fantasy of bisexuality, of course, as a continuum in the dream of *oneness* that presides over infantile desire. There is also the aspiration of being unisex as a way to blur our differences. The split between the sexes, which reveals the deficiencies within the genders, can idealize hermaphrodites as a representation of an elusive wholeness. Despite the advances in the women's lib movement, the idea of the "eternal feminine" endures—the angelic creature with the mythical halo. We see visions of the idealized and unrealistic female, a kind of imaginary good mother who, in order to remain as such, must be shielded from the unpredictability and harsh realities of life. Do we not often find this attitude toward women in certain ecclesial writings?[31]

Sexuality, a bedfellow of the ghosts of castration, also points to the untamed mythical thinking of transgression and punishment. Many of us are aware of how AIDS was seen by some as God's punishment and as a way to curtail the perverse freedom prevailing in recent times. This was never truer than when AIDS was seen as an exclusive homosexual problem.

The family, a space in which sexuality is configured, needs, like a few other institutions, the endorsement of the mythical. The myth of the united and happy family that periodically surfaces around Christmastime or is portrayed through touching stories in movies or other media. Or at the opposite end of the spectrum, the myth of the disappearing family institution, an idea that played out in the sixties with the countercultural philosophy of the hippy communes.

Myth as an idea of accessible sex education that relies on the fantasy of natural sexuality, unaware of sexual taboos. Or, on the other hand, myths of the necessary ethical accommodation to the laws of nature, as if nature did not also include the reality of the praying mantis that devours its male while copulating or the turtledove that, when it sees itself in front of a mirror, falls in love with its own image. And myth, of course, of a sexuality that is understood, explained, cataloged, and inventoried scientifically and can then be presented on television.

Myths of all types with their symbols and varying contexts. Madonna and Wilhelm Reich, two individuals advocating in their own way for sexual liberation. Prince and the English group Suede embodying our modern hermaphrodites. Sharon Stone and the Christian image of Mary serving as complementary ideals of the feminine myth, so ingrained in the male fantasy as the harlot and the virgin mother. A few years ago we also saw how the Spanish psychologist Dr. Elena Ochoa shared the myth of "sexuality without myths" through her television program *Hablemos de Sexo* [Let's Talk about Sex], made possible in part by advances in the field of psychology.

---

31. I contributed to an edited work with "Celibato, género y poder" [Celibacy, gender, and power] in *Cambio de paradigma, género y eclesiología* [Paradigm shift, gender, and ecclesiology], ed. Carmen Bernabé Ubieta, 109–30 (Estella: Verbo Divino, 1998).

Our own myths, which are not lacking in representation and analysis. We see them played out in great box-office hits, such as *The Last Tango in Paris*, *9½ Weeks*, and *Fatal Attraction*. Or, in equally impactful family films such as *Superman*, *Beauty and the Beast*, and *The Little Mermaid*, we see the great avatars of human psychosexual development lying dormant. We see them in great literary works, such as *Lolita* by Vladimir Nabokov or *Justine* by Marquis de Sade.

In short, myths, symbols, and legends showcase the varied needs of different social groups attempting to systematize, control, teach about, or understand a sphere that is seemingly beyond all technique, elucidation, and abridgment. Myths and legends, therefore, in which we find the soul of sexuality, while science merely tries to make sense of the outer shell. We are going to dedicate the following chapter to a reflection on the soul of sexuality—desire.

BIBLIOGRAPHY

Anzieu, Didier. "Freud et la mythologie." *Nouvelle revue de psychanalyse* 2 (1970): 114–145.

Bernardes, Jon. *Family Studies: An Introduction.* London: Routledge, 2008.

Bettelheim, Bruno. *The Uses of Enchantment: The Meaning and Importance of Fairy Tales*. New York: Knopf, 1976.

Bowlby, Rachel. *Freudian Mythologies. Greek Tragedy and Modern Identity*. Oxford: Oxford University Press, 2007.

Cameron, Devora, and Don Klulic. *Language and Sexuality.* Cambridge: Cambridge University Press, 2003.

Chodorow, Nancy J. *Femininities, Masculinities, Sexualities*. Lexington, Kentucky: University Press of Kentucky, 1994.

De Lauretis, Teresa. *Freud's Drive: Psychoanalysis, Literature, and Film.* New York: Palgrave Macmillan, 2008.

Devereux, George. *Ethnopsychoanalysis: Psychoanalysis and Anthropology as Complementary Frames of Reference.* Berkeley: University of California Press, 1978.

Foucault, Michel. *The History of Sexuality*, Vol. 1. London: Pelican, 1981.

Freud, Sigmund (1905c). *Jokes and Their Relation to the Unconscious.* In *The Standard Edition of the Complete Psychological Works of Sigmund Freud*, edited and translated by James Strachey, 8: 9–158. London: Hogarth, 1966.

——— (1905d). *Three Essays on the Theory of Sexuality.* In *Standard Edition*, 7: 125–245.

——— (1907a). "Delusions and Dream in Jensen's Gradiva." In *Standard Edition*, 9: 7–95.

——— (1909c). "Family Romances." In *Standard Edition*, 9: 205–226.

——— (1910c). "Leonardo da Vinci and a Memory of His Childhood." In *Standard Edition*, 11: 57–137.

——— (1911f). "Great Is Diana Ephesians." In *Standard Edition*, 22: 342–344.

——— (1912–1913). *Totem and Taboo.* In *Standard Edition*, 13: 7–161.
——— (1913f). "The Theme of the Three Caskets." In *Standard Edition*, 12: 289–302.
——— (1918a). "The Taboo of Virginity." In *Standard Edition*, 11: 193–208.
——— (1920g). *Beyond the Pleasure Principle.* In *Standard Edition*, 18: 1–64.
——— (1928a). "Dostoevsky and Parricide." In *Standard Edition*, 21, 169–172.
——— (1939a). *Moses and Monotheism.* In *Standard Edition*, 23, 1–137.
——— (1942/1906b) "Psychopathic Characters on the Stage." In *Standard Edition*, 7: 305–310.
Gagnon, John. *An Interpretation of Desire*. Chicago: University of Chicago Press, 2004.
Gagnon, John, and William Simon, *Sexual Conduct: The Social Sources of Human Sexuality*. Chicago: Aldine, 1973.
Gherovici, Patricia, and Manya Steinkoler, eds. *Lacan, Psychoanalysis, and Comedy*. New York: Cambridge University Press, 2016.
Godefroy, M. *Études de sexologie.* Paris: Bloud & Gay, 1965.
Green, André. *The Chains of Eros.* London: Karnac Books, 2002.
———. *The Tragic Effect: The Oedipus Complex in Tragedy*. Cambridge: Cambridge University Press, 1979.
Jackson, Stevi, and Sue Scott. *Theorizing Sexuality*. Maidenhead: Open University Press, 2010.
Jones, Ernest. *Hamlet and Oedipus*. London: V. Gollancz, 1949.
———. *Psycho-Myth, Psycho-History*, Vol. 1–2. New York: Hillstone, 1974.
Kapkan, Ann E. *Psychoanalysis and Cinema*. New York: Routledge, 1996.
Kimmel, Michael S., *The Sexual Self: The Construction of Sexual Scripts.* Nashville, TN: Vanderbilt University Press, 2007.
Lang, Birgit, Joy Damousi, and Alison Lewis. *A History of the Case Study: Sexology, Psychoanalysis, Literature.* Manchester: Manchester University Press, 2017.
Laplanche, Jean. *Freud and the Sexual.* New York: International Psychoanalytic Books, 2011.
Lebeau, Vicky. *Psychoanalysis and Cinema: The Play of Shadows.* London: Wallflower, 2001.
Lévi-Strauss, Claude. *The Savage Mind.* Chicago: University of Chicago Press, 1966.
Malinowski, Bronislaw. *Sex and Repression in Savage Society*. London: Kegan Paul, Trench, Trubner & Co., 1927.
Marcus, Laura. *Dreams of Modernity: Psychoanalysis, Literature, Cinema.* Cambridge, MA. Cambridge University Press, 2014.
Mead, Margaret. *Sex and Temperament in Three Primitive Societies*. New York: William Morrow.
Merck, Mandy. *The Sexual Subject: Screen Reader in Sexuality.* London: Routledge, 1992.
Nicolaïdis, Graziella, and Nicos Nicolaïdis. *Mythologie grecque et Psychanalyse*. Paris: Delachaux & Niestlé, 1994.
Parker, Ian. *Psychoanalytic Mythologies*. London: Anthem Press, 2011.
Richardson, Diane. *Rethinking Sexuality*. Thousand Oaks, CA: Sage, 2000.

Ricoeur, Paul. "Wonder, Eroticism, and Enigma." In *Sexuality and the Sacred*, edited by James B. Nelson and Sandra P. Longfellow, 80–84. Louisville, KY: WJK Press, 1994.

Rodowick, David. *The Difficulty of Difference: Psychoanalysis, Sexual Difference, and Film Theory*. London: Routledge, 2014.

Simon, William. *Postmodern Sexualities*. New York: Routledge, 1996.

Soldati, Lorenzo. "Psychanalyse et sexologie: antagonisme ou complémentarité?" *Rev Med Suisse* 24 (2010): 625–7.

Sztalryd, Jean Marie. "Psychanalyse et sexualité." In *Manuel de sexologie*, edited by P. Lopès and F. X. Poudat. Issy-les-Moulineaux: Masson, 2007.

Zajko, Vanda, and Ellen O'Gorman. *Classical Myth and Psychoanalysis: Ancient and Modern Stories of the Self*. Oxford: Oxford University Press, 2013.

Žižek, Slavoj. *Enjoy Your Symptom!: Jacques Lacan in Hollywood and Out*. London: Routledge, 2001.

Chapter Two

That Obscure Object of Desire

The more fundamental a human concept is, the harder to demarcate. This is certainly true of desire. It is difficult to talk about desire, even when variations of the same concept are in and of themselves easy to differentiate. Desire can be understood as a human structure that operates as a backdrop of perpetual longing or also like a sharp reality that is set in motion by a specific need, similar to what we would also refer to with terms such as wanting, craving, yearning, and so on. In this sense, we would need to determine whether desire was manifesting as a process or as a basic inclination (the *epithymia* of the Greeks as passion or lust and its Latin equivalent of *concupiscence*[1]) or desire as specific formulations of those same tendencies concerning someone or something.

However, *desire*, which is a core concept in contemporary psychoanalysis, did not appear among the terms that Freud offered a specific theory for, as he did with other related concepts such as *drive* or *libido*. Freudian terminology was not explicit and clear in this regard. The term frequently used by Freud, *Wunsch*, refers not so much to the explicit formulation of desire but the process that seeks to reproduce some basic satisfaction. It does not differentiate itself enough from other words also used, such as *Begierde* or even *Lust*, as processes of the appetites. Without a doubt, it was through Jacques Lacan's complex and polemical work where the term *desire* rose to prominence in the current language of analytical theory. This theorization will be taken into account in our reflections, without, on the other hand, using it in a reductionist way. Rather, we will follow the words expounded by Antoine Vergote in

1. The concept of *concupiscence* acquired its largely pejorative connotation (an expression meaning the dynamics of sin) only under the influence of Stoic philosophy. As we know, the corresponding Greek term *epithymia* is used in the New Testament to express a desire or wish that can also be applied to holy realities, such as, for example, the desire for God's revelation (Mt 13:17).

one of his last and most important works[2] in which the term *Triebwunsch*, or *instinctual desire*, captures the most essential aspects of the Freudian concept of the drive and, in particular, its intimate connection with the libidinal body. At the same time, the term *instinctual desire* should not be confused with the concept of something specifically sexual in the most erotic and genital sense.[3] Desire relates to pleasure, like the self-seeking satisfaction that is linked to a series of representations, like images, ideas, and memories throughout the life of an individual. The union of pleasure with its representation is expressed with terms such as "I like," "I want," and "I love," terms that express an active readiness toward those objects that have been indexed emotionally through our personal experiences. Instinctual desire is, therefore, a reality molded by representations and likes, which relate to the feeling of pleasure and alludes to willingness.

The term *instinct*, on the other hand, recalls the bodily dimension of the word *desire*, which is ultimately rooted in the biological. However, this concept of instinctual desire does not stray far from the Jungian conception of libido, understood as something of general interest, nonspecific, detached from its bodily strata. The concept of instinctual desire, then, offers an open dynamism, broader than the strictest understanding of sexuality but not as broad as Jung might imply with the term *libido*, likening it to a general interest. It becomes evident, then, that desire can be understood as that which seeks pleasure and avoids displeasure.

SEPARATION AT THE ORIGIN OF DESIRE

We can only come closer to understanding the origins of human desire by understanding our own reality as *separate beings* that stemmed from the birth process itself. Because, what might seem self-evident and demonstrable in the

2. Antoine Vergote, *La psychanalyse à l'épreuve de la sublimation* (Paris: Cerf, 1997), especially 96–113. Antoine Vergote differentiates between libido and sexuality. By libido, he means the carnal psychological dynamism that animates all bodily activities in order to find sources of pleasure. Libido is described as a biological need that becomes autonomous. For Vergote, defining the libido by the pleasure principle means describing the psyche as a system that is organized in such a way that it conjures up pleasure, which is its purpose. The object is what allows the realization of that purpose and what gives it explicit meaning. In that sense, the object, the goal it is linked to, is the cause of the drive activity. Not a mechanical cause because the libido does not belong to the field of sciences that work with that concept of cause. The libido is a psychic dynamism that allows and advances the system of life that is specific to humans: beings endowed with language. Understanding libido, instinctual desire, in this way, as something broader than sexuality, we can appreciate that, through narcissism and via the ego ideal, instinctual desire can be transformed on the one hand into a sexual drive and on the other hand into a dynamic that powers other activities. Individuals enjoy the latter so much that those recede from the needs that become limitations. Ibid. 258–59.

3. Vergote, *La psychanalyse à l'épreuve de la sublimation,* 111.

physical sense—*I am not you, you are separate and different from me*—is also the cause of the strongest sort of emotional resistance within us.[4]

What we have within us is essentially a longing for a holistic fusion, a wish to go back to an original state, a longing for the womb in which there is no separation or difference. We are thus inheritors of a mythical ideal. And what was a physical reality that occurred biologically on the day of our birth, that is, separation from the mother's body, will not come to completion on a psychological level until much later and only when one is willing to full-heartedly accept this most basic separation that occurred within the imaginary of the maternal. Indeed, as Nicodemus expressed it, man cannot re-enter the mother's womb and be born again. Jesus also stated that only through the spirit we are authentically reborn as humans because flesh is born from flesh, while spirit is born from spirit (Jn 3:6). In other words, it is only through a complex process that we can, via the biological separation that gave us life, manifest the psychic departure that allows us to be a fully autonomous individual. And, thus, we become distinct individuals with unending types of longing.

This all stems from an early separation that results in a detachment that becomes ingrained in us like a perpetual want, but a want that is so severe that it becomes unacceptable. To avoid feeling like a failure and accept that intolerable separation, the newborn imagines himself as that which satiates the vacuum created from the breach with the mother since what fulfills the desire of the other cannot in itself be faulty. But this pseudo-restitution of the lost prenatal unit imagined by the newborn functions in a hallucinatory way, as a temporary buffer from desire. A long and complex string of rational elaborations will become necessary so that the individual comes to accept the reality of separateness and incompleteness that will, therefore, result in some form of desire.

Through that long and complex journey, the Oedipus complex, as we will soon see, comes to embody the separation that took place through the birth process. By accepting and embracing that separation that came through that paternal symbol, we are now reborn as true human beings. The Oedipal condition thus becomes a means by which the formation of subjectivity and the understanding of oneself can take place.

However, that separation will continue to be an open fissure, a never fully healed wound, something bottomless, a type of insufficiency that activates that force that we call desire. A dynamism that, at the same time, defines us

4. Margaret Mahler's entire development theory also focuses on this important issue of separation. This great psychoanalyst explains psychic development in terms of the initial symbiosis and the process of separation-individuation that takes place. From a normal autistic phase to the symbiotic phase, to the four subphases through which the individuation process takes place. Margaret S. Mahler, Fred Pine, and Anni Bergman, *The Psychological Birth of the Human Infant: Symbiosis and Individuation* (New York: Basic Books Inc., 1975).

as individuals and generates a latent aspiration that seeks to recover what was lost. Spanish poet Agustín García Calvo intuits that man only sings about what is denied and lost to him.

IGNORED DESIRE AND ITS CONFLICTS

One of the fundamental, if not the most fundamental, aspect of psychoanalytic research on sexuality has been its capacity to bring out the unconscious. Instinctual desire sinks its roots below the reach of the conscious mind, becoming imperceptible, beyond our control according to whim or need. A difficult matter for us to accept, becoming a wound for the narcissistic side of us that believes it can understand and manage everything that happens to us. But as Paul Ricoeur so beautifully expressed, "ultimately, when two beings embrace, they don't know what they are doing; they don't know what they want; they don't know what they are looking for; they don't know what they are finding."[5] Indeed, a challenging subject for the so-called science of sexuality.

One's unique history, which outlines the distinctive affective-sexual configuration of each person, will force one to differentiate between the possible and impossible, between what is allowed and what is prohibited. From a series of processes that we will analyze later in chapter 4, instinctual desire will shift into the realm of the forgotten, relegated to the margins of conscience, unable to be verbalized. It is the realm of the Unconscious—it is like an immense iceberg that, submerged under the surface of the sea, reveals only a small part of what is actually there.

From the depths of the unconscious, however, desire will remain strong and furtively demand that its aspirations be known. However, desire will constantly be challenged by defense mechanisms and prohibitions, often in imperceptible ways. Conflict, then, is an inescapable part of the human sexual experience. A conflict that, as has been correctly stated, is to be expected and only becomes truly problematic when that conflict becomes the norm. That is when it significantly disturbs and hinders the two basic tasks that are the basis for our stability: work and love. Everything will depend on the various defense mechanisms that each one has developed within this challenging dynamic. But we must admit that a certain degree of conflict is inherent in the dynamics of affection and we must be able to come to an acceptance, as we will analyze in chapter 5, that the ongoing task of maturing will never be fully completed.

5. See Paul Ricoeur, "Wonder, Eroticism and Enigma," in *Sexuality and the Sacred*, ed. James B. Nelson and Sandra P. Longfellow (Louisville, KY: WJK Press, 1994), 141.

Conflict is then, to some degree, inherent in the dynamics of desire. The laws, the norms, and the prohibitions are eternal companions. Rules that will vary according to the times and places of different cultures, but that will always form part of the structuring and limitation that desire will require to be a part of society, to what we call human nature. We have come a long way from that ethnocentric delusion of the European anthropologists who, unaware that similar sexual precepts existing in their own culture, believed in the existence of the happy primitive who lived naturally and who spontaneously interacted with the world of desires without cultural limitation. Where there is sexuality, there is law. Where there is society and culture, there is limitation and order put upon instinctual desire. And the method by which desire and law are mediated will determine the way and the degree to which conflict results.

The world of desire is also inextricably linked to its opposite, an antidesire or counterdesire, understood as hatred and aggressiveness.[6] Desire is accompanied by these qualities from the start, becoming an ally or, even, submitting to it as an instrument for its own and conflicting objectives, as is seen with sadism or masochism. Within each individual, love and hate, life and death also become inseparable. And that profound ambivalence, which psychoanalysis recognized as one of the most distinctive features of human affectivity,[7] will simultaneously produce conflict and guilt. There is no desire without law, nor desire unaccompanied by the shadow of hatred and aggressiveness. We will revisit this later on in the book.

THAT OBSCURE OBJECT OF DESIRE

The unconscious nature of our drives means that, to a large extent, we live our lives without understanding the motivations, impulses, fears, and desires that inform our decisions and life choices. This is why it is so easy to go astray when emotions are involved. This awareness suggests that we can never be completely certain of reaching a balanced state. Where sexuality and feel-

---

6. For the moment we will overlook the range of problems related to the intrinsic, instinctive, biological nature of aggression and also the learned, sociocultural aspects. As we know, Freud felt that aggression had an originating, not secondary character, as he expressed in his book (1920g) *Beyond the Pleasure Principle*, in *Standard Edition* (London: Hogarth, 1966), 18: 1–64. Then, some see aggression as a result of frustration and social conditioning. See Melanie Klein and Joan Riviere, *Love, Hate, and Reparation* (London: Hogarth, 1937). Nicole Jeammet, *La haine nécessaire* (Paris: PUF, 1989); "Violence et destruction," *Revue Française de Psychanalyse* 48 (1984): 917–1093.

7. The concept of ambivalence appears in the analysis of the obsessive neurosis of the so-called "rat man." (1909d) "Notes upon a Case of Obsessional Neurosis," in *Standard Edition*, 10: 151–249.

ings are concerned, there are no guarantees. A fire that was believed to be extinguished could suddenly be relit; a seemingly peaceful clear day could be taken over by a sudden storm; or a facade of apparent strength, built with dedicated effort for years, could come crashing down at any given moment.

Moreover, we see that all those aspirations that were unconsciously rejected do not remain in a state of inertness or mere rest. From their latent state, those feelings linger in the background like a discreet director behind a curtain, unknowingly controlling the personal dynamics between individuals, coloring thoughts, generating attractions and rejections, or mobilizing defenses or mysterious sympathies and antipathies. It can be said that in few other areas of life can that which is ignored act so powerfully on our beliefs, prejudices, or values.

The title of the present chapter alludes to Luis Buñuel's last film, *Cet obscur objet du désir* (*That Obscure Object of Desire*, 1977). No other filmmaker managed to channel emotion in the way that this director from Aragon did, highlighting through powerful imagery the untenable seeking of desire after an object. Whoever wants to learn something about desire need look no further than Buñuel's filmography, more insightful than any other set of works available. It is no wonder that psychoanalysts have always been so keenly interested in his work.

It has been said, and rightly so, that Buñuel's films are about the subversion of values and that subversive seed finds fertile ground in the dynamics of desire, in its capacity to question the establishment that thwarts its progress. Religion, family, education, social conventions, living conditions, and repressive forces are always faulted as repressive agents of desire. Desire is what permeates Buñuelian writing, either directly by attempting to open the door to the unconscious, as he does in his first surrealist film *Un Chien Andalou* (*An Andalusian Dog*, 1929), or *L'Age d'Or* (*The Golden Age*, 1930), or indirectly by alluding instead to the traces of the impossible pursuit of desire through their dreams and symptoms. It is what we see in films like *Viridiana* (1961) or *El ángel exterminador* (*The Exterminating Angel*, 1962), in the splendid and little known *Él* (*This Strange Passion*, 1952), or, in his later creations *Le charme discret de la bourgeoisie* (*The Discreet Charm of the Bourgeoisie*, 1972), *Le fantôme de la liberté* (*The Phantom of Liberty*, 1974), or *That Obscure Object of Desire.* The Buñuelian narrative speaks simultaneously about the struggle of giving voice to desire and the possibility of identifying its obstacles and, through them, the possibility of tracing the topology of repression, which is nothing other than an inverted image of its zigzag pattern.

Indeed, as Buñuel so marvelously showed, the object of desire is obscure. Needs can be met and certain aspirations can be achieved. Desire, however, can only be metaphorically or metonymically fulfilled. In other words, only through substitutions, through the innumerable objects that appear in our life, can desire be satiated in some way, but always via approximations and replacements. These objects, a love, a project, an adventure, seem to present themselves in the image of the missing object of desire. Just when they come within reach it becomes evident that the desired object could never truly be grasped. It falls outside the reality that its symbols suggested. This is why all manner of satisfaction inevitably leads to a new dissatisfaction.[8]

However, even when our deepest desires have been granted to us, sources of frustration are never far away. We should take note that, in any pedagogical endeavor, one's upbringing is key in learning to tame feelings of frustration. This will alleviate tendencies toward violent reactions in response to the source of frustration or against oneself, in the form of self-aggression.

Needs are met. That is to say, an internal tension that was unleashed inside of us is eliminated by a specific action that procures the sought-after object. Food calms hunger. An object manages to restore the imbalance stemming from the needy tension. Water quenches thirst. But no object will permanently extinguish desire, and, for that reason, there are an infinite numbers of objects that may seem attractive to quench that thirst. The chain of need, fortunately, never ends. The desired object will never appear in our lives because, ultimately, desire is a type of ghost, harkening to an imaginary paradise, something that never existed outside our created myth. In this way, desire links us to a past that nothing in the present will satiate, although unlike momentary biological needs, it does not remain in the present, but opens us up and propels us toward the future and the other.

CHIMERAS AND HOPES IN THE DYNAMICS OF DESIRE

The Spanish philosopher Xavier Zubiri described human beings as "animals of reality," however, also doomed to illusions. And it is hard to heal from patterns that drag us to the illusory again and again without warning. The need that is inscribed in the very heart of our desire, that fissure and that wanting that nothing and no one can fill, is the origin of the inevitable alienation that is always ready to be reborn through a string of fantasies. Desire can be understood as the child of anguish and the father of illusion.

The object of desire is always at the ready with mirages presented to fulfill our expectations via various epiphanies, as if our relationship with reality was

8. This is how Freud understands the object of the drive's relativity. Ultimately, the drive is not defined by the object, but by the force itself that results from the attraction, independent of the object that could lead to satisfaction. See *Three Essays on the Theory of Sexuality*, in *Standard Edition*, 7: 125–245.

a necessary delirious pregnancy. The romantic relationship, especially during the period of falling in love, where one experiences such intense fascination with the other, is the ultimate example of that exciting dynamic of desire. We say with good reason that love is blind.

The Spanish word *ilusión* [illusion/excitement] has a very curious double meaning. The *María Moliner Spanish Dictionary* explains that *ilusión* can mean "a mental image of a non-existent thing" or "joy and happiness that is experienced with the possession, contemplation or hope of something."[9] *Ilusión*, then, can be a mental elaboration, the exclusive product of desire, or it can, on the other hand, be a balanced expression lying somewhere between desire for the illusory and hope for something achievable. To be looking forward to something is very different from being deluded about having something. And avoiding illusion is not the same as being disillusioned.[10]

In a work titled *Breve tratado de la ilusión* [Brief Treaty on Illusion],[11] Julián Marías discusses the odd semantic changes that the word *ilusión* has undergone in Spanish usage, drifting toward a more romanticized ideal. It is a change that Spanish dictionaries took time to acknowledge.[12] Marías remarked on how curious it was that a word that could start out meaning deceit, trickery, error, and uncertainty could eventually come to mean something entirely different, an innocent version of the word signifying something lively, confident, and loving toward life, especially toward one's endeavors.

One's attitude toward life is filtered through a hopeful or cynical lens, by which reality is interpreted. A reality that, let's not forget, is always skewed

---

9. *Diccionario de uso del español* (Gredos: Madrid, 1998), s.v. "*Ilusión.*"

10. In *Psicoanálisis y religión: diálogo interminable* (Trotta: Madrid 2000, 170–176) I stated that Spanish-speaking psychoanalysts should reflect on the bipolar nature of the term *ilusión*. From the Latin etymology that relates it to the world of games (*illusio*, comes from *illudere*, whose simple form is *ludere*, to play) it gradually acquired the connotation of *deception*. This can be seen in the *Tesoro de la lengua castellana o española* [Treasury of Castilian or Spanish Language], the first monolingual dictionary written in 1611 by Sebastian de Covarrubias, where *ilusión* is defined as "something appearing different than it is," and this is how it acquires strength throughout the Baroque literature of the Golden Age, especially in ascetic and mystical circles. The devil is a master in the art of creating illusions, clumsy deceptions for the unsuspecting soul.

11. Julián Marías, *Breve tratado de la ilusión* (Madrid: Alianza, 1984).

12. According to Julián María, it was Espronceda who took notice of the evolved meaning of "*la ilusión*." Dictionaries were slow to take on this new meaning. In 1845 the *Nuevo diccionario de la lengua castellana* [New Dictionary of the Castilian Language] by Vicente Salvá retains the concept of deception, as does the *Diccionario de la Sociedad Literaria* [Dictionary of the Literary Society]. Still today, *Le Petit Larousse* (Spanish edition) defines it as a mistake made by the senses or a general misunderstanding, relating *ilusionado* [excited/looking forward to] to "deceived." A first glimpse of the new meaning is found in Ramón Joaquín Domínguez's *Diccionario Nacional* [National Dictionary], where we see "Object conceived by fantasy, an imaginative delightful creation, which would bring happiness to the individual if it came true, but which almost always borders on the impossible." This lexical tradition was lost until Maria Moliner reincorporated the double meaning in 1967. *El Diccionario de la Real Academia Española* [The Dictionary of the Spanish Royal Academy] did not incorporate the more positive meaning until 1982. See Marías, *Breve tratado de la ilusión*, 10–37.

in some way. *Ilusión*, then, can mean a way of looking at life in a way in which the future appears promising, a way to fulfill one's dreams and expectations. One is looking forward to the future. One makes present through fantasy what has not yet occurred. Although this is accompanied by uncertainty, which is different than delirium, which means that there is always the chance of falling into the illusory realm.

Donald W. Winnicott astutely pointed out the need for hope in the development and maturation of personality in his study of what he called the *transactional object*.[13] From this perspective, "hopeful illusion," like a child of desire, fulfills a critical role in the development of our ideals and life plans. It is a powerful force in human psychic development and a source of creativity and well-being.

Continuing with this idea, desire should be viewed as that thrust that prevents us from lapsing into a state of inertness and becoming paralyzed by despair and apathy. Desire is the force that creates a tension between the wished-for and the found, thus becoming a fundamental source of vitality. It can also function as a support structure for our worries and the basis for the development of hope. It is the momentum that takes us from what is to what could be.

Evidently, beyond the field of psychology to which these reflections adhere, other anthropological fields should be investigated to bring us closer to "what is to be expected" and to assess whether these findings line up with the ultimate aspirations of human desire. Here, we can only point out that the dynamics of desire become the support system or infrastructure for the human quest for fulfillment, regardless of whether that search empowers one to find desired objects or one comes to the conclusion that desire is a useless passion, one that auto-destructs with its own desiring.

We should ask ourselves an important question from the vantage point of psychology, however—whether we can truly differentiate between the desire that leads to chimeras (not to mention the delusion or psychotic hallucination) and the desire that makes one hopeful and leads to possible life fulfillment. As we will see later, in the chapters dedicated to the subjects of the development and maturation of instinctual desire (4 and 5), only by the progressive acceptance of our condition as "separate beings"—that is, in recognizing the absence inscribed in the heart of our desire—can we free ourselves from the fantasies that delude us in order to access a dynamism that realistically imagines a better life. Only from the recognition of that separateness that defines us as individuals can the world open up to us like a horizon full of possibilities.

---

13. David Winnicott, *Human Nature* (New York: Schocken Books, 1988); Winnicott, *Playing and Reality* (London: Tavistock, 1953); David M. Wulff, *Psychology of Religion: Classic and Contemporary Views* (New York: John Wiley & Sons, 1991).

THE CHILDREN OF DESIRE

There is no accounting for taste, the saying goes, and this is certainly true, for tastes are as varied as people themselves. Desire results in a multiform blossoming of aspirations, wishes, cravings, endeavors, ambitions, moods, and whims that take individual form according to one's story line. Everyone is continually spinning his or her own particular fantasy, like in a film titled *La noche mas hermosa* (*The Most Beautiful Night*, 1984) by Spanish director Manuel Gutiérrez Aragón, which features an assortment of characters living out their most intimate and colorful fantasies in a curious night of cosmic phenomena under the Madrid sky.

The individual story has the last word, a word that will become cemented through the gratifications obtained and the fantasies achieved. From there, new and specific desires will spring forth from the various vicissitudes of one's biography and, most importantly, from relationships and interpersonal encounters.

But even if it is our personal story that has the last word concerning our desires, it will be challenging, if not impossible, to make sense of that message, not even by the individual who authors it. The authentic objects of desire can be continually ignored, split off from consciousness through repression. It will remain in the realm of the unconscious, revealing only some partial aspects in distorted form. A complex set of processes intervene so that the emergence of desire is sufficiently camouflaged. Only through dreams and neurotic symptoms can these ignored desires make a disguised appearance.[14]

It becomes costly, however, when the field of excluded desires becomes bloated. Inauthenticity reigns. It is then that we can say with certainty that we do not know what we want. And the danger lies in the possibility of our lives deviating in directions that are but expressions of mistaken desires. When we are invaded by the desire of others, we may end up ignoring our own desires. As an example, those aspiring to a religious vocation may be avoiding a deeper and forbidden longing to remain attached to the mother figure, or they may be ignoring homosexual leanings; desire for coupled life built according to ethical or ideological attunements might end up ignoring emotional incompatibilities that would prohibit a deep relationship; desire to choose a profession that aligns with the tendency to please the paternal desires might

---

14. Freud dedicated one of the most important (and also challenging) chapters of *The Interpretation of Dreams*, in *Standard Edition*, 4–5, 509–621, to understanding these unconscious processes in "Psychology of the Dreams-Processes." As we know, the central thesis of the work is that dreams, after their apparent chaos and confusion, are always masking an attempt to fulfill a desire, usually linked to childhood experiences with an indestructible nature. He found a similar concept of wish fulfillment in the formation of neurotic symptoms.

not respond to true abilities and aspirations, and so on. It becomes evident that these life missteps could multiply exponentially.

Unawareness of one's own desires not only leads to possible inauthenticity but also could result in damage to oneself or open conflict with others. Our truest aspirations can become incompatible tendencies that clash with each other. And, in this sense, it could be said that, to one degree or another, we are all capable of witnessing the desires within us and, therefore, experiencing a certain amount of internal conflict. But things can get so out of hand that the "children of desire" end up waging war within one's personality and the individual becomes like the backdrop of a battlefield, reduced to the suffering of a spectator. Not even the conscious aspirations will be able to call a ceasefire.

In a similar vein, the incompatibility of our desires can short-circuit and leave us paralyzed, unable to carry out our wishes. Legend has it that a good-natured fairy wanted to fulfill three wishes for a poor and unhappy couple who lived in abject poverty. Just then, the unhappy woman caught the scent of freshly cooked sausage. She was unable to repress her desire to have such tasty food, and her wish was granted instantly. Her husband, angry at the loss of one of the three splendid wishes to such a vulgar desire, was livid with his wife. His anger made him want his wife's nose to resemble the sausage she had requested. His wish was granted. The tragedy was on full display. The good woman was entirely disfigured while her unfortunate husband felt ashamed that his wife should have such a face. Only one wish remained for the couple, and, evidently, the only logical request was to have things return to normal. This was also granted to them, but their opportunity to improve their life condition came to naught. This comical tale reveals what frequently but rather tragically happens when we long.

BIOGRAPHY SUBSTITUTES BIOLOGY

As we mentioned in the previous chapter, one of the most important things to understand about instinctual desire is the critical nature of the biographical and historical narrative that shapes it. The way that psychology has described instinct in the biological sense in relation to the behavior of animals falls short when we try to understand human behavior in the affective-sexual domain. This goes far beyond the sphere of the reproductive biological sexual instinct aimed at species survival; it is a force, a push that, as instinctual desire, aspires to that untenable fusion that we have previously spoken about. This point is critical in helping us to understand affection, emotion, and desire in the broadest sense.

Frank Beach has been one of the most significant researchers in recent times in the field of sexual behavior. He theorizes that sexual arousal is enormously varied and complex and, as one moves up the phylogenetic tree, the variety of sexual behaviors in which more complex animals engage is correlated with the development of their cerebral cortices. Hormonal control in lower animals gives way to neurological control in higher animals. In a sense, Beach affirms that, through evolutionary progression, the degree to which sex hormones control sexual behavior progressively recedes so that human behavior becomes relatively independent from this influence.[15] Experiments using surgical castration carried out by Beach and other researchers illustrate this progressive increase in sexual complexity. In lower animals, castration results in the practical annulment of sexual functions. As you move up the tree, these interventions become less effective, to the point where, when we arrive upon man, castration does not result in loss of sexual interest or reduction in the frequency of copulation and pleasure.[16] The influence of the environment thus becomes increasingly important in the determination of sexual behavior. As progress is made in the evolution of sexual patterns, they are no longer stereotyped or guided by specific signals—they are almost totally dependent on individual learning. As Clarence Arthur Tripp affirms, with each bit of progress that the brain makes, the less physiological control we see exerted over the sexuality of the organism.[17] The sexuality of man displays the most progress—the ability to imagine an opportunity, to plan it, and to be ready before it happens.

In close agreement with these findings, psychoanalysis has also revolutionized the concept of human sexuality. Indeed, it has ceased to be understood as a biological urge driven primarily by the need of species survival but has gone on to be considered as a force that, originating from the organism, aspires to the satisfaction of an impossible desire—a fusion, a fulfilling merger. The specific direction that this force will take in each subject will be shaped primarily by the particular vicissitudes of life.

As we shall explore further on, not even psychosexual orientation in heterosexuality or homosexuality will be an instinctual or biological matter. In his *Three Essays on the Theory of Sexuality*, Freud states that "psychoanalysis considers that a choice of an object independently of its sex . . . is the original basis from which, as a result of restriction in one direction or the other, both the normal and inverted types develop."[18] Such early indication of a distinction between the drive and its object coincides with the aforementioned biological findings, the progressive relaxation of sexuality's control

15. Clellan S. Ford and Frank A. Beach, *Patterns of Sexual Behavior* (New York: Harper & Row, 1969), 266.
16. Fred S. Keller and William N. Schoenfeld, *Principles of Psychology* (East Norwalk, CT: Appleton-Century-Crofts, 1950).
17. Clarence Arthur Tripp, *The Homosexual Matrix* (New York: McGraw-Hill, 1975).
18. Freud (1905d), *Three Essays on the Theory of Sexuality*, in *Standard Edition*, 7: 145. Note added in 1915.

factors, which among other things could involve the consideration that a subject's masculinity and femininity does not depend so much on biological imperatives as on cultural and psychological conditioning. From this early disconnect between the drive and the object, heterosexuality does not then appear to be something merely spontaneous, but explainable based on context. To this end, Freud affirms, "Thus from the point of view of psycho-analysis the exclusive sexual interest felt by men for women is also a problem that needs elucidating and is not a self-evident fact based upon an attraction that is ultimately of a chemical nature."[19] Biography, history, and environment will, therefore, be the prime determiners in understanding that vast reality that we call instinctual desire and that has so surprisingly surpassed sexual instinct in the human species.

When we analyze and try to make sense of instinctual desire, we must avoid what Carlos Castilla del Pino has termed the "biological fallacy," especially when it comes to evaluating the male and female aspects—the epistemological error that occurs when we extrapolate the purely biological to the psychological and social. He says, "What doubt is there that biological differences exist. Women have genitals that are completely different from those of men. Women have a whole endocrine system that works differently than in men, qualitatively, anatomically, and physiologically. So then, to bring the biological differences between men and women, that is, those genital aspects, to the psychological and social differences, that is the biological fallacy."[20] Being genetically male or female does not necessarily mean being masculine or feminine, categories that are much less rigid and far more complex than the words suggest. "[We] must conclude that what constitutes masculinity or femininity is an unknown characteristic which anatomy cannot lay hold of," Freud correctly pointed out.[21]

Instinctual desire, then, can be thought of as a heterogeneous force that opens up an array of possibilities to both evil and virtuous ends. That is the ambiguity that results from the enormous wealth that nature provided to the individual. The field of objects to which instinctual desire can turn its attention to is very broad. Unlike the animal world, there are many possible expressions that instinctual desire can channel.

THE VARIOUS EXPRESSIONS OF DESIRING

The central role of desire in molding the human subject and the contingency of the objects of desire through the various manifestations resulting from our

19. Freud, 146.
20. Carlos Castilla del Pino, "Femenino-Masculino," *Argumento* (Oct. 1979), 23.
21. Freud (1933a), *New Introductory Lectures on Psycho-Analysis*, in *Standard Edition*, 22: 114.

particular psycho-biographical incidences and sociocultural conditions result in that force of desire spreading through all aspects of human activity. That is why—understandably so—we attempt to carry out a type of hermeneutics of desire wherever we may find it. Not everything will be about desire, but desire will be present in just about everything an individual endeavors to do.

It is hard to argue that desire is not present in a very basic and direct way in our affective-sexual world. Even with this understanding—one generously granted by psychoanalysis—desire remains linked to the specific corporal realm of the human being. There, it finds its genesis where it develops in a primordial and significant way. It is through sexuality that we can aspire to achieve a fusion that shatters the boundaries imposed by our individual differences. The search for the other through sexual encounter ultimately aims, as Plato expressed with his myth of the divided human being in the *Symposium*, to the return of an earlier state in which there is no duality and separation imposed by differences of the sexes.

But the search for another person with whom to lessen the feeling of separation—that separation that we came into the world with—can also express itself in many different ways through personal relationships. Even while coupling with the opposite sex is seen as the norm, it is not the only way in which human desire expresses its primal need. Same-sex relationships have always been and will continue to be a way by which desire is expressed—in a thousand ways, in all cultures, and throughout history. Homosexuality, as we will later see, is a dimension present in all human desiring and will become a critical force in the psychodynamic orientation of many individuals.

Besides the more explicitly erotic and sexual intention, instinctual desire will likewise encourage the warm, intimate bonds that individuals seek through friendship. Desire will be the force that facilitates communication and encounters between human beings that go beyond the differences or similarities that might exist between the sexes. A special bond offered freely, that friendship will be animated through the vigor of desire and will result in a type of ethical commitment, a noble outcome of this important expression of desire.

The love that is animated through desire will not stop short of expressing itself at the individual level. Narcissism and self-esteem are both expressions of that love that comes with their benefits and also with all the possible risks. Because—as we will see later on—whether through narcissism or self-esteem, there are "loves that kill."

From that initial place where it is configured, desire unfolds into significant and complex mutations, via the different associations an individual establishes through his surroundings. But the great human passions for knowledge, power, or ownership are also impregnated by desire, which finds within them and their respective sociocultural formations, channels for their seeking and finding. Desire is thus articulated through various types of demands and corresponding satisfactions with the inevitable frustration. Art, science, religion, economics, and politics are areas in which desire becomes more perceptible and expressed differently. The sublimation of instinctual desire thus plays a critical role in helping us become those representatives of civilization and culture.

Among these "sublime" fields of human experience, it is religion that offers the best vehicle to pursue desire's deepest aspirations. Through union with God, desire can manifest as the highest form of loving fusion, a merging without limitation. It is the mystical experience, where desire nobly embodies its ultimate ambition of wholeness—the elimination of any separation with the beloved object.[22]

We can conclude then that there are numerous and varied expressions of instinctual desire. And many sociocultural incidences mark the peculiarities of these diverse expressions of desire. Each era and each culture leaves its mark on these varying voices: through family, coupled life, homosexual relationships, friendships, and so on—they are strongly conditioned by the cultural identifiers of each era. It is worthwhile, then, to reflect on the changes that have taken place with our affections, loves, and passions in recent times.

BIBLIOGRAPHY

Beirnaert, Louis. *Aux frontiers de l'acte analytique*. Paris: Seuil, 1987.

Bowly, John. *Attachment and Loss*, Vol. 1 and 2. New York: Basic Books, 1969/1982.

Buñuel, Luis. *My Last Sigh.* Minnesota, MN: University of Minnesota Press, 2003.

Cameron, Devora, and Don Kulick. *Language and Sexuality.* Cambridge: Cambridge University Press, 2003.

De La Colina, José. *Objects of Desire: Conversations with Luis Bunuel*. New York: Marsilio Publishers, 1994.

Delgado, Manuel, and Alice J. Poust. *Lorca, Buñuel, Dalí: Art and Theory*. Lewisburg PA: Bucknell University Press, 2001.

Dolto, Françoise. *Solitude*. Paris: Gallimard, 1994.

Domínguez-Morano, Carlos. "Ciencia, ilusión y creencia." *Revista Portuguesa de Filosofia* 59 (2003): 431–53.

———. "La soledad." *Sal Terrae* 95/8 (2007): 639–50.

Ey, Henri, ed. *L'Inconscient.* Paris: Desclée de Brouwer, 1996.

Freud, Sigmund (1900a). *The Interpretation of Dreams*. In *Standard Edition*, 7. London: Hogarth, 1966.

——— (1905d). "Three Essays on the Theory of Sexuality." In *The Standard Edition of the Complete Psychological Works of Sigmund Freud*, edited and translated by James Strachey, 7, 125–245. London: Hogarth, 1966.

22. I explored this subject in depth in my work titled *Mística y psicoanálisis* [Mysticism and Psychoanalysis] (Madrid: Trotta, 2020), where further bibliographical information can be found.

——— (1915e). "The Unconscious." In *Standard Edition*, 14: 159–66.
——— (1920g). *Beyond the Pleasure Principle*. In *Standard Edition*, 18: 1–64.
——— (1923b). *The Ego and the Id*. In *Standard Edition*, 19: 1–66.
Fromm, Erich. *Escape from Freedom.* Oxford: Farrar & Rinehart, 1941.
Galanaki, Evangelia P. "The Origins of Solitudes: Psychoanalytic Perspectives." In *The Handbook of Solitude: Psychological Perspectives on Social Isolation, Social Withdrawal, and Being Alone*, edited by R. J. Coplan and J. C. Bowker, 71–89. New York: Wiley & Sons, 2013.
Green, André. *The Fabric of Affect in the Psychoanalytic Discourse*. New York: The New Library of Psychoanalysis, 1999.
———. *The Chains of Eros*. London: Karnac, 2002.
———. *Key Ideas for a Contemporary Psychoanalysis: Misrecognition and Recognition of the Unconscious*. London: Routledge, 2005.
———. *The Work of the Negative*. London: Free Association Books, 1999.
Klein, Melanie. "A Contribution to the Psychogenesis of Manic-Depressive States." *International Journal of Psychoanalysis* 16 (1935): 145–74.
———. "Symbol Formation in Ego Development." In *The Selected Melanie Klein*, edited by J. Mitchell, 95–111. London: Penguin Books, 1986.
Lacan, Jacques. *Écrits: The First Complete Edition in English.* New York: Norton, 2007.
———. *Formations of the Unconscious: The Seminar of Jacques Lacan, Book 5*. Malden, MA: Polity Press, 2017.
———. *The Four Fundamental Concepts of PsychoAnalysis, Book 9.* New York: Norton, 1978.
Mahler, Margaret. *The Psychological Birth of the Human Infant Symbiosis and Individuation.* New York: Basic Books, 2000.
María, Julián. *Breve tratado de la ilusión*. Madrid: Alianza, 1984.
Masotta, Oscar. *Ensayos lacanianos*. Barcelona: Anagrama, 1976.
Nasio, Juan D. *Le livre de la douleur et de l'amour*. Paris: Payot, 1996.
Rosolato, Guy. *Essais sur le symbolique*. Paris: Gallimard, 1969.
———. *La relation d'inconnu*. Paris: Gallimard, 1978.
Roudinesco, Elisabeth. *Lacan: An Outline of a Life and History of a System of Thought.* New York: Polity, 1999.
Smith, Joseph H., and William Kerrigan, eds. *Interpreting Lacan.* New Haven, CT: Yale University Press, 1983.
Symons, Stephane. "Lacan's Concept of Desire and Its Vicissitudes." *The American Journal of Psychoanalysis* 68 (2008): 379–98.
Vasse, Denis. *Inceste et jalousie: la question de l'homme.* Paris: Seuil, 1995.
———. *Les temps du désir*. Paris: Seuil, 1969.
Winnicott, Donald W. (1958). "The Capacity to Be Alone." *International Journal of Psychoanalysis* 39 (1958): 416–20.
———. *Human Nature.* London: Routledge, 2015.
———. *Playing and reality*. Oxford: Penguin, 1971.

Chapter Three

Current Transformations in the World of Desire

Desire is channeled and expressed in numerous ways, as numerous as the opportunities for encounter and union that life offers us. Because of its disruptive force, it is erratic at times; other times, it is ambiguous—desire molds our personality. It opens doors; it closes them too, coloring ideas and outlooks, illuminating and blinding according to one's individual experience.

As we have seen, we had to adjust our idea of *sexuality* based on that panorama of the ambiguous reality that psychoanalysis laid out for us. As analytical research progressed, the participation of desire became evident in more aspects of human behavior. At the same time, it was increasingly moving him away from the restrictive field of biology. We have bodies—of that there is no doubt—but that body seems to serve mainly as a platform by which to unfurl a dynamism that is essentially geared toward relationship, relationship with others, relationship with the world, relationship with one's fantasies and internal representations. Our affective evolution is, therefore, more dependent on our personal history and biography than on mere instinctual biological mechanisms.

In our personal history, early parental and family relationships play a major role. We will come back to this later. But, through this primary framework that is the nuclear family, our affective dynamic also reflects the impact of the social and cultural references of our environment. The makeup of our instinctual desire is not disconnected from the social and cultural forces around us. The impulses of each individual are crafted according to social context, and each human group configures and structures particular ways of channeling and expressing these impulses. Instinctual desire is also fundamentally conditioned by these sociocultural structures. It is understood that the myths, rites, taboos, and ideas of the Middle Ages, the Renaissance, or the Victorian era, for example, were different from those of today.

Frequently, there are even factors, originally alien to the world of desire, that also end up causing significant changes and mutations. And, if we can say that psychoanalysis has been instrumental in how we view and experience sexuality in our culture,[1] other factors have also played an important role. The result is that men and women nowadays think, feel, and experience sexuality in a very different way than their closest ancestors might have. Few areas of human behavior have changed as fast and as profoundly as sexuality has, which is understood in this broader sense as what we call instinctual desire. It is worth reviewing these other factors that have had such a deep impact on our lives.

CURRENT CHANGES IN THE IDEAS AND REALITIES OF SEXUALITY

Along with psychoanalysis, other scientific disciplines have also played an important role in the transformation of both the concept and experience of sexuality. Psychophysiology has shown, for example, that sexuality is moving away from being reproduction focused and tied to neurohormonal mechanisms and is rather becoming more dependent on the central nervous system and the functions that are proper to man, like language and symbolization. Reproduction will undoubtedly continue to be an essential function for sexuality and also for human life, but, already overflowing the limits of the animalistic, it is only one of its functions and can no longer be defined solely in this way.[2] Sexuality, from its intimate connection with the central nervous system, also becomes something more than pleasure received in exchange for the burdens inherent in procreation—it becomes a vital function with a much broader reach.

From the fields of ethnological and anthropological studies, we were also taught that, throughout the centuries and in the various continents, societies have conceived, practiced, and structured sexuality in ways as varied and distinct as other human endeavors. Here, too, it was noted that reproduction,

1. Philip Rieff, *Freud: The Mind of the Moralist* (New York: Viking Press, 1959); Luigi Zoja, *Ethics and Analysis* (College Station, TX: A&M University Press, 2007); Henri Ellenberger, *The Discovery of the Unconscious: The History and Evolution of Dynamic Psychiatry* (New York: Basic Books, 1970); Erich Neumann, *Depth Psychology and a New Ethic* (Boston: Shambhala, 1990); Thomas Szasz, *The Ethics of Psychoanalysis* (New York: Basic Books, 1965); Arnold I. Davidson, *The Emergence of Sexuality* (Cambridge: Harvard University Press, 2004).

2. See John Money, *Sex Research: New Developments* (New York: Holt, 1965); M. Godefroy, *Études de sexologie* (Paris: Bloud&Gay, 1965); Lynn Margulis and Dorion Sagan, *Origins of Sex* (New Haven, CT: Yale University Press, 1986).

while essential, was not the main or sole consideration in the social functions that societies imposed on sexuality.[3]

From a different vantage point, we have the social criticism of the family undertaken from Freudian-Marxist positions, which made a mark on the concept of sexuality with large sectors of the population. The work of Wilhelm Reich,[4] for example, had a strong belated echo in the so-called sexual revolution of the sixties, along with that of thinker Herbert Marcuse of the Frankfurt School. The work of the latter, titled *Eros and Civilization: A Philosophical Inquiry into Freud*[5]—in which he advocates for the possibility of a nonrepressive society—became a latent seed for revolutionary ideas in Berkeley, Paris, Berlin, and Madrid student revolts of the sixties. If Prometheus was the giver of the progress that we have so far enjoyed, it would now be Orpheus and Narcissus that would put an end to all repressive institutions and achieve a *rationality of satisfaction*. Herbert Marcuse thus proclaimed the advent of a nonrepressive society and encouraged others to facilitate its arrival. Regardless of whether these ideas have materialized or not (for it does not seem that Narcissus manifested quite in the way Marcuse foresaw), there can be no doubt that these ideas played a transformative role in the experience of a generation's sexuality. The impact is felt to this day.

All of this social criticism has had significant repercussions on our social movements, mobilizing against what has been called the "rebellion against the father." Paternal figures fall from their pedestals (despite the inevitable repressive and regressive currents that history brings), and, with that fall, a potent method for maintaining sexual control also collapses. Freedom and autonomy progressively replace the role previously played by authority and obedience.

There has always been an intimate relationship between sexuality and power, a relationship where sexuality is represented as the privileged symbol of authority and domination. The term *impotent* suggests—as we very well know—the one who is incapable in both respects. As Jacques Pohier has pointed out, sexuality rises above other human dimensions as

---

3. See Claude Lévi-Strauss, *The Elementary Structure of Kinship* (Boston: Beacon Press, 1969); Margaret Mead, *Sex and Temperament in Three Primitive Societies* (New York: William Morrow, 1959); Bronislaw Malinowski, *Sex and Repression in Savage Society* (London: Kegan Paul, Trench, Trubner & Co., 1927), and *Sex, Culture, and Myth* (New York: Harcourt, Brace & World, 1962); Martine Segalen, *Historical Anthropology of the Family* (New York: Cambridge University Press, 1986).

4. See Wilhelm Reich, *The Function of Orgasm* (New York: Cambridge University Press, 1973); *Character Analysis* (New York: Farrar Straus and Giroux, 1990); *The Sexual Revolution* (New York: Farrar Straus and Giroux, 1974).

5. Herbert Marcuse, *Eros and Civilization: A Philosophical Inquiry into Freud* (New York: Beacon Press, 1974).

the privileged ground of self-vindication against those who might withhold certain freedoms.[6]

Thus, the act of taking on an unquestionable position of authority will always suppose, in the primordial sense, to situate oneself with the capacity to control and subvert the other's capacity for pleasurable self-affirmation. Every type of social, political, or religious tyranny has intuited this profound dynamic derived from our psyche. Sexual repression, therefore, has always made them inseparable elements. In it, they have found a key element for maintaining their own power structures.

Nowadays, the emergence of very explicit sexual and erotic manifestations of desire in political realities like post–Soviet Russia, or post-Franco Spanish democracy, or the tendencies that can be seen in Cuba today, which run parallel to the cracks that are opening up in the system. At the same time, the political opening through the sole channel granted by the capitalist system also reveals the commercialization of sex and its terrible effect, witnessed in all the countries of our globalized culture.

Along these lines, neither can one forget the role that the progressive secularization of Western society has played in the collapse of old sexual norms. The legal inclinations of current Western governments seem to demonstrate this—even when they are conservative and aligned with the religious institutions of their countries, they are openly opposed to the religious position on important issues such as divorce, abortion, homosexuality, cohabiting, and the use of contraceptives. Religious institutions are slowly losing ground on issues that are so directly tied to the world of desire.[7]

At a deeper level, we must consider that previous positions and attitudes toward sexuality were maintained thanks to religious representations that were socially enforced and individually internalized. With a "God is dead" attitude and, above all, with the practical atheism and the religious indifference of the masses, many pillars that upheld the structure of sexual behavior have fallen. Religious representations are no longer the controlling factors of sexual morality, as they were decades ago. Today's parents and grandparents look at their children's sexual behavior in a surprisingly different way than they did in their younger years.[8] In this sense, they are much more permissive, based on the conviction that what their own experiences were was not all that positive. They do not want their children to go through the

---

6. Jacques Pohier, *Au nom du Père* (Paris: Seuil, 1972), 192.

7. Carlos Domínguez-Morano, *Experiencia cristiana y psicoanálisis* (Santander: Sal Terrae, 2006), 131–48.

8. See Patricia Neff Claster and Sampson Lee Blair, eds., *Gender, Sex and Sexuality among Contemporary Youth* (London: Emerald, 2018); Chris Harris, Nickie Charles, and Charlotte Davies, "Social Change and the Family," *Sociological Research Online* 11 (2006), http://www.socresonline.org.uk/11/2/harris.html.

same difficulties that they now see as senseless and without merit, if not outright harmful.

Even those who maintain their religious beliefs and practices today have very different ideas about sexuality. It is a well-known fact that every day the chasm grows wider between the tolerance of sexual behaviors practiced by Catholics and the approaches that remain acceptable to the ecclesiastical hierarchy. Current sociological studies bear proof of this reality, where the new generations differ from the official norms of the Church leadership.[9] Their values regarding masturbation, premarital relationships, the use of contraceptives, homosexuality, and so on become progressively more alien to the ideals of the Church.

There are a growing number of practicing believers who, even with conservative views, disregard the moral orientations of the hierarchy. It is not uncommon to find married couples belonging to traditional apostolic movements who, adhering to the strictest Catholic norms in other aspects of their life, openly confess that, where sexuality is concerned, they feel free to adjust their behavior according to their own conscience. They have been progressively distancing themselves from the moral discourse of church authority. This situation, no doubt, poses serious problems to the moralist and also to the theologian. We cannot delve into this issue in depth here.[10] Suffice it to say that these profound changes, regardless of how we may morally judge them, have greatly influenced the world of desire. Later, we will reflect on, through the lens of psychology, these transformations and their positive or negative implications. We will explore these lights and shadows.

THE IMPACT OF SOCIOECONOMIC TRANSFORMATIONS

Many authors have insisted that the changes that have taken place have not only happened due to reflection on sexuality itself but rather are a result of the influence of a series of transformations in the social fabric that go beyond sexuality and its possible ethical implications.[11]

---

9. Marion Maudet, "Religion and Sexuality in France from the 1970s to the 2000s," *Population-E* 72 (2017): 671–96.

10. I reflected on this topic in the following article: "Sexualidad e institución. Hacia una nueva moral sexual," *Selecciones de Teología* 33 (1994): 231–37.

11. See Alex Liazos, *Families: Joys, Conflicts, and Changes* (New York: Routledge, 2016); Christina L. Scott and Sampson Lee Blair, eds., *Intimate Relationships and Social Change* (London: Emerald, 2017); K. Calvo and José Ignacio Pichardo, "Sexualities Transformed? Inside Visions of Sexual, Social, and Political Change in Spain," *Sexualities* 14 (2011): 503–508.

One of these factors has been the lengthening of life expectancy, thanks to advances in medicine, biology, chemistry, and other sciences. Starting in the 20th century, the benefits experienced have been remarkable, and the effects felt in the sentimental and sexual areas, profound.[12]

Among other things, longer lives have come to mean a qualitative transformation for the female sexual experience, with a definite impact on the couple, families, and love relationships in general. Until recently, the entire sex life of a woman was dedicated to the functions of procreation and parenting. Women often died shortly before or after menopause and their marital life was practically reduced to a succession of pregnancies—the average was five or six children due in large part to high infant mortality, frequent pregnancies, and the economic need to have extra helping hands in the family. Currently, however, the period between marriage and the birth of the last child may last only four years, after which there will normally be a long period (the possibility of celebrating a golden wedding anniversary is not far-fetched) in which the couple will live through some critical exchanges of emotional and sexual communication that will have nothing to do with the procreative functions.

In summary, if in the past a woman's sex life lasted an average of less than twenty years, of which practically every moment was defined by a succession of pregnancies, today, a woman's sex life can last well beyond fifty years, of which only six or seven will be occupied by two or three pregnancies. This has an immediate impact on the experience of instinctual desire. A couple's emotional and sexual life becomes a project of an entirely different nature. The world of desire ceases to refer exclusively to procreation and becomes wider, deeper, and more personal. The effect this has had on the ways of representing the coupled life has been significant. Without the intervention of any particular theory, ethical consideration, or deep reflection, procreation has been but on a back burner, while the affective and interpersonal dimensions have come to occupy the preeminent position, with all the risks, fears, or excitement that they may bring.

The plethora of contraceptive methods and the possibility of artificial insemination have also made an impact on our industrialized world in how we view sexuality—offering increased means by which to separate reproduction and sex. They become options that, independent of moral considerations, did not exist a century ago and that substantially change how sex is experienced. Even if a couple adheres to the precepts of the ecclesiastical leadership, their way of perceiving the relationship will also change. They know that it could

12. See Hillard Kaplan, Kim Hill, Jane Lancaster, and A. Magdalena Hurtado, "A Theory of Human Life History Evolution: Diet, Intelligence, Weed Knowledge and Longevity," *Evolutionary Anthropology* 9, no. 4 (2000): 156–85; Lawrence I. Conrad, *The Western Medical Tradition* (New York: Cambridge University Press, 2006), 137; Elizabeth Arias, Jiaquan Xu, and Kenneth Kochanek, "United States Life Tables 2016," *National Vital Statistics Report* 68 (2019): 1–66.

be otherwise, that there is a wide range of alternatives available that will affect the outcome of sexual activity. It will be through personal choice and not destiny that the couples embark on this procreative journey.

Another important factor of social transformation in the West over the past century has been the transition from an essentially agricultural to an industrial society, together with the largely parallel phenomenon of urbanization. This sociocultural transformation has also played a substantial role in family life and the rhythms of affective and sexual life—they have seriously impacted family models.

In industrial urban societies, members of the individual family unit become practically the only means of emotional support, unlike the broad and complex family and social structure of peasant life offered. Marriage for love, which seems so natural and obvious to us now, is not, as family historians have pointed out, but a "19th-century invention." This was mainly due to social and economic considerations that until that moment had been essential in the establishment and formation of a family. A look at some of the swashbuckling film comedies about the Spanish Golden Age would confirm that love was not exactly exclusive to the sphere of marriage but rather ran through those other tributaries that took the form of love affairs and adultery.

In current times, couples form relationships based on the desire for communication and loving exchange, and this is yet another reason these relationships are no longer viewed in terms of procreation. In the long, complex, and intense life of the couple, procreation will be seen only as a chapter, important no doubt, but secondary to what sexuality in its broadest sense can and should provide to that common life project.

TODAY'S LIGHTS AND SHADOWS

Thus, through the complex changes that have taken place in the conception of sexuality, we have noticed that both psychoanalytic and other human science research coincide in the following: sexuality and procreation in the human species seem to be two separate realities that, according to the field of biology, are inextricably intertwined but which cease to be so when they enter the realm of the human.

Also, the sociocultural and economic transformations that seem to have increased the gap between sexuality and procreation, already apparent through phylogenetic evolution, have made this reality all the more obvious. With the increased access and variety of birth control, possibilities of artificial insemination, and evolved awareness in how families and relationships are viewed, there is an ever-growing number of people who experience sex as a dynamism that, beyond the biological and procreative objectives, allow for new dimensions of joy and encounter. What nature has allowed, culture has consolidated.

Thus, behaviors such as masturbation, premarital relationships, homosexuality, and the use of contraceptives are experienced and appreciated differently. They are approached with a new mentality and sensibility. Many of these sexual behaviors are seen as completely normal and with the certainty that sexuality is a dimension of life that does not have to be questioned merely because it is a source of pleasure but only in the context of possible detriment to self or other. These new ways of thinking and experiencing sexuality and pleasure have also had an important impact on how to address childhood and adolescent education. We no longer live in the age of concealment and denigration of sexuality that was so damaging for many, having been brought up in an environment, both at home and at school, full of threats and taboos.

There is no doubt that the repression experienced in times past caused serious psychological problems. Many are the individuals who still painfully recall the experiences of sickly guilt experienced in their young years, the terrors to which they were subjected with threats of all kinds (earthly and beyond), the catastrophic effects that it had on other areas of their lives, and the emotional scarring that resulted. For most, sex was not an aspect of their instinctual desire to be channeled toward the natural unfolding of life but rather a source of neurotic conflict and submission to dark forces of power. It appears self-evident that, in the past century, the changes in how sexuality is comprehended and approached have been healthy and beneficial.

That said, not everything that derives from the new ways of thinking about and experiencing sex should be lauded as the advent of a new age of sexuality. At least from a serious psychoanalytic perspective, one cannot fall into the naive notion that everything has already been remedied and that sexuality, at last, is exempt from neurotic mechanisms, allowing it to reach a state of fullness and freedom.

As we saw in the previous chapter, psychoanalysis demonstrated the conflictive power that instinctual desire holds over the human species. This cannot be sidestepped through certain social tweaks, such as being more open-minded toward certain sexual behaviors. These same behaviors can respond to very diverse dynamics and are not always free of conflict or even pathology. The same "modern" and "open" patterns of sex education can also be impregnated with very dark tendencies but now camouflaged with a thin layer of scientific veneer. To give an example, among possibly many, being naked before one's children can be a sign of a healthy body awareness or of underlying exhibitionist tendencies that give rise to early erotization, as it is also possible to seem permissive toward certain sexual behaviors and simultaneously feel terribly and irrationally guilty about them, without even being consciously aware of this inconsistency.[13] The conscious-level initiatives and goals are not always easily followed by the complex and obscure dynamics of the unconscious.

Instinctual desire is accommodated through the channels that social dynamics provide. Each era and each culture provides a few lanes for some, hinders others, propels interests, offers objects of seduction, and fascinates with proposals of different sorts. Desire, in its drive and search for gratification, manifests in each society according to where the forbidden fruit appears. Our globalized and commercial society has masterfully designed such a place—the place of consumerism. Desire in its erratic form easily succumbs to the seduction that consumerism offers.

CONSUMING AND OWNING: A PERVERSE OFFSHOOT OF DESIRE

Desire today tends to get easily derailed. It has shifted to a fetishistic world of objects; it disperses into blanket anxiety about ownership and consumption, of hoarding and accumulation, in which it tries to satisfy what interpersonal relationships do not. This opens a current of regressive voracity in which people and the world, in general, are seen as a kind of nourishing bosom, forced to provide food and perpetual satisfaction.

Desire becomes frenzied in a state of unending discontent. Refusing to recognize limits, there is always something new that society is ready to display so that our need multiplies at the rate of the capacity for production. The car we own will never be the best, our computer will never have the latest features, our house will never provide all the comforts that would satisfy our desired quality of life, our clothes will never be as stylish as we would like, reflecting the social status we aspire to.

As Pascal Bruckner has elucidated, the supermarket has become our "Garden of Earthly Delights."[14] Not even Bosch could have imagined such a profusion of tempting offerings. Torrents of light, kilometers of shelves, infinite color—it is the victory of capitalism over scarcity. One cannot fully take in the cornucopia of goods. Being a consumer means knowing that there will always be more

13. It is illuminating, in this sense, to look back at how masturbation was viewed from the medical perspective in the 18th and 19th centuries. Doctors and enlightened thinkers (some of them avowedly antireligious and anticlerical) considered that this behavior was the catalyst for a whole series of physical and mental illnesses (such as madness or suicide) that today would make any specialist smirk. Undoubtedly, unconscious guilt was categorized as an illness when it couldn't be called a sin. See Francisco Álvarez-Uria, "The Sex of Children," *Psychoanalytic Series* 4 (1983): 55–93.

14. Pascal Bruckner, *The Temptation of Innocence: Living in the Age of Entitlement* (New York: Algora Press, 2000), 48.

on display that can be purchased, an immense nourishing breast, overflowing, uncontainable. We can choose to spend over $3,000 on a bottle of whiskey when an average price would only be about $30 (although few people would likely afford it, although this is not the point). What is astounding is that anything that could possibly be needed is available, and more than we could ever wish for. For this reason, people sometimes go to the mall not to buy but to verify that everything is within reach or that there will always be more than what could be hoped for. In this way, the possible becomes desirable and the desirable becomes necessary. Desire is thus perverted in an evil displacement toward material possessiveness, unleashing a genuinely perverse dynamic. Bruckner says, "The empire of consumerism and entertainment have added the right to regress to the general inventory of human rights."[15]

In this global situation, money becomes desire's main fetish. It is never a purely economic, rational, or useful relationship. Money also implicates the "problem of love," as psychoanalysis has shown us. Here, we also find an important branch of desire. We uncover one of desire's most important expressions in our current world. This shows, among other things, that, as happens in areas related to sexuality, money also results in duplicity, insincerity, and hypocrisy. Speaking about money can sometimes be as cumbersome as talking about sexual matters.[16]

Through a perverse love of money, it is no longer a matter of *having something* but of *having oneself* in a centripetal dynamic. It is about enclosing oneself inwardly while shutting out the outside world. The individual tries to cover over an internal lack and to attain a feeling of security, but, in fact, it results in the most insecure position that one can imagine because as Erich Fromm expresses in his analysis of ownership, "If I am what I have and if I lose what I have, who then am I?"[17]

Our desire is not immune, of course, to the sociocultural dynamics in which it develops naturally, grows, and is compelled to find objects of satisfaction. This is why we must take into account the current economic dynamics that can branch out through the tree of desire. Desire stimulates the most regressive aspects of these behaviors related to money. For this reason, one could concur with Otto Fenichel that it is money that influences and conditions the relationship with perverse eroticism, for it is the social conditions that influence the scope and intensity of the instinctive tendencies of reten-

15. Bruckner, *The Temptation of Innocence*, 86.

16. Along these lines, see Sigmund Freud (1913c), "On Beginning the Treatment," in *Standard Edition*, 12:131. Additionally, I reflected on the relationship that psychoanalysis established between money and libido in *Belief after Freud: Religious Faith through the Crucible of Psychoanalysis* (London and New York: Routledge, 2018), 207–17.

17. Erich Fromm, *To Have or to Be* (London and New York: Bloomsbury, 1997), 107.

tion. Childhood drives are transformed into a desire to become wealthy only under specific social settings.[18]

To this, we should include Fromm's observations that highlight the profound human alienation that results from Western modes of consumption. Consuming has ceased to be meaningful; it has become a way of satiating artificially induced fantasies, fantasies that are alien to our true and unique self. We eat and drink the fantasies that propaganda feeds us. Consuming has become an end unto itself, an end that is compulsive and irrational, where *being* is replaced with *having*, to the point, wherein today's society, a perverse identification occurs in which the subject could avow confidently that "I am what I consume."[19] And, as a consumer, interpersonal relationships also take on that perverse dynamism. Hysterical and perverse tendencies are imposed on the interpersonal sphere.

CAMOUFLAGED HYSTERIA AND PERVERSION MANIFESTED

Hysteria is the mental conflict that speaks par excellence to the erratic voices of desire. In no other conflictive situation does instinctual desire become so involved. In a way, hysteria is a problem that results from desire. Therefore, perhaps psychiatry and clinical psychology found it, and still find it, a challenge to define, to trace its boundaries, to identify within it its various forms and manifestations. It is as if it were diluted everywhere and, therefore, could not be clearly defined anywhere. It is changing, plastic, infinitely moldable, like the capacity of water to adapt itself to any vessel or bypass with its own rhythm and strength any obstacle that tries to interrupt its flow. It is a disturbance like no other, which adapts so effortlessly to the sociological and cultural changes of each epoch.

The great and striking hysteria of Freud's time is no longer so easily found, particularly, those spectacular hysterical conversion disorders in which the body channeled the mental conflicts into blindness, paralysis, aphasia, and so on—these have disappeared almost entirely. Hysteria today is subtler, more cultured, less strident in its manifestations. And yet hysteria, as the most dramatic expression of instinctual desire, still lingers and continues to influence the relationships and behavior of our society.

Hysteria has even gone through a name change. It no longer appears as *hysteria* in the great manuals and handbooks of psychiatry and

18. Otto Fenichel, *The Psychoanalytic Theory of Neurosis* (New York: Norton, 1995), 545.
19. See Erich Fromm, *To Have or to Be* (London and New York: Bloomsbury, 1997).

psychopathology.[20] *Hysteria* does not seem to be a politically correct term, having such negative associations to the repressed damsels of the Victorian era. When diagnosing a US Marine, we prefer to talk about *posttraumatic stress disorder*, although the underlying problem is inextricably linked to symptoms of hysteria.

But hysteria, operating like the disease of desire, lives on. Moreover, today, many social aspects seem to propel hysteria into ways of behaving individually and within relationships. We may no longer find the manifestations of conversion disorder resulting in blindness or paralysis or in the great hysterical attacks (those that Buñuel portrayed so brilliantly in films like *Nazarín*); today, hysteria is camouflaged in other forms of spectacle where the intention of the desire remains intact—seduction, exhibitionism, attention seeking, the need to be looked at and praised; the culture of ostentatious seduction in marketing, of the public spectacle, of perverse exhibitionism. Never before have the most intimate affairs of man been thrown into the public spotlight. They are trumpeted on television programs or splashed over gossip magazines. We are thus turned into characters that become part of the drama that hysteria builds up.

Not without reason, it has been said, that today we have gone from the sexuality of the elephant to the sexuality of mandrills,[21] that is to say, from sexuality that, according to San Francisco de Sales, is a model of modest behavior particular to elephants[22] toward a morality that seems to coincide with that of the sexual behavior of the mandrills, which boast of their nakedness, insolently expose themselves, and touch and satisfy themselves in plain sight.

Many authors have already explored the social manipulation of sexuality.[23] Suffice it to say that the sexual model of baboons that has its social equivalent in the idea of sex for sale everywhere responds to a particular hysterical dynamic that, paradoxically, attempts to escape the anguish and uncertainties of sex itself, sex that is readily available and detached, avoiding the deeper implications of intimacy.

In this way, the superficial and uncompromising manipulation of others, which is at the essence of hysteria, becomes the means of social encounter.

---

20. It is telling that hysteria is no longer one of the disorders listed in the DSM-5 (*Diagnostic and Statistical Manual of Mental Disorders*) of the American Psychiatric Association.

21. See Francisco Álvarez-Uria, "The Sex of Children," *Psychoanalytic Series* 4 (1983): 91–92.

22. According to the saint, the elephant never changes partners; it tenderly loves the one it chooses. But the male is with the female only every three years, for only five days, and with so much secrecy that he never lets himself be seen in the act; on the sixth day, he is seen looking for a river in which he may wash his body, not wanting to return to the flock until he has been purified. See Francisco de Sales, *Introducción a la vida devota* [Introduction to the Devout Life, III] (Barcelona: Librería Católica de Pons y Co, 1878), 356–57.

23. See, for example, the aforementioned Herbert Marcuse in his work *Eros and Civilization* (New York: Beacon Press, 1974). The current search for a regressive fusion situation that seeks to exclude any type of regulation is analyzed by Jean Claude Sagne, "La mutation des modèles de l'echange sexuel dans une societé en changement," *Le Supplement* 111 (1974): 480–89.

The other cannot be turned into a controllable object, like another product on the market. The network of interpersonal relationships is directly affected by the aforementioned consumer mentality. A utilitarian and uncompromising ideology is imposed, avoiding any kind of commitment in personal relationships. The consumerist mentality of disposable products permeates the ways of viewing relationships, which are becoming easier, more numerous, and increasingly superficial. The current fever of internet chat, defined already by clinical psychology as addictive, is quite illustrative.[24] Never before were there so many people we could communicate with and never was it easier to do so with such detachment. It is the channel-surfing culture in which everything is consumed and very little is metabolized.

There is a pattern of emotional detachment in the relationships that seek to avoid feelings of instability, disappointment, or unrestrained passion, which can lead to suffering. By avoiding meaningful commitment, vulnerabilities are also avoided. Casual sex is also a way of circumventing the torment of jealousy or the tendency toward anxious possessiveness. Perversion becomes evident when sex becomes purely and exclusively merchandise, something that becomes detached from the person. Individuality is completely annulled in order to convert the body into a pure object of pleasure, where there are no norms nor limits.[25] The increase in child pornography, trafficking of women, and the sex tourism industry demonstrates that sex is increasingly becoming a product available to anyone, beyond rules and ethical considerations, in the infinite possibilities that the market now offers—the internet serving as the current platform of opportunity.

This is what Tony Anatrella tried to explain in his work *Le sexe oublié*,[26] a work that generated controversy and confusion in his seeming critique of homosexuality. Anatrella argues against a sexuality that is pressured by the sociocultural environment into ignoring its emotional dimension. The perverse and sadistic elements are imposed on this supposedly "liberated" society, leading to a paradoxical amnesia toward the sex that distresses and conflicts. The impulsive behavior that keeps the individual in the narcissistic and in the Oedipal search for the lost incestuous object becomes normalized. In this way, the opening toward the other's unique individual nature is obstructed.

In short, barriers are erected against emotions and affective intensities that emanate from the force of desire. This makes it more difficult to feel empathy

24. To this end, see R. Gubern, *El eros electrónico* (Barcelona: Taurus, 2000); Silvia Vianzon, "Internet sessualità e benessere," *Rivista di Sessuologia Clinica* 24 (2017): 23–38; Nicola M. Döring, "The Internet's Impact on Sexuality: A Critical Review of 15 Years of Research," *Computers in Human Behavior* 25 (2009): 1089–1101.

25. See Piera Aulagnier et al., *Le désir et la perversion* (Paris: Seuil, 1967).

26. Tony Anatrella, *Le sexe oublié* (Paris: 1990). The work, which some people find debatable in its arguments, and others suspicious in its intentions, illustrates, however, that impossible neutrality that affects both the writer and the reader regarding sex.

in relationships, to recognize what others are feeling, to capture their unique sensibilities and feel moved by the experiences of the other. Add to this, as with hysteria, the great difficulty in experiencing guilt because of the resistance of the fragile ego.

And while in a state of hysteria we find it difficult to accept the differences between the sexes,[27] in our culture, we also clearly perceive the longing for the bisexual, for the undifferentiated, to dismantle the profiles that separate and define. There, in the place beyond the genders, lives a fantasy of primal fusion to which hysteria aspires.

The hysteric displays of victimization are also reflected in the social context. We are all becoming children, Pascal Bruckner insists, spoiled children, children who, because they feel entitled to everything and are not forced to do anything, are unable to handle challenges and feel immediately victimized when something is denied to them. Today, there is a surprising tendency to feel a sense of identification with the victims of the Holocaust—Pascal Bruckner asks himself.[28] The Western individual feels unjustly mistreated and violated in his fundamental rights the moment the slightest thing goes awry. Hence, as Bruckner himself says, it seems that the most common pastime nowadays is lamenting oneself, a typically hysterical symptom as an expression of a never satisfied desire. A constant state of complaint, then, a continuous grievance, a sustained dissatisfaction—serving as fuel for that hysterical dynamic that our society seems to stimulate and favor.

Thus, springing from one's family history and biographical vicissitudes as well as social influences, the world of instinctual desire takes shape in each individual, leading to fulfillment and satisfaction, or dead ends, or internal breakdowns in a dramatic and hellish fashion. Madness exists as a paradigmatic expression of desire that could not coexist with reality and find a way to channel through it. Desire strayed so far that it became an "independent state," overtaking the individual like a devastating hurricane. The madman is a body swept up in the gusts of desire.

In the case of perversion, desire did not stop with the individual but forced him to submit to its dictate, adopting the power of an incorruptible tyrant. The sadist, the masochist, the voyeur, or the exhibitionist operates in this way, shaped by a few detours imposed at certain stages of his personal journey. We will not be addressing perversion or insanity in this work, but we will now be zeroing in on the key moments of emotional development and, when a state of maturity has been reached, to what type of desire leads to a creative and inspired life.

---

27. See Sigmund Freud (1908b), "Hysterical Fantasies and Their Relation to Bisexuality," in *Standard Edition* 9: 159–66.

28. Pascal Bruckner, *The Temptation of Innocence: Living in the Age of Entitlement* (New York: Algora Press, 2000), 228–31.

BIBLIOGRAPHY

Álvarez-Uria, Francisco. "El sexo de los niños." *Serie Psicoanalítica* 4 (1983): 55–93.

Arias, Elizabeth, Jiaquan Xu, and Kennet Kochanek. "United States Life Tables 2016." *National Vital Statistics* 68 (2019): 1–66.

Bauman, Zygmunt. *Life in Fragments: Essays in Postmodern Morality*. Oxford: Blackwell, 1995.

Bruckner, Pascal. *The Temptation of Innocence: Living in the Age of Entitlement*. New York: Algora Publishing, 2000.

Butler, Judith. *Bodies That Matter: On the Discursive Limits of "Sex."* New York: Routledge, 1993.

———. *Excitable Speech: A Politics of the Performative*. New York: Routledge, 1997.

Calvo, Kerman, and José I. Pichardo, "Sexualities Transformed? Inside Visions of Sexual, Social, and Political Change in Spain." *Sexualities* 14 (2011): 503–508.

Davidson, Arnold. I. *The Emergence of Sexuality*. Cambridge, MA: Harvard University Press, 2004.

Domínguez-Morano, Carlos. *Belief after Freud*. London and New York: Routledge, 2018.

———. *Experiencia cristiana y psicoanálisis*. Santander: Sal Terrae, 2006.

———. "La alteridad difuminada." *Proyección* LI (2004): 347–67.

———. "Sexualidad e institución. Hacia una nueva moral sexual." *Selecciones de Teología* 33 (1994): 231–37.

Ellenberger, Henri. *The Discovery of the Unconscious: The History and Evolution of Dynamic Psychiatry*. New York: Basic Books, 1970.

Fenichel, Otto. *The Psychoanalytic Theory of Neurosis*. New York: Norton, 1995.

Foucault, Michel de. *Histoire de la sexualité*. Tome 1: "La volonté de savoir." Paris: Gallimard, 1976.

Freud, Sigmund (1908d). "'Civilized' Sexual Morality and Modern Nervous Illness." In *The Standard Edition of the Complete Psychological Works of Sigmund Freud*, edited and translated by James Strachey, 9: 177–204. London: Hogarth, 1966.

——— (1930a). *Civilization and Its Discontents*. In *Standard Edition*, 21: 59–145.

Fromm, Erich. *To Have or to Be*. London and New York: Bloomsbury, 1997.

Giddens, Anthony. *Transformation of Intimacy: Sexuality, Love, and Eroticism in Modern Societies*. Cambridge, MA: Polity Press, 1992.

Horkheimeer, Max. "Egoism and the Freedom Movement: On the Anthropology of the Bourgeois Era." *Telos* 54 (1982): 10–60.

Hunt, Lynn, ed. *The Invention of Pornography: Obscenity and the Origins of Modernity, 1500–1800*. New York: Zone Books, 1993.

Johansson, Thomas. *The Transformation of Sexuality: Gender and Identity in Contemporary Youth Culture*. London and New York: Routledge, 2007.

Kaplan, Hillard, Kim Hill, Jane Lancaster, and A. Magdalena Hurtado. "A Theory of Human Life History Evolution: Diet, Intelligence, and Longevity." *Evolutionary Anthropology* 9, no. 4 (2000): 156–85.

Kinsey, Alfred C., Wardell B. Pomeroy, Clyde E. Martin, and Paul H. Gebhard. *Sexual Behavior in the Human Female*. Philadelphia and London: Saunders, 1953.

Laumann, Eduard O., John H. Gagnon, Robert T. Michael, and Stuart Michaels. *The Social Organization of Sexuality: Sexual Practices in the United States*. Chicago and London: University of Chicago Press, 1994.

Lawrence, Conrad I. *The Western Medical Tradition.* New York: Cambridge University Press, 2006.

Lévi-Strauss, Claude. *The Elementary Structure of Kinship.* Boston: Beacon Press, 1969.

Liazos, Alex. *Families: Joys, Conflicts, and Changes.* London and New York: Routledge, 2016.

Lipovestky, Gilles. *Le bonheur paradoxal. Essai sur la société d'hyperconsommation.* Paris: Gallimard, 2006.

———. *L'ère du vide: Essais sur l'individualisme contemporain.* Paris: Gallimard, 1983.

———. *Métamorphoses de la culture libérale. Éthique, médias, entreprise.* Montréal: Édition Liber, 2002.

———. *Plaire et toucher. Essis sur la société des séductions*. Paris: Gallimard, 2017.

Lyotard, Jean François. *La condition postmoderne*. Paris: Editions de Minuit, 1979.

Malinowski, Bronislaw. *Sex, Culture, and Myth.* New York: Harcourt, Brace & World, 1962.

———. *Sex and Repression in Savage Society*. London: Kegan Paul, Trench, Trubner & Co., 1927.

Marcuse, Herbert. *Eros and Civilization*. New York: Beacon Press, 1974.

Margulis, Lynn, and Dorin Sagan. *Origins of Sex.* New Haven, CT: Yale University Press, 1986.

Mead, Margaret. *Sex and Temperament in Three Primitive Societies*. New York: William Morrow, 1959.

Money, John. *Sex Research: New Developments.* New York: Holt, 1965.

Neff Claster, Patricia, and Sampson Lee Blair, eds. *Gender, Sex, and Sexuality among Contemporary Youth*. London: Emerald, 2018.

Neumann, Erich. *Depth Psychology and a New Ethic*. Boston: Shambhala, 1990.

Pohier, Jacques. *Au nom du Père.* Paris: Ed. du Seuil, 1972.

Reich, Wilhelm. *Character Analysis.* New York: Farrar Straus and Giroux, 1990.

———. *The Function of Orgasm*. New York: Cambridge University Press, 1973.

———. *The Sexual Revolution*. New York: Farrar Straus and Giroux, 1974.

Rieff, Philip. *Freud: The Mind of the Moralist.* New York: Viking Press, 1959.

Scott, Christina L., and Sampson Lee Blair, eds. *Intimate Relationships and Social Change*. London: Emerald, 2017.

Segalen, Martine. *Historical Anthropology of the Family.* New York: Cambridge University Press, 1986.

Sigusch, Volkmar. "The Neosexual Revolution." *Archives of Sexual Behavior* 27 (1998): 331–59.

———. "On Cultural Transformations of Sexuality and Gender in Recent Decades." *German Medical Science* 2 (2004): 1–31.

Szasz, Thomas. *The Ethics of Psychoanalysis.* New York: Basic Books, 1965.

Zoja, Luigi. *Ethics and Analysis*. College Station, TX: A&M University Press, 2007.

Chapter Four

Desire's Long Journey

BIRTH IS SEPARATION

Instinctual desire journeys far during the life of each individual. From the start, there will be factors that will determine the unique adventures and explorations that instinctual desire will live out through each person. Genetic variables will also have a say in the direction and stratagems that instinctual desire takes, though this is not an area that the field of psychoanalysis delves into deeply. But it would be naive and foolish to forget that biology plays an important role in our global psychodynamics. Freud never forgot that; he was always quick to point out the joint role that physiology and environment play in shaping the different aspects of affective life. His followers, however, were less sensitive to that aspect of inherited and biological constitution, which is interlaced with the psychodynamics of personality. We will not focus here on those genetic aspects either. But we wish to be clear that those genetic factors are always present, even if only as a predisposition over which certain circumstantial possibilities will be facilitated or hindered.

There is not much reliable information about the psyche of the fetus. However, there is a growing belief that during pregnancy there are cognitive processes at play that influence the world of desire. Both the interpretation of dreams and the analysis of certain mental conflicts led Arnaldo Rascovsky to venture a hypothesis about the fetal psyche, which he saw as a type of nirvana, a hallucinatory experience where all needs are met. Several recent pathophysiological pregnancy studies suggest, however, that intrauterine life may also present problems and imbalances of various kinds.[1] In any case, the

1. See Juan Rof Carballo, *Biología y psicoanálisis* (Bilbao: Desclée de Brouwer, 1984); Fred M. Levi, *Psyche and Brain: The Biology of Talking Cures* (London: Routledge, 2011); Bianca Faveret

fetal state serves as an allegory for desire. An allegory that, at the level of primitive fantasy, mirrors the myth of a paradise where existence is free of otherness, a happy and undifferentiated oneness. Many origin myths refer to this idealized fantasy in one way or another.[2]

The birth process, therefore, is similar to the account of the expulsion from paradise.[3] At the moment when the umbilical cord is cut, we become essentially *separate beings*, forever. As mentioned in chapter 2, this becomes the defining dynamic of human desire. We had not previously been *separate beings*—we were, together with our mother, an indivisible reality. This is the defining moment for our feelings and sense of longing. The navel will be the mark of our *closure*, a witness, therefore, of our *individual* reality and our distinct constitution.

There is still far to journey before this separation that is innate in us and triggers the deepest desire within us can be integrated and intellectually processed. The newborn will still experience long periods in which, through the hallucinatory experience, he believes he is one with the mother. The steps that define the internalization of the physical separation that took place on the day we were born are progressive and complex, as we will see. Along this path, we will encounter, first, the smile and then speech, attempting to bridge that which separates us. Thus, if the navel signifies a type of closure, speech creates an opening that offers the possibility of spanning that innate separation.[4]

It seems clear. We will forever dwell in a state of extreme wistfulness, wishing to eliminate the distance and the difference between us, always in search of something with whom or with what to alleviate our sense of estrangement, people, things, fantasies—anything that can become an object through which to revive, however fleeting, that feeling of embryonic union. Lovers, passions, mergings of a mystical sort, are the expressions of desire—the preferred ways by which each one attempts to calm his extreme and primal "lack of being." This process will be complicated and slow, until,

---

and María Sanchez, "Psychoanalysis and Biology: An Epistemological Re-Discussion," *International Forum of Psychoanalysis* 11 (2002): 202–208.

2. Along these lines, see Antoine Vergote, *Interpretation du langage religieux* (Paris: Seuil, 1974). According to the Jungian point of view, the traces of the great archetypes of the collective unconscious would already be present in the fetal psyche.

3. The birth process creates a rupture of the flow of life present in the intrauterine environment. Now, the heart changes rhythm, the lungs begin to breathe, the digestive functions start to operate fully, and so on. The external world also presents itself as a reality in which satisfaction and frustration alternate in a way incomprehensible to the newborn. See Bernard This, *Naitre* (Paris: Aubier-Montaigne, 1973). Within psychoanalysis, Otto Rank highlighted the anguish of birth as a fundamental source of all subsequent anguish: *The Trauma of Birth* (New York: Dover, 1993). Freud, who recognized the value of Rank's theory, distanced himself from it when the author started to see the role of that primordial anguish as the source for all human anguish. See Sigmund Freud (1926d), *Inhibition, Symptom, and Anxiety*, in *Standard Edition* (London: Hogarth, 1966), 20: 75–172.

4. Denise Vasse alludes to this in her appropriately titled work *L'ombilic et la voix* (Paris: Seuil, 1974).

finally, that separation can be assimilated so that those infatuations, passions, and encounters do not lead to disappointment or self-denial tainted with resentment because of that division that turns us into nostalgic beings. This is the process that we will be exploring henceforth.

INCORPORATING OTHERNESS

Breastfeeding becomes the best way to maintain that primordial union. It is the ultimate method for instinctual desire to achieve its unifying purpose. Therefore, through suckling, the baby not only satisfies its need for nourishment, but it derives significant pleasure from it, which will later be sought out for its own means. Thus, the biological need for nourishment is accompanied by a need to merge with the other and the gratification and pleasure that come with it.[5]

The mouth thus becomes a source of pleasure, a pleasure that far exceeds the need to be fed. The pacifier, the finger, the blanket, anything will serve as a way to revive the hallucination of the desired union with the maternal. Even while sleeping, the baby at times appears to be sucking. It no longer needs that external body to simulate the unifying and fulfilling pleasure of the good object—the mother's breast.[6]

In short, the act of breastfeeding goes way beyond the function of satisfying the biological need for nourishment. It is the opportunity to merge with the maternal object—the breast, which, beyond a physical body part, thus becomes an object of the psyche, a *partial object.*[7] The external is *incorporated*, that is, integrated as part of one's own body, as part of one's individual reality. The breastfeeding baby is fused; it gets confused, thus, with the maternal process to the extent that it no longer knows whether it is mouth or breast, the wanting that receives or the fullness that gives. So fused, so con-fused, the baby experiences its first encounter with otherness.[8]

---

5. See Sigmund Freud (1923a), "Two Encyclopaedia Articles," in *Standard Edition*, 18: 240–59; and (1940a), "An Outline of Psycho-Analysis," in *Standard Edition*, 23: 23–207.

6. See Françoise Dolto, *Psychanalyse et pédiatrie* (Paris: Seuil), 31–35; Isabel Sanfeliu, *Karl Abraham: The Birth of Object Relations Theory* (London: Routledge, 2014), 195–216.

7. This is how Melanie Klein sees the mother-child relationship, which avoids the emotional ambivalence that marks its relationship with the total object. Partializing the relationship allows the infant to experience an exclusively positive, "good" relationship, shielding it from negative feelings. See R. D. Hinshelwood, *A Dictionary of Kleinian Thought* (Northvale, NJ: Aronson, 1991), s.v. "Partial objects."

8. These early oral relationships are established independent of an actual breast or bottle. Pediatricians and psychoanalysts tend to recommend breastfeeding, seeing it as something very positive and preferable to the alternatives, although we shouldn't speak in absolutes. A well taken care of bottle-fed baby who receives warmth and affection is certainly in a better position than a poorly breastfed baby whose mother is experiencing anxiety and feelings of rejection.

The prospect of eating or being eaten will become a central theme of early childhood fantasy and will leave its mark on the unconscious realm of the adult. Grown-ups will often play the game of "eating" their little ones, provoking both great fright and joy on the child's part.[9] Many are the myths, legends, and children's stories that demonstrate that primitive fantasy and illustrate the anxieties associated with this dual pursuit, so undifferentiated in the first stages of life. From Cronus to Dracula, from the totemic meals to the wolf of Little Red Riding Hood, eating and being eaten has always played an important role in the most profound human fantasies.

But the support that desire finds in the act of nourishment will forever be marked by this activity. Eating will always be equated with something more than sustenance, just as the union with the beloved body will always have echoes of orality and food. The relationship with food will become something more significant than just satisfying a biological need. Additionally, the emotional aspect will play an important role in this basic biological function. *Eating with*, in all times and cultures, has always been and will always be an act of *coming together*.

The associations with the maternal world will, however, be the most significant of all. Eating will continue to be, in some ways, like incorporating portions of that primitive good object that represents the mother's breast, even more so if there has been a great degree of fixation or regression in relation to that first stage of libidinal development. It was through food, explained a psychotherapy patient, where he felt most closely the presence of his recently deceased mother. That is also why, instinctively, many men compare their mothers' food with their wives'. At a deeper level, when certain pathological aspects intervene, serious disorders, such as anorexia and bulimia, could surface.[10]

Along with eating, many other oral-focused activities will reconnect with those primal satisfactions of desire. Drinking, smoking, taking drugs, or medicating oneself, all of these can become substitutions for those early attempts to merge with the maternal object. They calm, relax, and provide a sense of well-being. The individual who feels the need to carry around a pillbox and instantly feels anxious when the medication is misplaced is burdened with something more significant than chemical compounds. The individual is finding relief from anxiety by having a *good object* nearby that can provide oral tranquility. And in those cases in which the separation from the *good breast* is unbearable, the addiction to these substitute objects can have devastating

9. See Sigmund Freud (1918b), *From the History of an Infantile Neurosis*, in *Standard Edition*, 7: 7–122.

10. Obviously, among these food-related issues, there are also, as we know, other determining factors, such as culture. See Anita Fedirici and Allan Kaplan, "Overview over Biopsychosocial Risk Factors Underlying Anorexia Nervosa," in *Evidence-Based Eating Disorders*, ed. Ida Dancyger and Victor Fornari (New York: Nova Biomedical, 2014), 3–19.

consequences. Through the mouth, then, we introduce breasts that annihilate and kill, be they tobacco, alcohol, medication, or drugs.

But, if eating or ingesting things through the mouth harkens back to that primal oral affection, the world of emotion and eroticism will also harken back to this old relationship with food. The mouth becomes an important erotic object, and the fantasy of oral merging plays a significant role in sexual relations, activating the lowest strata of the affective world. Because of this, the relationship of the erotic object with food and eating is reflected in many ways. Language is one of them. The old expression *he is a tall drink of water* suggests that someone is both attractive and worthy of intake. We often say that someone is sweet; we use the word *honey* as a term of endearment. There are many such cases in songs and sayings where edibles represent an object of desire.

PRIMITIVE ANXIETIES

During these first stages of life, the baby lives in an imaginary, symbiotic, and fused relationship with the world. Reality does not yet exist. You could say that he is everything and everything is he. The child thus relates to the world in an illusory way, and the elements that surround it serve only to respond to his impulses and needs.

In this context, the relationship with the mother (or whoever takes her place) gets to the core of what Spanish physician Rof Carballo called the *primary warp* (*urdimbre primaria*). This can be understood as an integral and guiding reality, like a plot from which an understanding of self and others is defined.[11] Because, in truth, when the child drinks from the breast or the bottle, the child is also taking in the face—the mother's whole reality. The type of relationship established with her will be vital. In some way, the world will take on that maternal countenance. Therefore, if the early years are imbued with positive emotion, the child will feel safe and protected. But, if these experiences are negative, the *bad objects* will dominate one's internal reality.[12] That *primary warp* that Rof Carballo refers to is a "transactional reality," a state in which both the child and the mother simultaneously

---

11. See Juan Rof Carballo, *Urdimbre afectiva y enfermedad* (Barcelona: Labor, 1961); Consuelo Martínez Pelayo, "Affective Warp and Education: An Approach to the Pedagogical Thought to Juan Rof Carballo," *Estudios sobre Educación* 28 (2015): 139–54.

12. René Spitz researched children who, having been raised in certain medical institutions, grew up without the proper attention and emotional care. He described what he called *anaclitic depression*, also called *hospitalism*. The children displayed serious personality issues: anorexia, deep states of sadness, varied physical problems with great resistance to healing, and so on. See René Spitz, *Anaclitic Depression: Psychoanalytic Study of the Child* (New York: International University Press, 1946); *No and Yes: On the Genesis of Human Communication* (New York: International University Press, 1948); *The First Year of Life* (New York: International University Press, 1965).

influence each other—what the baby awakes in the psyche of the mother, whether anxiety, guilt, joy, or possessiveness, for example, will inevitably reverberate back to him and shape him in relation to the world. Definitively, we find ourselves in a complex world, one in which we continually stumble upon deep anxieties that are rooted in the challenges of accepting that early separation that defines us from birth.

Although the early oral relationship represents an attempt to maintain a feeling of union with the other, denying this "otherness" does not prevent that feeling of separation that took place at birth from being felt in other ways. That perfect lasting union is no longer feasible. The maternal breast is present as a good, unifying object but not in a continuous way. There is an alternation of maternal presence and absence that reflects the built-in nature of separation, a separation that the newborn cannot understand nor, therefore, fully assimilate. He only understands that the desire for union has been frustrated, that he is hungry and does not receive his food immediately, he is thirsty and his thirst does not get quenched, he is cold or hot and does not receive the comfort needed, he feels anxious and cannot find a soothing voice, and so on. Therefore, the mother is not the *absent chest* but rather the *bad chest*, tormenting, hostile, and dangerous. The world, suddenly, becomes a threatening reality. Separation in these early stages is perceived through a purely negative lens. A forceful and threatening negativity invades the inner world since the baby is not yet capable of differentiating its own reality from that of the external world. A nagging sense of anguish becomes embedded in the newborn, a reflection of that intolerable separation. Because it is incomprehensible, it must simply be suffered through.

The psyche of the newborn is thus split between a good world and a bad world, a good mother and a bad mother, or, more concretely, a *good breast* and a *bad breast*. As these realities alternate, the loves and the hates are felt instantly. This is what Melanie Klein called the *paranoid-schizoid position*,[13] where we encounter the most serious mental conflicts as well as many mythical representations, such as witches, fairies, evil stepmothers or kind mothers, gods or demons. Also, a certain Manichean way of thinking takes root here. Incapable of nuance, the psyche divides, seeing reality in stark black and white terms.

Depending on the type of relationship established in these early stages, between the fourth and the sixth month, we encounter the initial *paranoid-*

13. This position was described by Melanie Klein in 1946 and greatly influenced later psychoanalytic theorizations. Melanie Klein, *Envy and Gratitude and Other Works 1946–1963* (London: Hogarth, 1975). As an introduction to the thought of this important psychoanalytic figure, see Julia Segal, *Melanie Klein* (London: Sage, 1992); Claude Geets, *Melanie Klein*, (Paris: P.U.F., 1971); Harry Karnac, *Melanie Klein and Beyond: A Bibliography of Primary and Secondary Sources* (London: Routledge, 2009).

schizoid position (since time is relative, Melanie Klein prefers to speak of *position* rather than *stage* or *phase*), to progress through to the *depressive position*, when it becomes possible to accept that separation. The baby will realize that there is no *good mother* who assists and cares for him and another *bad mother* who abandons or persecutes him. There is only the only reality, which now begins to be perceived in a more integrated manner as a total object and not partial. She is present and then goes away, something that gratifies and frustrates, but she is no longer the imagined perfect good mother nor the evil mother who was feared and who the baby wished to lash out at. A period of mourning takes place—the fantasy of a totally good object must be given up as well as the other hated identity, the one that frustrates and endangers. The integrated perception of that specific reality leads to more mature relationships and an increase in the caring and altruistic feelings that benefit the welfare of the maternal object.[14] The relationship with that maternal object progresses from the condition of primitive fusion to a more refined, what we could call, *dual* and in which the separation is gradually being accepted. However, the baby will still project its own image of the mother following its own needs and desires. The infant is not yet capable of imagining or accepting that the mother is a separate object, in other words, that she has her own independent wants and needs.[15]

SEPARATIONS AND LOSSES

That ingrained feeling of separation, however, continues to linger. Weaning plays an important role. It is not always easy since it implies renouncing direct contact with the mother. Eating will now approach the satisfaction of a biological need, although, as we have already seen, it will always be impregnated with deep emotional traces.

As the processes of separation progress, the body will be a guiding force. The maturation of the sphincters will allow for a new biological process, that of defecation, which will reflect interests and explorations laden with significant emotional meaning. It is a new activity that the child discovers, with

---

14. Melanie Klein spoke of "reparation" as a mechanism that expresses the primitive guilt generated by the imaginary damage that the baby subjected the "bad mother" to. Depending on the degree to which the good or bad object ends up influencing the avatars representing these positions, feelings of envy or gratitude will develop in relation to life and to others. See Melanie Klein and Joan Riviere, *Love, Hate and Reparation* (New York: Norton, 1964).

15. As we already pointed out in chapter 2, Margaret Mahler's theory insisted on detaching from the motherly object as the central axis of development. See Margaret Mahler, *The Psychological Birth of the Human Infant Symbiosis and Individuation* (New York: Basic Books, 2000). See also Margaret Mahler, Fred Pine, and Anni Bergman, *La Naissance Psychologique de L'être Humain—Symbiose Humain Et Individuation* (Paris: Payot, 1980).

the benefit of being controllable by his own will. Within libidinal development, it initiates what the field of psychoanalysis has deemed the anal phase. During this time, the child's interest shifts from the oral area, which was the focus throughout the first year of life, to this new area of the body. Although defecation serves primarily as a biological function, the child will also find a source of pleasure in it. A new challenge surfaces in the world of desire. The polarity of expulsion-retention, both sources of pleasure, is now established as a paradigm for relating to objects.[16]

This moment is also important because it ushers in the first standards of hygiene. Until then, the child's behavior was driven by the pleasure principle. Now, a new reality comes to the fore, an outside world that displays hostility toward the child's natural impulses. It is forced to become a *clean animal*, a civilized and cultured being.

Faced with the limitations that these rules now impose, the child will react differently according to how he relates to his environment. He will either cordially accept the renunciation of pleasure or will oppose and rebel against it. In the best-case scenario, the renunciation of pleasure will not cause an aggressive reaction toward those who deny that pleasure. All anal sexuality has a tinge of aggression that, like in oral scenarios, has echoes in some of the profanities that makes reference to these acts. Obtaining pleasure and pain coincide in the act of defecation.

In this way, the aggressive components associated with desire (let us recall that these traits became apparent through biting and eating in the oral phase) become particularly obvious with anal eroticism[17] and, sometimes, go beyond it. Rof Carballo was very insightful in mentioning how the word used in coarse language to indicate the act of making love is also used to express the destructive tendencies that we wish upon our fellow being or that we fear may beset us. "This mixture of physical love, the undisputed root of the highest forms of love, along with the anal aggressive component, should be more carefully studied by philologists, novelists, psychoanalysts, and historians."[18]

In this moment of libidinal development, there is another key aspect worth highlighting. Along with aggressive entanglement, anal affectivity is also marked by the seal of omnipotence and narcissism. The child feels proud of this newly available power (hence, the reason the beginning of this phase has been called *megalomaniacal*). He now finds that he has an important weapon

16. See Freud (1908b), "Character and Anal Erotism," in *Standard Edition*, 9: 167–75; (1913k) "Preface to John C. Bourke's *Scatological Rites of All Nations*," in *Standard Edition*, 12: 335–37; (1917c) "On Transformations of Instinct as Exemplified in Anal Erotism," in *Standard Edition*, 17: 128–31; (1916–1917) "Introductory Lectures on Psycho-Analysis," in *Standard Edition*, 15.

17. See Carmelo Monedero, *Psicología evolutiva y sus manifestaciones psicopatológicas* (Madrid: Biblioteca Nueva, 1972), 201–202.

18. Juan Rof Carballo, *Rebelión y futuro* (Madrid: Taurus, 1970), 117.

of self-affirmation, whether through submission or rebellion, that he can exercise at will. But, also, far from expressing disgust toward the excrement, the child considers it of great value, insofar as it is like a part of his body that has become detached, as valuable as himself. Only later will the sense of disgust and repugnance develop, also as a defense mechanism for tendencies that must be repressed. (For example, in severe cases of schizophrenic psychosis, we may encounter coprophagy, which indicates an inability to confront anality.) The inclination shown by children to play and manipulate every dirty thing they encounter is a displacement that allows both the satisfaction and the renunciation linked to anality. Later, many of these anal components will become associated with other objects,[19] particularly with money, as mentioned in the chapter dedicated to the current transformations in the world of desire (chapter 3). The dynamic of retention-expulsion, which defined the genesis of anal activity, thus spreads out into the world of emotions in relation to objects. The dynamics of masochistic submission or sadistic control are also typical of this phase and may extend to interpersonal relationships. Submission, or control through domination, are both attitudes that relate to these stages of libidinal development.

THE LAW OF DESIRE

Desire's long journey, channeled through the libidinal body, will be greatly impacted and shaped through its focus on genitality. Gender awareness will take place between the third and fourth year of life. We speak of discovery in the most literal sense because until that moment both girls and boys had lived with the conviction that there was only one sex. In reality, they had yet to fully comprehend the concept of male or female. They viewed everyone as simply people.

The discovery of two different physical realities is perplexing for children and arouses great curiosity and interest. It was something unexpected, some unforeseen new reality has appeared before their eyes. The spheres of genitality cause polarization, which is also expressed through sexual behaviors, such as masturbation, erotic games, and so on. In conversation, therefore, they will return to the subject again and again, as if trying to find a reason for the inexplicable. The feeling that "something" is missing in the female sex generates serious concern for both the boy and the girl.[20] It will take a while

19. I explored this topic in my work *Belief after Freud* (London: Routledge, 2018), 207–17.

20. Much debate has ensued in the psychoanalytic field and beyond about the definitions and understandings Freud gave to the feminine and the value attributed to the penis in relation to sexuality. Reference may be made to "La castration et le fémenin dans les deux sexes," *Revue Française de psychanalyse* 57 (1993); "Filiations fémenines," *Revue Française de Psychanalyse* 58 (1994);

before it is understood that having a penis is not the same as being the possessor of a phallus (as a symbol of potency and fertility, example par excellence of desire),[21] and that, therefore, the male with his penis, like the female with her vagina, is fated to accept a *lack*, which will be a type of symbolic castration, that is, the acceptance of a fundamental limitation in the world of desire—nobody can have it all, nor can anyone be everything they want to be. In other words, nobody is the phallus; rather each one is limited in capacity and potential, whether in the form of a penis or a vagina.[22] This also amounts to saying that all human desires (oral, anal, visual, and so on) will be forever tainted by the knowledge of having to accept the dissatisfaction of desire.

Disappointment in desiring a sense of wholeness. Wanting to feel whole by seeking out the elusive soul mate. Looking for that other half through varied means, never exactly finding that perfect match that allows one to feel complete. Difference will get in the way of perfection, and the separate nature that defines us will make itself evident, demonstrating the hopelessness of producing that whole. The fantasy of sexual nondifferentiation appears, however, in myths and legends and in dreams and fantasies and certain social situations (such as unisex trends). It is the denial of difference, the denial of the other, the dream of hermaphrodite oneness. In a more pathological sense, that difference of the sexes is denied through fetishism.[23]

It is the law of desire—it cannot be satiated—a law that one is forced to accept and that within the Oedipal structuring finds its most defining and significant moment. We made reference to it in chapter 3. On the long journey that desire embarks on in order to be structured as human desire, the individual has had to differentiate between the possible and the impossible, the allowed and the forbidden. The oral and anal phases we already forced into renunciations, separations, and losses. This was necessary to develop and mature the sense of desire, the desire that in childhood expressed omnipotent objectives, with possibly devastating effects when failing to recognize limits. Now, in the Oedipal phase, it must face an essential norm and limitation as a requirement for accessing the human dimension. The total object of desire (represented for the child subject in the mother or father) is excluded from the field of satisfaction. Neither can we forget that in the global structure of the Oedipus

---

Janine Chasseguet-Smirgel, *La sexualité fémenine* (Paris: Payot, 1964); Janine Chausseguet-Smirgel, ed., *Female Sexuality: New Psychoanalytic Views* (Ann Arbor: University of Michigan Press, 1970); Silvia Tubert, *La sexualidad femenina y su construcción imaginaria* (Madrid: El Arquero, 1988).

21. See Jacques Lacan, *Formations of the Unconscious: The Seminar of Jacques Lacan, Book 5* (Cambridge: Polity, 2017).

22. See David Nasio, *Enseignement de 7 concepts cruciaux de la psychanalyse* (Paris: Rivages, 1988); Bernard Penot, *Passion for the Human Subject* (London: Karnac, 2008), 93–104; Russell Grigg, "Semblant, Phallus, and Object in Lacan's Teaching," *A Journal of the Unconscious* (2007): 130–37.

23. Sigmund Freud (1905d), *Three Essays on the Theory of Sexuality*, in *Standard Edition*, 7: 145.

there is also a current that links desire in relation to the same-sex parent. It is the inverted or homosexual side of the Oedipus complex.[24] *Oedipus complex* for the psychoanalyst, *the prohibition of incest* for the anthropologist, these are the terms that correspond to the diverse ways of viewing a reality that profoundly affects human sexuality.

In this sense, the Oedipus complex goes beyond triangular history, best expressed in the mythical sense by the Sophocles tragedies, and becomes like the great crossroads between desire and reality, between child omnipotence and the Law, the passage from the imaginary to the symbolic, from nature to culture, the bridge to the world of symbol, of the word, of reality. And it is clear that this formative human experience can function within the family paradigm, thus accommodating the story line extracted by Freud from the Sophocles tragedies or through other cultural paradigms happening now or in the future. Its argumentation or dramaturgy might coincide with that account to a greater or lesser degree. But this is, to some extent, secondary. The fundamental issue lies in the structure of the individual through channels where love and hate, desire and law, rebellion and submission intersect in a sometimes multiform historicity.

But we must not forget that the law that shapes and manages desire in the Oedipal situation does not only represent negative and prohibitive characteristics. Through its observance, the individual can form an identity and enter the relational field. In this sense, the Superego, which Freud referred to as the *heir of the Oedipus complex*, plays a leading role. The superego suggests the internalization of the law that prohibits incest and, from there, the laws, ideals, and moral principles that define the nature of social groups.

Through the renunciation of one's parents, a person becomes a distinct individual, a link in the continuity of the generations, and will embody a name that becomes an identity for the self and in the eyes of others. As we saw earlier, the Oedipal situation becomes an important moment in the formation of subjectivity and the shaping of oneself. In this sense, as the French philosopher Louis Althusser rightly expressed, the Oedipus complex is the adventure whereby a little animal born of a man and a woman becomes a human being,[25] a human being who has the right to love and procreate according to the terms of the law that desire defines. That being renounces the desired totality of being the phallus and becomes satisfied with both the possibility and the potentiality of having a penis or a vagina. That is what psychoanalysis intends when it uses the expression *symbolic castration*. It is a severing that is produced by an act that separates and dissociates the imaginary and narcissistic link between the mother and child, a law that breaks the illusion

24. Sigmund Freud (1927b), "*Fetishism*," in *Standard Edition*, 21: 147–57.
25. Louis Althusser, *Freud et Lacan* (Paris: La Nouvelle Critique, 1965).

of being a possessor; it stops the identification with that imaginary omnipotence.[26] The Oedipus consecrates, then, on a higher level, that essential separation that took place through birth. It is that critical moment in the acceptance of our reality as *separate beings*.

Separated beings, and also fortuitous, in that they could have been born . . . or not, of being called to fragility and limitation, and finally, to the inevitability of death. The omnipotent narcissism, previously projected onto the parental figures to the point of conferring them attributes of divinity (parents know everything, can do everything, are infallible and good without exception), now no longer seem to measure up in the same way. The Oedipus also supposes, in this sense, a critical step in the renunciation of childhood omnipotence.

Children's concern for issues related to birth and fertilization plays an important role in all this.[27] But, as Freud indicates, behind these matters, there is another more pressing question with a tinge of the metaphysical, that is, the origin of life. It is the passion for understanding our origins. Such a question, however, corresponds only to the metaphysical. It is driven by narcissism and the feelings of omnipotence that derive from it. The beginning and end of life, birth and death, are matters that damage this omnipotence that wishes to exist beyond limitations and derides uncertainty. But birth and death are the ultimate unknown. Hence, the child struggles to understand and accept that his parents, reflections of his omnipotence, may originate from other people who are linked to a succession of generations. Children find it especially difficult to accept death. "My 'I' cannot be stolen," a child would be likely to say, just as the Spanish philosopher Unamuno in his struggle with mortality.

All of the confusion felt in the Oedipal situation can be resolved in only one way—renunciation—resigned to inhabit the role of father or mother, to accept the "symbolic castration" and settle for occupying a position, a place within the family constellation, to accept being a mere link in the chain of generations, with a beginning and an end, with a desire that drives toward something that is never found. Luis Cernuda poetically expressed that desire in a question that nobody has an answer for.

LATENCY AND OPENINGS

Renouncing Oedipal incestuous desires will liberate one from instinctual desire beyond the primitive and narrow interests of early childhood. Now,

26. Jean-Tristan Richard, *Clinique de la castration symbolique* (Paris: Harmattan, 2001); David Nasio, *Enseignement de 7 concepts cruciaux de la psychanalyse* (Paris: Rivages, 1988).

27. Sigmund Freud (1908), "On the Sexual Theories of Children," in *Standard Edition*, 9: 205–26. In the *Three Essays on the Theory of Sexuality*, Freud refers to the *drive for knowledge* (*Wissentrieb*), which comes into sharp focus during this time in relation to sexuality.

throughout later childhood and until puberty, desire will broaden its horizons and show interest in many different things. It is a period of relative calm that occurs between two stages of great intensity related to the sexual. *The latency phase* was the name given by psychoanalysis to highlight the dormant state in which the great searches and erotic aspirations will remain until puberty.[28] This latency will play a critical role, however, in the configuration of the human being as a cultural being since sociocultural interests will find a unique opportunity in the postponement of the most primitive interests to graft their own buds onto the tree of desire. In this stage, the tree of desire will find an opportunity for expansion and will branch out in different directions. The specific values that come from the social environment will thus direct its growth.

Because, in its origins, instinctual desire formed the unifying tree trunk, we will now see differentiation that will allow it to pursue its base objective of encounter and union through diverse expressions. Of note, instinctual desire will be forced to differentiate explicitly erotic and sexual aspects from those that are simply tender, affective, and warm. The introjection of the law of desire, the acceptance that the mother and father are excluded from the field of sexual interest, will begin to develop toward them an intense love but completely inhibited from erotic intentions. The love for the parents is "platonized," and the erotic tendencies remain latent until a later time when they can redirect themselves toward different objects outside the family environment. Following the Oedipal stage, the erotic and the tender tendencies will thus be clearly differentiated as branches that splinter off from the trunk of desire.

Simultaneously, the tree of desire will take on the various interests that the social environment tries to graft onto it. In this way, instinctual desire transforms and absorbs the values that culture feeds it. From there, and through the mediation of language and symbolization, the object of its seeking changes, as will the type of satisfaction that may be found in it. It is the process that psychoanalysis calls sublimation and, as a key expression of desire, to which we will later dedicate a chapter.

In this period of life, from the fifth or sixth year, these sublimation processes play an essential role in the life of desire. The family horizon widens to allow other sociocultural institutions to have an influence, and schooling plays a fundamental role. Other life aspects will now concern and interest the child. This will become an ideal time to undertake various types of learning, to join numerous collective projects, to reinforce one's identity in accordance with the environment, to establish new affective bonds through friendship.

However, sharply erotic and genital urges during this period of latency are not uncommon. Applying the boy's or girl's instinctive energy toward

---

28. The term *phase* or *latency period* was coined by Wilhelm Fliess. Freud refers to it in the first section of the second essay on child sexuality. See *Three Essays on the Theory of Sexuality* in *Standard Edition*, 7: 177–78.

cultural values is still a rearing ideal, from which, as Freud indicates, the development of the individual is almost always diverted at some point and, in many cases, frequently—"From time to time a fragmentary manifestation of sexuality which has evaded sublimation may break through; or some sexual activity may persist through the whole duration of the latency period until the sexual instinct emerges with greater intensity at puberty."[29]

The relationships with classmates at school also play an important role in this latency stage, shaping the individual's world of desire. It is not always easy to integrate into an environment that due to its role as a complex organizational apparatus is often experienced as a threatening and dangerous reality. A child must apply a range of social skills to merit the approval, affection, or admiration of others. And not everyone is equally successful. But, at the same time, school life also allows (beyond the academic content and social values that it offers) the reinforcement of the Self, through identification with peers as well as through competition and rivalry with others. The "gang" of friends, a common social formation at this stage, will serve as a channel for conveying kindness and affection as well as aggression.

For their part, educators will exhibit myriad forms of affections, fundamentally dependent on the type of parental transfers that they are subjected to. In a society in which, as we discussed in chapter 2, there is an exaltation of the narcissistic and that seems averse to any type of ideal or norm, the teacher, the necessary bearer of ideals, becomes a figure to be perceived with a sense of rejection and the most violent animosity. The figure that, fifty years ago, was generally praised and valued in society, today becomes a punching bag that gathers all the aggressiveness that the group feels toward limitation. These are bad times for those whose basic function is to represent and envision cultural ideals, as it seems that today's instinctual desire rejects any type of limitation that seeks to organize and structure it.

REACTIVATIONS AND RESOLUTIONS

After the relative tranquility of the latency period, a wave of more overt sexual desire enters the individual, disturbing the emotional balance that was enjoyed throughout the grade school years.[30] Biological factors are clearly at play. This period brings hormonal changes that produce the biological maturation of sexuality, with the development of its primary and secondary char-

29. Sigmund Freud, *Three Essays on the Theory of Sexuality*, in *Standard Edition* (London: Hogarth, 1966), 7: 179.

30. Erik Erikson, *Identity: Youth and Crisis* (London: Faber, 1968); José Luis Lillo, "La censura de la adolescencia," *Temas de psicoanálisis* 4 (1999): 103–30; Hans Zulliger, *Die Pubertät der Kanben* (Vienna: Hans Huber, 1972); Hans Zulliger, *Die Pubertät der Mädchen* (Bern: Hans Huber, 1976).

acteristics. This causes an invasion of the instinctive sexual force that will, like a transcript of the psyche, reactivate the old themes of instinctual desire.

To a greater or lesser degree, the general dynamic of personality comes into conflict, leading to either a healthier, more perverse or more neurotic situation, depending on the environment and conditions that instinctual desire encounters during this time. But, in general, the Ego, which had been strengthening throughout early childhood, will now be threatened again by the forces of the It, now awakened by hormonal development. On the other hand, the demands and ideals of the Superego will also play an important role in restructuring the balance or by further accentuating the conflict. When the Ego is beset by the demands of a tyrannical Superego, it will be filled with somewhat unconscious feelings of anguish and guilt. When it is the It that imposes itself over the Ego, however, there will be a tendency to compulsively search for sexual and aggressive gratifications that will not be exempt from intense feelings of guilt. The intensity of the crisis and the outcome will depend, then, on the strength of the impulses of the It, the Ego's degree of tolerance toward erotic drives, and the nature of the defense mechanisms, however adequate, as well as the type of environmental pressures and influences.[31]

This new psychodynamic situation must also be understood from the perspective of the revival of the childhood Oedipal themes during this time. During the latency phase, they are somewhat dormant, but now they resurface with force in order to find a definitive resolution. It is a time when the world of desire will take shape, although mainly determined by the previous psychobiographical events.

This reactivation of the Oedipal contents and the need to finally accept the law of desire while renouncing incestuous bonds is what operates as the nucleus of the emotional shock of adolescence. It is to say goodbye to the old objects of love, which sometimes caused depression, as well as activating the prototypical adolescent manic defense.

This is why the adolescent is so often a sad being, one who does not understand the reasons for the feelings of grief nor comprehends the manic defenses with which he tries to escape from his depression, his singing, laughing, and jumping in order to avoid crying and falling apart.

Masturbation, so typical of this period, often brings back unconsciously unresolved issues of childhood Oedipal conflict. It is there that we can find an explanation for guilt (not always conscious) that this type of behavior so easily awakens. Masturbation produces many ghosts that cause fears, anxieties, and guilt in the unconscious realm. In this sense, it is illuminating to revisit the views of the medical field on this subject, beyond the areas of morality. Masturbation was associated with endless mental and physical illnesses, with

31. See Anna Freud, *The Ego and the Mechanisms of Defense* (London: Karnac, 1933).

theories that make us smile today, but that in their time enjoyed great prestige and credibility among scientists.[32] Based on his statements on the subject, we see that Freud himself was an inheritor of prejudices and objections that betray the ghosts that were nestled in the mentality of his time. In his work *Heredity and Aetiology of Neurosis* (1896),[33] for example, he sees onanism as a cause for neurasthenia. And, in the prolonged debate on the topic that began in 1912 within the Vienna Psychoanalytic Society, almost everything was focused on the harmful nature of masturbation and, above all, "A fixation of infantile sexual aims may be made possible, and a persistence of psychical infantilism. Here we have the disposition for the occurrence of a neurosis."[34] It will take time for the psychoanalytic field to view masturbation as a phenomenon that, corresponding to a variety of behaviors, can be placed within the range of normality as well as pathological symptomatology.

Only the investigation of the fantasies that accompany it (conscious or unconscious) can we clarify the meaning to which said sexual behavior corresponds. Sometimes, masturbation is simply an attempt at self-affirmation, a kind of self-assertion in the face of authority that the youth sees as antagonists to his desire. But, in this period, it generally responds to an attempt to move from a narcissistic to an object-focused dynamic. From the dense autoerotism where the adolescent dynamic dwells (favored by the rapid transformation of the boy's or girl's body into the body of a man or woman), the young person also tries to navigate the sea of love objects. The imaginary world that accompanies masturbation reveals that attempt to seek and face what is beyond self and family, what previously preoccupied the youth's interest.[35] As earlier stated, the Superego's tolerance for the erotic pulls will also correlate to the conflict that results from this type of behavior. It should be noted that masturbation that becomes compulsive is likely manifesting a childhood conflict that has not been resolved and could lead to narcissistic stagnation. In any case, the problem does not lie so much in the masturbatory activity itself but rather in the latent conflicts that it points to.

When looking at the psychodynamics of adolescent desire, the homosexual dimension (which we will discuss in an upcoming chapter) should also be considered. It is more externalized than in other periods of life and highlights that Oedipal revival (in its inverted dimension) that is characteristic of this time as well as the difficulty that the adolescent experiences in approaching the other sex. The "intimate friendships" characteristic of this

32. Francisco Álvarez Uría, "El sexo de los niños," *Serie psicoanalítica* 4 (1983): 55–93.

33. Freud (1896d), "Heredity and Aetiology of Neurosis," in *Standard Edition*, 3: 143–56.

34. Freud (1912f), "Contributions to a Discussion on Masturbation," in *Standard Edition*, 12: 243–54.

35. An interesting study was done by André Alsteens, *La masturbation chez l'adolescent* (Bruges: Desclée de Brouwer, 1967).

stage reveal that latent homosexual current, with great discretion and exhibitionist nuances, as well as in the jealousy and possessiveness that characterizes these type of friendships. Same-gender friendships give stability and offer protection against the discomforts that the opposite sex arouses in the adolescent.

Sometimes, there can be explicitly homosexual behaviors (usually in the form of mutual masturbation) that do not have the power to reorient the emotional-sexual dynamics in that direction. Moreover, the alarmism and drama that this type of situation has produced on occasion seems clearly counterproductive. If a structuring of desire has not already been configured along those lines, these behaviors will hardly lead to a definitive homosexual orientation.

The ghosts that relate to the opposite sex are also those that spring forth from the platonic crushes so characteristic of this age. The beloved figure is filled with an aura of perfection that brings the youth closer to the parental images lingering in the inner world itself. That is why these platonic loves are also limited to the purely tender and affective components, leaving aside the most explicitly erotic and genital elements. It has been said, and rightly so, that the first love during these stages unconsciously has a lot to do with the first true love—the one that took place in the Oedipal stage with the figure of the mother or father. The separation between the tender and erotic aspects is what most clearly harks back to the parental representations. The challenge that arises for the adolescent, then, is to reunify those two aspects that had to be separated by the Oedipal situation in order to encounter the love object and conquer it outside the realm of the familial. This will be one of the key points in the maturation of desire, which we will focus on in the next chapter.

BIBLIOGRAPHY

Ajuriaguerra, Juan. *Psychiatrie de l'enfant*. Paris: Masson, 1971.

Baldwin, Alfred L. *Behaviour and Development in Childhood*. New York: Dryden Press, 1951.

Bereczki, Tamas, and Petra Gyuris. "Oedipus Complex, Mate Choice, Imprinting: An Evolutionary Reconsideration of a Freudian Concept Based on an Empirical Study." *Mankind Quarterly* 1 (2009): 71–94.

Blasi, Carlos H., and David F. Bjorklund. "Evolutionary Developmental Psychology: A New Tool for Better Understanding Human Ontogeny." *Human Development* 46 (2003): 259–81.

Block, Jack. *Lives through Time*. Berkeley, CA: Bancroft Books, 1971.

Blos, Peter. *On Adolescence: A Psychoanalytic Interpretation.* New York: Free Press, 1962.

Blum, Gerald S. *Psychoanalytic Theories of Personality.* New York: McGraw-Hill, 1953.

Bornstein, Marc H., Deborah L. Vandell, and Karen S. Rook. *Lifespan Development: Infancy through Adulthood.* Boston: Cengage Learning, 2010.

Bowlby, John. *Child Care and the Growth of Love. London: Penguin Books, 2014.*

———. *Maternal Care and Mental Health.* Northvale, NJ, and London: Jason Aronson, 1995.

Buss, David M. Evolutionary Psychology. New York: Wiley, 2005.

Carducci, Bernardo J. *The Psychology of Personality: Viewpoints, Research, and Applications.* Hoboken, NJ: John Wiley & Sons, 2009.

Chausseguet-Smirgel, Janine, ed. *Female Sexuality: New Psychoanalytic Views.* Ann Arbor: University of Michigan Press, 1970.

Dolto, Françoise. *Séminaire de psychanalyse des enfants.* Paris: Seuil, 1985.

Erikson, Erik H. *Childhood and Society.* London: Hogarth, 1965.

———. *Identity: Youth and Crisis.* New York: Norton, 1968.

———. *The Life Cycle Completed.* New York and London: Norton, 1988.

Freud, Sigmund (1905d). *Three Essays on the Theory of Sexuality.* In *The Standard Edition of the Complete Psychological Works of Sigmund Freud*, edited and translated by James Strachey, 7: 125–245. London: Hogarth, 1966.

——— (1908b). "Character Anal and Erotism." In *Standard Edition* 9, 167–75.

——— (1908c). "On the Sexual Theories of Children." In *Standard Edition* 9, 205–16.

——— (1912f). "Contributions to a Discussion on Masturbation." In *Standard Edition* 12, 243–54.

——— (1916–1917). *Introductory Lectures on Psycho-Analysis.* In *Standard Edition,* 15.

——— (1918b). *From the History of an Infantile Neurosis.* In *Standard Editio,* 17: 7–122.

——— (1923a). "Two Encyclopaedia Articles." In *Standard Edition,* 18: 235–59.

——— (1940a). *An Outline of Psycho-Analysis.* In *Standard Editio,* 23: 23–207.

Hurlock, Elisabeth B. *Developmental Psychology.* New York: McGraw-Hill, 2001.

Kastembaum, Robert, ed. *Encyclopedia of Adult Development.* Phoenix, AZ: Oryx Press, 1993.

Klein, Melanie. *Envy and Gratitude and Other Works 1946–1963.* London: Hogarth, 1975.

Klein, Melanie, and Joan Riviere. *Love, Hate and Reparation.* New York: Norton, 1964.

Kohut, Heinz. *The Analysis of the Self.* New York: International Universities Press, 1971.

———. *The Restoration of the Self.* New York: International Universities Press, 1977.

Lacan, Jacques. *Formations of the Unconscious: The Seminar, Book 5.* Cambridge, UK: Polity Press, 2017.

Lebovici, Serge, and Michel Soulé. *La conaissance de l'enfant par la psychanalyse.* Paris: PUF, 1973.

Lerner, Richard M. *Concepts and Theories of Human Development.* London: Psychology Press, 2001.

Mahler, Margaret. *The Psychological Birth of the Human Infant Symbiosis and Individuation.* New York: Basic Books, 2000.
Migone, Paolo, and Giovanni Liotti. "Psychoanalysis and Cognitive-Evolutionary Psychology: An Attempt at Integration." *International Journal of Psychoanalysis* 79 (1998): 1071–95.
Monedero, Carmelo. *Psicología evolutiva y sus manifestaciones psicopatológicas.* Madrid: Biblioteca Nueva, 1972.
Mussen, Paul H. *The Psychological Development of the Child.* Englewood Cliffs, NJ: Prentice-Hall, 1963.
Piaget, Jean. *Intelligence and Affectivity: Their Relationship during Child Development.* Palo Alto: Annual Reviews, 1981.
———. *Psychology and Epistemology: Towards a Theory of Knowledge*. Harmondsworth: Penguin, 1972.
Rank, Otto. *The Trauma of Birth*. New York: Dover, 1993.
Rascovsky, Arnaldo. "Beyond the Oral Stage." *International Journal of Psychoanalysis* 37 (1956): 286–89.
———. *El psiquismo fetal*. Buenos Aires: Paidós, 1960.
Rof Carballo, Juan. *Urdimbre afectiva y enfermedad.* Barcelona: Labor, 1961.
Slavin, Michael Owen, and Daniel Kriegman. *The Adaptive Design of the Human Psyche: Psychoanalysis, Evolutionary Biology, and the Therapeutic Process*. New York: Guilford Press, 1992.
Spitz, René. *Anaclitic Depression: Psychoanalytic Study of the Child.* New York: International Universities Press, 1946.
———. *The First Year of Life.* New York: International Universities Press, 1965.
———. *No and Yes: On the Genesis of Human Communication.* New York: International Universities Press, 1948.
This, Bernard. *Naitre*. Paris: Aubier-Montaigne, 1973.
Vasse, Denis. *L'ombilic et la voix.* Paris: Seuil, 1974.
Winnicott, Donald W. *The Child and the Family*. London: Tavistock, 1957.
———. *Collected Papers: Through Paediatrics to Psychoanalysis.* London: Tavistock, 1958.
———. *Playing and Reality.* London: Tavistock, 1971.
Zulliger, Hans. *Die Pubertät der Kanben.* Vienna: Hans Huber, 1972.
———. *Die Pubertät der Mädchen*. Bern: Hans Huber, 1976.

Chapter Five

Accepting the Absence

It is a long journey. Endless in some ways because the primal aspiration to eliminate all manner of separation and difference is also never ending. But desire's aspirations can and should be guided so that those dynamics can become a propelling force for life and not a cause for destruction. Desire, as we explained earlier, can manifest as false illusion or as hope, as delirium and insanity, or as *a breath of life*, as the exhilaration that opens a creative doorway to reality. To achieve this, we will have to gradually accept our condition as *separate beings* until we fully recognize our lack of being, that very absence that is etched into the heart. Only in this way can we liberate ourselves from the illusion that deceives us, to access a dynamism grounded in a reality that can envision something greater. It is not an easy road, nor can it be easily described. Therefore, before attempting to do so in these pages, we should attempt a thorough analysis of the various concepts of the said process.

MATURITY: A CHALLENGING CONCEPT

Many difficulties arise in trying to define maturity. This is probably one of the reasons the field of psychoanalysis has used this term so cautiously. Various interpretations throughout time and in different cultures alert us to the many possible meanings. Being wise or just might have been the ideals of a mature person in Greek or Jewish cultures. In the Middle Ages, however, spirituality, contemplation, and aestheticism were prioritized. Being moderate has been an ideal of maturity within the Stoic tradition, the idea surfacing time and again throughout history from antiquity until the Renaissance. The force of reason and the notion that man should be guided by this principle became the prominent ideal during the Age of Enlightenment. In modern times, we find that maturity becomes notably psychologized, losing some of the moral connotations of times past.[1] Now in postmodern times where individualism has become the norm, maturity revolves around the concept of self-esteem, a subject that we will look at more closely in the chapter dedicated to narcissism.

In reality, concepts and ideas about maturity are heavily conditioned by sociocultural beliefs and biases. This makes finding an appropriate definition quite a challenge, as does diagnosing and evaluating it. Whether consciously or unconsciously, individuals may include their own highest ideals and values for life in their concept of maturity: pleasure, happiness, mysticism, intelligence, altruism, and so on.

Groups and institutions also tend to develop parameters to determine who is mature, making a judgment about individuals based on whether they fall within the norms explicitly or implicitly understood. At times, there may even be individuals who, through a normal process of maturation, will question the group or institutional dynamics. They will then be labeled as immature or unbalanced and referred to a psychotherapy specialist who will use the norms of the institution to indoctrinate the individual. There will be no shortage of specialists willing to carry out this exercise in conformity.

Besides, it is important to point out that personal growth always involves a complex set of processes at various stages. In effect, maturity involves some basic biological components without which development on higher levels would not be possible (it would be hard to argue, for example, that a child can emotionally mature in the anal stage if he has not previously reached the necessary control of the sphincter that permits the control of defecation). Cognitive, social, and other processes are implicated and mutually interact—they progress at different rates, making it difficult to provide an overall assessment. When a young person has matured in the cognitive areas (according to Jean Piaget, at fifteen, youth can already make use of logical thought), he is still far from achieving some key traits of social or emotional maturity. We are thus forced to surmise that maturity is a process that is never fully completed. It is a *utopia* that should encourage us to persist on this unseen path while striving to reach the elusive finish line. Nobody is ever fully mature. Furthermore, accepting that each of us is a product of our past that has marked us with indelible

1. An overview of how the understanding of maturity has evolved can be found in Juan José Zacarés and Emilia Serra, *La madurez personal. Perspectivas desde la psicología* (Madrid: Pirámide, 1998). See also Domenic Antonucci, *Maturity Models* (London: Kogan Page, 2014).

joys and tribulations will perhaps be the surest sign that we are on the right track to personal maturity.

THE PSYCHOANALYTIC CONCEPT OF PSYCHOSEXUAL MATURITY

Concepts related to maturity are scarce in psychoanalytic literature. It is telling that *maturation*, as well as related terms, seems to be missing in psychoanalytic dictionaries and encyclopedias (in contrast to the treaties or manuals related to humanist psychology, for example). Sometimes, we find references to human growth and development along the lines described in the previous chapter. But in this description of development, the goal of such a process is not defined, only the possible hindrances that could slow or derail such a process. That is, only possible fixations, regressions, or conflicts are addressed. But, in general, the final objective of such an evolution is not stated, or, in some cases, it is mentioned in a very general way. For example, Austrian-American psychoanalyst Ludwig Eidelberg defines maturity as the gradual development of the psychic apparatus that is determined simultaneously by the central nervous system in direct relation to the environment. A fully mature person would be one that is relatively independent of external objects.[2] In other cases, maturity has been understood in essence, as an adaptation to the circumstances of an individual's everyday environment, regardless of whether the environment is a healthy one or not. As Eliane Amado Levy-Valensi affirmed, the goal of psychology is not to force the individual to conform to his environment as if this were a given reality but rather to encourage the dynamics of personal evolution within and beyond that environment.[3] This is the type of psychoanalysis that has been used, especially in North America, as yet another type of social control. As we have seen, beliefs and biases have also impregnated the psychoanalytical lack of interest in the idea of maturity.

Freud's take on this subject is worth considering. Without a doubt, it is in his *Three Essays on the Theory of Sexuality* where we find our first clues. Here, we learn about a final stage of libidinal development, which he considers key for attaining sexual maturity. This would be the *supremacy of the genital stage* and the parallel convergence of the other partial childhood drives. Freud affirms, "The complete organization is only achieved at puberty, in a fourth, genital phase."[4] One may say that this stage indicates maturity, or at the very least, that

2. Ludwig Eidelberg, *Encyclopedia of Psychoanalysis* (New York: The Free Press, 1969), s.v. "maturation."

3. See Eliane Amado Lévi-Valensi, *Les voies et les pièges de la psychanalyse* (Paris: PUF, 1971).

4. Sigmund Freud (1940a), *An Outline of Psychoanalysis*, in *Standard Edition* (London: Hogarth, 1966), 23: 151.

maturity is now possible. There is not much more to it than that. To Freud, adult sexuality is nothing but the achievement of the unification of the various infantile urges, which were previously independent, partial, and autonomous in their quest for satisfaction, such as the oral, anal, phallic, exhibitionist, voyeuristic, sadistic, and masochistic drives and so on. As we will later see in the chapter dedicated to homosexuality, psychoanalysis in later times had to rethink how that criteria for unification called *genital organization* was understood. In some ways, despite the revolution in thinking that was happening during Freud's time, he continued to be influenced by ideas of sexuality that were prevalent in his time, where the norm was based on biological instinct and, therefore, in the capacity for sexual relationships that lead to procreation.

Nevertheless, from the Freudian perspective, it is evident that adulthood and a developed sense of desire mean something more than simply being capable of having sexual relations based on physiological readiness followed by the subordination of the so-called *partial drives*. That ultimate *genital stage* goes beyond sexual competence on a physical level. In one of his writings titled "*Wild" Psycho-Analysis*,[5] Freud remarked that there were many "crazy people" out there who made love daily, and he squarely negated the type of psychoanalytic treatment that merely prescribed the maintenance of sexual relations. If one forgets about the emotional aspect, which Freud refers to as *psychosexuality*, one strays far from the true psychoanalytic vision.

The so-called *supremacy of the genital stage* involves a whole series of profound dimensions of the psyche that are not always easy to assimilate. In either case, instinctual desire, as previously defined, must encompass other aspects beyond mere physical sex in order to evolve. Within this expansive backdrop where sexuality emerges, there should be other similarly expansive aims through which maturation and adequate expressions of desire can take place.

It is interesting to note that Freud defined the aim of psychoanalytic treatment as early as 1904, saying that it "will never be anything else but the practical recovery of the patient, the restoration of his ability to lead an active life and of his capacity for enjoyment."[6] Years later, in 1923, he persists, in more detail, with the same idea, "The aim of the treatment is to remove the patient's resistances and to pass his repressions in review and thus to bring about the most far-reaching unification and strengthening of his ego, to enable him to save the mental energy which he is expending upon internal conflicts, to make the best of him that his inherited capacities will allow and so to make him as efficient and as capable of enjoyment as is possible."[7]

In other words, Freud viewed love and work as the foundation that allows a person to achieve balance and maturity. These two elements will serve as

5. Freud (1910b), "'Wild' Psycho-Analysis," in *Standard Edition*, 11: 221–27.
6. Freud (1904), "Freud's Psycho-Analytic Procedure," in *Standard Edition*, 7: 253.
7. Freud (1923a), "Two Encyclopedia Articles," in *Standard Edition*, 18: 251.

a springboard for reflecting on the challenging concept of maturity. It is here where we will find our way to desire in a ripened form, aware of what we have experienced until that moment. In subsequent chapters, we will explore particular ways of maturing within the various expressions of desire.

LOVES THAT KILL

These two dimensions of balanced adulthood are not independent of each other. Work and love, or in broader terms, desire and goals, are intimately connected—they exhibit a mutual interdependence within individuals. As we will explore in the chapter dedicated to sublimation, the work, understood as a project for the transformation of one's reality, is fed by both work and life, which could also be called a *labor of love* (with the risk of becoming an infantile, neurotic, or perverse love). This will be discussed in more detail in a subsequent chapter, but, for now, we will focus on the maturation of desire, that is, in the capacity to have interpersonal relationships, in the ability to love and be loved.

But first, we must preface this discussion by mentioning that *love*, in Freud's estimation, is one of the most misunderstood concepts.[8] When we say love, we might be referring to relationships maintained solely for sexual satisfaction (sometimes referred to as *making love*), or the positive feelings between parents and children or between siblings, or in broader terms we might be referring to altruism or love for humanity as a whole. Or, as is often spoken about nowadays, of self-love. Love can manifest in a wide variety of ways, anywhere from relationships with other individuals to interactions with the sacred (love of God) or even with how we relate to ideas and things.

But just as our love objects can manifest in various ways, so can the methods by which we express that love. Love, in the purest psychodynamic sense, is a wish for union, a want for closeness, and with that, a desire to eliminate all the separation and differences that interfere. For this reason, love is vulnerable to tremendous ambiguity. *There are loves that kill*, goes a wisdom-filled Spanish saying. The clinical psychologist has the opportunity to attest to this in his practice on a daily basis.[9] Love can be a search for oneself through the mirror image of another, it can express itself as a somewhat latent wish for closeness and strong need to be appreciated, it can manifest as desire for passive and dependent bonding, or

8. See Freud (1930a), *Civilization and Its Discontents*, in *Standard Edition*, 21: 102.

9. See "L'amour," *Revue Française de Psychanalyse* 60 (1996); André Green & Gregorio Kohon, *Love and Its Vicissitudes* (London and New York: Routledge, 2005); Leon L. Altman, "Some Vicissitudes of Love," *JAPA* 25 (1977): 35–52; Ignacio Gárate Martínez, "Del amar y sus riberas," *Clínica y análisis grupal* 22 (2000): 69–81.

as a form of dominance and control (alongside aggression), all within the same dynamic that we continue to refer to as *loving*. It can also represent a strategy and a shield (as in a *reaction formation*)[10] in the face of great conflict. Or one can look for the experience of love purely for the sake of loving, for the feelings it invokes, using the subject as a mere instrument to obtain satisfaction. Hysteria is not proof of loving another; it is love for the sake of loving itself, even when it involves sacrifice, with an apparent selflessness almost to be admired. It has been said, and not without reason, that nobody loves like a hysterical person. But we can't forget that we are talking about a love that undermines the very condition needed for maturation: a respect for individuation and difference. Therefore, the capacity for love does not equate to maturity; rather, we must specify which type of love we are talking about. To that end, we will dedicate some words in the following reflections.

RENOUNCING TOTALITY

It must be stressed once again, that it is only through the acceptance of our condition as *separate beings* that desire can evolve. Only through the laborious task of recognizing our separateness, of the acceptance of lack that constitutes us and that initiates the stage of symbolism and language (like the stage that propels us into the unavoidable presence-absence), can we be motivated by desire. Only then can we be liberated into the search of its realizations (always partial) and through it live a more dynamic life, while avoiding the delusions, which when taken to the extreme, become a type of insanity.[11] For it is only from the acceptance of absence, from the acceptance of the solitude of which we are made, that a world of possibility opens up, making it possible to have the type of love that gives life, which unlike hysteria, mutilates and kills.

That recognition of lack (which would perhaps be a good indicator that the psychoanalytic process has concluded) does not lead to, despite what we might expect, to look upon life with a sense of absurdity or disappointment. On the contrary, it is that lack that allows us to know ourselves, to know others and reality itself. It is a true encounter, for it is no longer born of a necessity to devour and annihilate the one who changes or grows further

10. This is the term used to describe the defense mechanism by which one behaves contrary to one's true unconscious desire.

11. The difficulty in accepting that separation can be expressed in many ways. The psychosomatic realm is very telling. It is the body that, many times, reveals the resistance to separation, voicing what the conscience will not. "All my asthma problems disappeared when I sent my mother to hell," explained a psychotherapy patient, an only child, who was told that he had no siblings so that he could be the sole recipient of everything his parents had to give. On this subject, see the theory of José Bleger, *Symbiosis and Ambiguity: A Psychoanalytic Study* (New York: Routledge, 2013).

apart. A true encounter results from a desire that recognizes this lack, and from there, manifests as a petition to another who is free and unique. It is not about blindly imposing one's self on another, oblivious of the other's language or unconscious mind. From the recognition of the absence, the other can blossom, as a man or as a woman, and they can become companions on the journey of life. The world becomes a springboard for creation, meaning, and possibility.

In effect, we are referring to the acceptance that we will never be everything to anyone, nor will anyone be our all. As distinct beings, our greatest opportunity is to be companions to one another, supportive of one another in the various ways in which one can be caring, in the passionate love of couples, in the intimate commitment of friendship, in the solidarity of brotherhood, always, however, with the understanding that those companions will never try to eradicate the separateness and difference that reflects our innermost need. All encounter and communion between two subjectivities is simultaneously presence and absence, opaqueness and transparency.

Desire's temptation to create a love fusion means, in the long term, destruction of that love because fusion implies the destruction and disappearance of the individuals who exchange that love. Desire is always born as the possibility of a true encounter in the person who is well grounded in their subjectivity, that is, in those who have been able to accept their fundamental deficiency, those who have avoided getting lost in the maelstroms of pursuits that pacify one temporarily. Only in this way will one be able to approach another, accepting them as *other*, in other words, as separate and unique.

At the same time, it will now be possible to have an intimate encounter with one's own self because the *good internal objects* prevail over ones of a threatening nature, ones that cause a perpetual escape from reality. In this way, one even learns to love solitude, for it facilitates an encounter with the self, with a type of communion, one that is a fountain of internal wealth and a method for more authentic encounters with others.[12] Antonio Machado said it best with the following verses: "I converse with the one who is always by my side / he who speaks alone hopes to speak to God someday / my soliloquy is conversation with this good friend / who showed me the secret of philanthropy."[13] For only those who are capable of being in touch with their internal world will be able to have meaningful exchanges with others.

Charles Blondel apparently said that psychoanalysis turned human beings into pigs, miserable pigs. Through this statement, psychoanalysis is perceived as a mere invitation to liberate the instinctive tendencies—this is far from a cor-

12. Along these lines, it is worth looking at Françoise Dolto, *Solitude* (Paris: Gallimard, 1994); Carlos Domínguez-Morano, "La soledad," *Sal Terrae* 95, no. 8 (2007): 639–50.

13. Antonio Machado, "Retrato," in *Poesía Completa. Campos de Castilla* (Madrid: Espasa-Calpe, 1979), 132.

rect understanding of the objectives of the analytical process. Let us recall once more Freud's critique in *"Wild" Psycho-Analysis* of how analytical therapy could be wrongly understood.[14] Although the statement attributed to Blondel does highlight an important part of the analytical process, which is a process of being let down, so to speak, which is confused with its final goal or objective. There is a whole process of mourning in psychoanalytic treatment—that is to say, grieving over letting go of the fantasies that made life bearable but which hampered the relationship with life itself. It is normal then to go through a "healthy depression" in order to face one's own existence, with all its potentialities and limitations. This would also be a requirement for accepting others, beyond the claims of totality attributed and demanded of them. From that starting point at the end of the analytical process, the world opens up as a potential for creativity and encounter.

LEAVE THE HOUSE OF YOUR MOTHER AND FATHER

But we have already seen that only after a long and complex process it *is* possible to accept the responsibility of that innate lack. And during the long journey, an Oedipal scenario presents itself at the level of the psyche, one where physical separation at birth and the cutting of the umbilical cord culminates and becomes consecrated. We saw it in the previous chapter—in some way, at the Oedipal level we are reborn, by accepting and owning the separation that takes place through the mediation of the paternal symbol. As it was with Abraham in Genesis, whom God instructed to leave his father and mother's house and go unto an unknown land. In essence, it is a personal story that unfolds as a creative encounter between self and others.

To leave the father and mother's home behind is thus a great achievement in the evolution of desire. But the process is never easy nor can it be done overnight because we are talking about something more significant than just leaving a physical place. It is about severing those early parental ties, to the old loves and hates associated with those parental representations, in such a way that future relationships are not conditioned by the aspirations of those representations and thus prolonging them.

Throughout life, many substitutions are made for those primary representations that define our childhood emotional landscape. From early on, teachers formed a link in the chain of parental transfers. Later, they became mythical figures, heroes or social leaders, perhaps a boss, higher-ups, or figures of authority in general (doctors, priests, healers) or even, as we will see later on, our friends, or even our spouse. Our initial source of attachment was thus pro-

14. Freud (1912b), "'Wild' Psycho-Analysis," in *Standard Edition*, 11: 221–27.

longed and condensed into these other relationships. This transference won't always be through a codependent lover relationship. It can also take place within a rebellious and aggressive relationship. In either case, both scenarios make it difficult to extricate oneself from the internal representations in order to achieve autonomy, independence, and liberty in our current relationships. Simultaneously, the other will never truly be another. He or she will become a ghostly parental representation, whether loved or hated, blurring the line between self and other.

However, the departure from the parental home will not be possible if those early established relationships did not allow for the introjection of some *good objects*,[15] strong enough to allow for encounters with what is distinct and different. Said in another way, if the *good mother and father* are not incorporated parts of oneself, an eventual external search for their substitutions will be unavoidable.

Metaphorically, a good maternal object would provide a basis for a cohesive narcissism, balanced, which, as we will see in the chapter dedicated to this subject, would also be a wellspring of self-esteem and confidence.[16] A good internalized paternal object will enable the meeting of goals, ideas, future projects, and personal development, said another way, the synthesis of the ego-ideal, which is worthy of pursuit yet reasonable. That ego-ideal would have to maintain an appropriate separation between the ego's realistic goals and its idealized ambitions, to have a healthy tension between *what is* and *what should be*, without creating an unrealistic chasm between the possible and the ideal. As Freud pointed out, "we see people falling ill just as often when they discard an ideal as when they seek to attain it."[17] In the cases in which the tension is excessive, the ego succumbs to a state of frustration, vulnerable to feelings of inferiority. The individual feels that he is not living up to the goals that ego-ideal has put forth.[18]

An aspect that is intimately related to the paternal metaphor and the ego-ideal is the feeling of guilt, one of the great challenges the human mind has to grapple with. Unfortunately, this is a complex issue that goes beyond the

---

15. These terms, important in post-Freudian psychoanalysis like the Melanie Klein school of thought, denote an unconscious experience or fantasy of a concrete object physically located inside the ego, which has its own motives and intentions toward the self and toward other objects. The existence of good or bad internal objects is mainly driven by encounters with external objects. Internal objects are, so to speak, mirrors of reality. But they also reflect, through projection, the experience and perception of these same external objects. See Robert Douglas Hinshelwood, *A Dictionary of Kleinian Thought* (Oxford: Free Association Books, 1998), s.v. "Internal Objects."

16. Heinz Kohut and Miriam Elson, eds., *The Kohut Seminars: On Self Psychology and Psychotherapy with Adolescents and Young Adults* (New York and London: Norton, 1987); Heinz Kohut, *The Restoration of the Self* (New York: International Universities Press, 1977).

17. See Freud (1912c), "Types of Onset of Neurosis," in *Standard Edition*, 12: 234.

18. See Freud (1930a), *Civilization and Its Discontents*, in *Standard Edition*, 21: 59–145.

scope of this book.[19] Suffice it to say that the relationship between desire and guilt are intimate and profound. Specifically, within the vast area of desire, the erotic and sexual easily produce the feelings of guilt that, so often, are purely unconscious. There is no sex without law, and as such, feelings of guilt can easily pervade sexual encounters, despite the changes in how we think and experience sexuality—as previously described in the chapter dealing with the social aspects of desire. A sense of guilt that is impervious to rational arguments, like the issue of masturbation that we saw in the previous chapter because it is tied to a variety of unconscious defenses foreign to the logic of the conscious mind. A guilt that in many cases is not even consciously felt but rather seeps into other areas of experience, seemingly outside of morality. Certain fears, phobias, problems of a psychosomatic nature, and frustrated acts of destructiveness are often expressions of a guilt linked to the world of desire that have never expressed themselves as such in the conscious mind. Therefore, the task of properly managing feelings of guilt is complicated, difficult, and continuous.

When we speak, then, of incorporating an internal paternal object that promotes adequate ideals and manages feelings of guilt, we are referring to a critical step in the evolution of desire. Of knowing how to express guilt when one has been hurtful (because the purpose is obviously not to completely bypass feelings of guilt) and knowing how to activate mechanisms of reparation for that damage caused. Also, knowing how to not be overly critical about oneself after a rational analysis of one's actions. In short, the ability to negotiate one's feelings of guilt, the ability to express conformity or nonconformity with them, agreement or disapproval, is a critical task for an adult. This task implies having attempted to incorporate the paternal metaphor that, on the one hand, accepts the separation that the paternal symbol represents and, on the other, avoids the need to resort to external sources through which to attain a verdict of guilt or innocence.

THE RENUNCIATION OF CHILDHOOD OMNIPOTENCE

Leaving the father and mother's home and the incorporation of the paternal and maternal aspects as guiding internal life objects implies renouncing the totality that typifies childhood desire. Desire that has not been organized, structured, or limited by law has perilous aspirations. *Everything now!* Goes the childhood mantra. However, the appropriate incorporations of the paren-

---

19. I have delved into this subject in my work titled *Belief after Freud* (London and New York: Routledge, 2018), 119–44.

tal figures mean an acceptance of one's limited capabilities, that chance and limitation are the parameters within which we must operate in this life.

Limitation and circumstance, acknowledging that we could have been born or not, because our very existence is based on the desire of others (a tough concept for childhood desire to swallow). The finite also, which conveys the impossibility of achieving the satisfaction of so many of our individual desires, and at times for much of humanity, the lack of the most basic of necessities. Circumstance in the face of nature, of the corporal, health and illness, and with the context within which our lives have unfolded. Circumstance and limitation, that of being inescapably bound to death, as the greatest denial of the ultimate aspirations of desire, which insist on rejecting the human condition time and again. "What, we ask, is the attitude of our unconscious towards the problem of death? The answer must be: almost exactly the same as that of primaeval man. . . . Our unconscious, then, does not believe in its own death; it behaves as if it were immortal."[20] This is how Freud expressed himself in a text titled *Thoughts for the Time on War and Death.*

Giving up childhood omnipotence, renouncing that unrecognized but important wish to be gods, it is that condition that truly empowers us to be human—limited, dependent, and finite. The only one that has been given to us and, on the other hand, the only one that gives us access to the plenitude that can be ours. The only one that is also capable of converting our desire into a wellspring of balance, focus, and well-being and not the force that when unchecked sweeps us into a whirlwind of emotion.

Diverging from the psychoanalytic perspective, Spanish physician, historian, author, and philosopher Pedro Laín Entralgo brilliantly expressed what the renunciation to the infantile omnipotence supposes. When he was asked what human maturity meant, he responded like this: "It is to recognize that much of one's potential will never come to fruition, to know that one cannot be reborn tomorrow, to feel that death can arrive at any moment and for no particular reason, and in fully experiencing what one is in the moment or might still be."[21]

The renunciation of that childhood omnipotence, of the secret yearning to be a god, becomes most apparent in how we tackle the various frustrations that life unexpectedly confronts us with and in how we avoid lashing out against the sources of frustration or ourselves. When constrained, the omnipotent childhood desire fights back against the sources of limitation (parents or educators) or redirects the rage or anger toward oneself. The child, *his sovereign majesty*, does not accept limitations placed on his desire. Growing up and maturing implies the serene acceptance that our desires can

20. Freud (1915b), "Thoughts for the Times on War and Death," in *Standard Edition*, 14: 296.
21. Pedro Laín-Entralgo, *Sobre la amistad* (Madrid: Revista de Occidente, 1972), 230–33.

be hindered, denied, reduced, all the while subduing the destructive violent reactions that could unfold.

Violence has accompanied desire from the start. Sucking became biting during breastfeeding. Later on, the obligatory acceptance of the hygienic norms during the anal phase became intertwined with forms of aggressiveness of a sadistic or masochistic sort. The need to conform to the law that reigned in the incestuous desire during the Oedipus stage caused a violent synthesis of love, hatred, and guilt. In its reactivation during adolescence, violence resurfaced in the form of nonconformity, aggressive self-affirmation, and also guilt and depression—all as types of self-aggression. Aggression, then, intersects with desire in complicated and significant ways throughout life.[22]

At times, it seems as though aggression rules desire and desire becomes aggression's lackey for its destructive ends. That vitality then becomes bitterness, resentment, cruel irony that is reflected in the sinister characters portrayed so artfully in literature or cinema. The management of the aggressive components that accompany desire, like it or not, plays an important role in an individual's psychodynamics and ability to become emotionally balanced. These aggressive components will flow in various unexpected directions, depending on our ability to renounce the primitive omnipotence that appeared to be ours.[23]

In this sense, we should recognize that a sense of humor is one of the unmistakable signs of maturation in the process of accepting the limitations and contingencies of reality. Therein lies a paradoxical victory over that reality to which one has submitted, as a necessity for survival. Through the lens of humor, the dissatisfaction that causes the renunciation of one's own desires in order to accept reality becomes a pleasure and a type of *revenge* over those limitations.

Freud made an astute observation in a brief and suggestive text on the subject.[24] He explains that, through humor, the ego buffers one from offense and delays suffering caused by reality—it insists on not being affected by the traumas of the outside world. At times the ego even attempts to turn those experiences into sources of pleasure. "Humour is not resigned; it is

---

22. These issues are explored in Erich Fromm's work *The Anatomy of Human Destructiveness* (New York: Holt, Rinehart, and Winston, 1973); also Juan Rof Carballo, *Violencia y ternura* (Madrid: Espasa, 1988); Françoise Neau, *Cruautés* (Paris: PUF, 2014); "Violence et destruction," *Revue Française de Psychanalyse* 48 (1984): 917–1093; Hede Menke-Adler, "Violence-Destruction-Transformation," *Revue Française de Psychanalyse* 81 (2017): 255–58; James Gilligan, "Toward a Psychoanalytic Theory of Violence, Fundamentalism and Terrorism," *International Forum of Psychoanalysis* 26 (2017): 174–85.

23. We will not delve into the possibility of original destructive drives here, as formulated by Freud (1920g) in *Beyond the Pleasure Principle*, in *Standard Edition*, 18: 1–64.

24. Sigmund Freud (1927d), "Humour," in *Standard Edition*, 21: 159–66.

rebellious,"[25] Freud tells us. In this refusal to submit to the circumstances of reality, humor would seem, from a psychopathological perspective, to show a regressive and reactionary side. And yet, by not ignoring or distorting reality (through hallucination) but contemplating it from another perspective (that of a loving and protective superego, says Freud), the rejection of suffering becomes possible—lifting the Ego above the outer world and able to astutely and triumphantly sustain the pleasure principle. Humor thus becomes an intelligent and nonpathological means of rejecting the real. The result is a beneficial and euphoric release.

Humor shows us that being in contact with and accepting reality does not obligate us to adopt a stoic and resigned philosophy. Rather, we can develop a relationship with humor where desire opens up a greater array of possibilities than what mere childhood fantasy could provide us.

OPENING ONESELF TO THE PRESENCE

Indeed, the previous set of reflections on the impulses of desire and the conditions for its evolution could lead us to believe that the key to maturity lies essentially in renouncing, abandoning, and limiting desire and accepting rules and laws. In short, a somewhat negative way of looking at individual maturation. However, we cannot lose sight of the fact that, although it is necessary to carry out this important task of renunciation and dispossession, all of this has a very positive end goal—having an epiphany about the other, the manifestation of otherness, the opening to presence, which arises only when the mists of omnipotence and childhood narcissism from which we all originate vanish. Because instinctual desire does not only expose our *lack of being* but also our *appetite for being*.

When we have reached the recognition of our *lack of being*, it essentially opens up the possibility of having a true encounter with the other, with that uniqueness of a free and distinctive self. The *other* is no longer an object of partial satisfaction, a breast or a mouth with which to savor a taste or calm a hunger. He is an *individual*, an integral reality that, with a unique subjectivity and, with liberty to respond, can say yes or no. In short, that person can be an object of satisfaction but also of frustration since the individual does not necessarily match the fantasy of a *total good object*, which always and fully satisfies. It is the perpetual novelty of the other's desire.

In essence, the ability to encounter an individual with newness and freshness implies having overcome that need to reduce the other to being a mere object of dependence or something for domination and control. In an adult

25. Freud, 163.

position, the other ceases to be looked upon as a source that supplies while one passively receives nourishment, all the while overlooking one's own capacity for offering and giving. In the same way, the other cannot be reduced to a mouth that must receive what an individual, representing a good and powerful chest, insists on giving. Both ways of relating to one another within relationships indicate depressive or manic dispositions in which the most primitive oral components of affectivity are activated in these different modalities. The adult capacity to love is established only when a mutual exchange is possible, in freedom, in the gifting and in the requesting, in the offering and in the petition.

This free exchange also skirts the enormous temptation to convert or reduce the other to an object of domination and control, a relationship in which the other's freedom is seen as a threat to the possessive urges that seek to enclose them, thus forcing the other into the object of his desire. In this situation, the relationship is tinged with a markedly aggressive and destructive dimension. The desire of the other is experienced as a danger, so an attempt is made to reduce it to a minimum and, if possible, to eliminate it altogether. Pleasure is related to the suffering of others. But, also, there can be complicity that results in a relationship that is impregnated with a sadomasochistic flavor, sometimes overt and sometimes more subtle, and in which the active sadistic and passive masochist alternate roles. Furthermore, these types of relationships are not always as obvious as they are in Buñuel films. Frequently, within even the most refined areas of culture or spirituality, we witness the types of relationships where the other is annihilated, controlled, or dominated. Or one may submit unconditionally by denying one's own will and desire.

The types of relationships established from either dependence or domination and control exhibit traces of the primitive stages of development, those that in the previous chapter we saw related to the oral and anal phases of libidinal development. Only then, in overcoming these stages and being able to integrate what Freud called the *genital stage* is it possible to encounter the other in a way that honors the separateness and the difference between them, in a relationship of interdependence that overcomes infantile dependence and allows for the establishment of a relationship that is cooperative and in harmony, one where there is a healthy degree of give and take.

But, as we already saw, the genital stage to which Freud refers goes beyond the mere ability to establish a fulfilling sexual relationship. It assumes the subordination of the so-called *partial impulses* (oral, anal, exhibitionist, and so on) in light of that global encounter that is established and the subordination, therefore, of the feelings and affections that correspond to those first stages of libidinal evolution. From this position of adulthood, this encounter acquires a global character. It is the individual who, as an integrated being, seeks out the other, who is also an integrated being, distinct and free. A deeply empathetic communication can be established with this other because by respecting the separation that helps keep confusion at bay, one can see oneself in another's shoes. It is as if one becomes the other person momentarily while knowing that this can never be.

Within this type of encounter, the sexual relationship can embody all the dynamism inherent in the world of desire. It expresses that fundamental aspiration to eliminate the separation that defines us as *separate beings*. But, at the same time, in a sexual relationship established from this level of maturation, the other is not confused with an object that is incorporated or acquiesces. And although that melding of bodies comes to represent the most explicit realization of the desire for union, those bodies know that they are defined by language, which expresses the separation they are forced to recognize. In his film *The Last Tango in Paris*, Bernardo Bertolucci masterfully showcases the harm that can result when bodies try to kill the language by which those individuals recognize each other as distinct individuals, free and unique in their ability to give and receive.

In the sexual encounters that occur from a place of maturity, however, the deepest, oldest, and most primitive strata of instinctual desire also plays a role. Contents that have to do with the first stages of the libidinal evolution, that is to say, all the feelings of oral or anal nature, with their specific impulses and longings, come into play in the encounter with the other. Displays of exhibitionism and sadism or masochism can also intervene. But they do so in a way that is subordinated to that discovery of a wholeness and uniqueness seen in the other. The encounter attempts to bridge the distance that separates them; to suppress the limits that confine them; and, at the same time, to recognize that it is impossible to eliminate those differences and distances. The sexual relationship and the mystical experience (which is often expressed in terms of erotic and intimate encounters) are both attempting to reveal desire's greatest aspiration for union, which in effect defines us all and, at the same time, acknowledging the impossibility of that union erasing the separation and uniqueness that define us.

From the place of adult affectivity, that is, of a desire that has previously been organized by law, a place that accepts the difference of the sexes and that has clarified one's psychosexual identity, pleasure is not seen as a threat that forces a withdrawal. By not aspiring to the totality and absolute supremacy that was maintained during childhood, an individual understands the opportunity and right to experience pleasure without anguish. Sexual dysfunctions like frigidity, impotence, and premature ejaculation would not find a place in mature affection. Likewise, from the assimilation of that law of desire that separated the tender feelings toward parents and the erotic, we can now experience union with the other who is no longer a mere reflection or substitution for those parental figures. With this other, therefore, the unification of tenderness and erotic sexuality becomes possible while avoiding the situation described by Freud, where, as he says, those who are loved cannot be desired, and those who are desired cannot be loved.

Thus, by leaving the father and mother's house and embarking on the unknown journey, that is, the adventure that is willing to take a risk from that place of loneliness common to us all, we can then get a glimpse of other beings, each unique and singular, wherein desire in its various forms finds its joy and satisfaction. Let us tackle, then, those diverse expressions where desire sets off in search of its object.

BIBLIOGRAPHY

Altman, L. L. "Some Vicissitudes of Love." *Journal of the American Planning Association* 25 (1977): 35–52.

Antonucci, Domenic. *Maturity Models.* London: Kogan Page, 2014.

Bleger, José. *Symbiosis and Ambiguity. A Psychoanalytic Study* (Hove, UK, and New York: Routledge, 2013).

Bowlby, John. *Attachment and Loss.* Vol. 1, *Attachment.* New York: Basic Books, 1969.

Bruner, Jerome S. "Nature and Uses of Immaturity." *American Psychologist* 27 (1972): 687–708.

Dolto, Françoise. *Solitude*. Paris: Gallimard, 1994.

Domínguez-Morano, Carlos. "La soledad." *Sal Terrae* 95, no. 8 (2007): 639–50.

Erikson, Erik H. *Identity: Youth and Crisis*. New York: Norton, 1968.

Erikson, Erik H., and Joan M. Erikson. *The Life Cycle Completed.* New York and London: Norton, 1982.

Fierro, Alfredo. "Dimensiones de la personalidad sana." *Revista de Psiquiatría y Psicología Médica de Europa y América* 16 (1984): 373–371.

Freud, Sigmund (1904a). "Freud's Psycho-Analytic Procedure." In *The Standard Edition of the Complete Psychological Works of Sigmund Freud*, edited and translated by James Strachey, 7: 247–54. London: Hogarth, 1966.

——— (1910k). "'Wild' Psycho-Analysis." In *Standard Edition*, 11: 221–27.

——— (1915b). "Thoughts for the Times on War and Death." In *Standard Edition*, 14: 273–300.

——— (1915c). "Instincts and Their Vicissitudes." In *Standard Edition*, 14: 109–40.

——— (1919e). "A Child Is Being Beaten." In *Standard Edition*, 1: 175–96.

——— (1923a). "Two Encyclopaedia Articles." In *Standard Edition*, 18: 235–59.

——— (1924c). "The Economic Problem of Masochism." In *Standard Edition*, 19: 155–70.

——— (1927d). "Humour." In *Standard Edition*, 21: 159–66.

——— (1930a). *Civilization and Its Discontents*. In *Standard Edition*, 21: 59–145.

——— (1940a). *An Outline of Psychoanalysis.* In *Standard Edition*, 23: 139–207.

Fromm, Erich. *The Anatomy of Human Destructiveness.* New York: Holt Rinehart & Winston, 1973.

Gárate Martínez, Ignacio. "Del amar y sus riberas." *Clínica y análisis grupal* 22 (2000): 69–81.

García-Monge, José Antonio. *Treinta palabras para la madurez.* Bilbao: Desclée de Brouwer, 1997.

Green, André, & Gregorio Kohon. *Love and Its Vicissitudes.* London and New York: Routledge, 2005.

Gilligan, James. "Toward a Psychoanalytic Theory of Violence, Fundamentalism, and Terrorism." *International Forum of Psychoanalysis* 26 (2017): 174–85.

Heath, D. H. *Fulfilling Lives: Paths to Maturity and Success. The Jossey-Bass Social and Behavioral Science Series.* San Francisco, CA: Jossey-Bass, 1991.

Kiefer, Christie. *The Mantle of Maturity: A History of Ideas about Character Development.* New York: State University of New York, 1988.

Kohlberg, Lawrence. *The Psychology of Moral Development.* New York: Harper & Row, 1984.

Laín-Entralgo, Pedro. *Sobre la amistad.* Madrid: Revista de Occidente, 1972.

"L'amour." *Revue Française de Psychanalyse* 60 (1996).

Lévi-Valensi, Eliane Amado. *Les voies et les pièges de la psychanalyse.* Paris: PUF, 1971.

Menke-Adler, Hede. "Violence-Destruction-Transformation." *Revue Française de Psychanalyse* 81 (2017): 255–58.

Neau, Françoise. *Cruautés.* Paris: PUF, 2014.

Rof Carballo, Juan. *Violencia y ternura.* Madrid: Espasa, 1988.

Sheldon, Kennon M., and Tim Kasser. "Getting Older, Getting Better? Personal Strivings and Psychological Maturity Across the Life Span." *Developmental Psychology* 37 (2001): 491–501.

Smelser, Neil J., and Erik Erikson, eds. *Themes of Work and Love in Adulthood.* Cambridge MA: Harvard University Press, 1980.

"Violence et destruction." *Revue Française de Psychanalyse* 48 (1984): 917–1093.

Zacarés, Juan José, and Emilia Serra. *La madurez personal. Perspectivas desde la psicología.* Madrid: Pirámide, 1998.

Part II

EXPRESSIONS OF DESIRING

Chapter Six

Love and Couples

It is the most basic manifestation of desire. It wells up through the experiences of love and romance and is buoyed by the needs of biology and society.

The biological dimension, which is the bedrock of instinctual desire, undoubtedly strengthens the alliance between the genders that ensures the survival of the species. The evidence brought forth by evolutionary psychoanalysis might even lead us to believe that behind the romantic ideal of the couple's union there is nothing but a biological need for survival of the species. From one perspective, the pairing behavior between humans seems much more akin to that of lower animals than we would like to admit. Hence, how we have come to this markedly Darwinian way of understanding the human pairing phenomenon.

Theories such as those espoused by David M. Buss have had a significant impact on how we think about this subject.[1] He conducted a study on the matchmaking process between more than ten thousand people from thirty-seven different cultures. In his study, he addressed sexual strategies, how to attract a partner and hold on to that person, the conflict between the sexes, and more; these criteria are all seen as fitting into the biological molds that ensure survival and propagation of the species according to evolutionary needs. In short, the ultimate motivations of seemingly tender and romantic behaviors,

1. David M. Buss, *The Evolution of Desire* (New York: Basic Books, 1994). A thorough study was done by Jacques Ruffié, *De la biologie à la culture* (Paris: Flammarion, 1976). Also recommended, Bianca Acevedo et al., "Neural Correlates of Long-Term Intense Romantic Love," *Scan* 78 (2012): 145–59. These sociobiological theories have had many adherents and have even inspired numerous television documentaries. Henri Laborit's theory was used as the basis for the script of the famous Alain Resnais movie, *My American Uncle* (1980), in which we simultaneously witnessed the protagonists in a typical love triangle and the behavior of some mice subjected to "analogous" scenarios in the laboratory. As some commentators have pointed out, it is as though not even the director of the film believed in his cowriter Henri Laborit's theories.

in reality, would only correspond to mechanisms imposed by the biological instinct of species survival. There are clear parallels between animal and human behavior (shocking sometimes, but simultaneously a good antidote to human pride), and the differences are not as many as we might think. However, it also seems evident that the transformations that society and culture have imprinted on biological instinct would lead us to believe that, here too, there has been a real qualitative leap relative to other species. This qualitative leap became possible by the same biological structures in their dialectical relationships with the environment.[2]

Simultaneously, the pairing methods in different cultures have been molded and configured according to the specific interests of the group. Economic, political, and religious interests that go beyond the purely biological are critical. For this reason, the union between man and woman has never been a private matter but rather a public event that has striven to uphold the prevalent societal norms.[3]

Instinctual desire, then, is expressed in this realm by those two basic biological and sociocultural pillars. We will set these aside, however, to focus specifically on the longing that underlies the biological stratum and runs through the institutional and cultural dimensions. And, where longing is concerned, we find the phenomenon of falling in love as the launching pad for the couple (as is the case for homosexual pairs, which we will address in the next chapter), whether this becomes socially recognized as a marriage or a domestic partnership or whether opting out of any formalisms.

THE "MADNESS" OF FALLING IN LOVE

There is no phenomenon in life that so vividly reveals the workings of instinctual desire as falling in love. Indeed, this phenomenon starkly reveals that lack within us and, at the same time, the desire to satiate that lack. Instinctual desire, therefore, imposes itself in a way that everything else, the external world with all its complexities and demands, becomes secondary. The psyche of the lover is fully absorbed by the sensation of being in the presence of the ideal good object that has arrived to fulfill all of his or her expecta-

---

2. The cephalic explosion that occurred in the 500,000 years after the appearance of *Homo erectus* was the consequence, rather than the cause, of new behaviors that required problem solving beyond the purely instinctive. The use of objects, the birth of language, and the division of labor were critical to the transformation of the anthropoid brain in man, thus making it possible for ecology to make its way to culture. See José L. Pinillos, *Principles of Psychology* (Madrid: Allianza, 1975), 52–55.

3. See André Burguière, dir., *Histoire de la famille* (Paris: Armand Colin, 1986), also Margaret Mead's classic *Sex and Temperament in Three Primitive Societies* (New York: Harper Collins, 2019) where she demonstrates how many things attributed to the biological instinct are, in reality, sociocultural products.

tions, to satisfy his or her shortcomings, to embody the hope for a perfected communion. Freud affirms that in the culmination of a love relationship one loses interest in the outside world; the lovers themselves are sufficient—"In no other case does Eros so clearly betray the core of his being, his purpose of making one out of more than one."[4]

But we all know that love is blind. That is to say, that the lovers' sense of affection operates in a world of illusion where the perception of the loved one is colored and transformed by one's own need and demand for union without end. It is the illusion, the great illusion, of eliminating once and for all that separation and difference that define us as *distinct beings*. There is, in this sense, a break from reality that seems to uphold that wise old saying that "love is blind." Nor is Freud exaggerating when he describes falling in love as "the normal prototype of the psychoses"[5] because there is, like in a state of psychosis, an obvious disconnect from reality. When lovers meet, the external world dissolves and almost disappears, completely absorbed in the intense experience of communion. In each other, they create the means to promote and experience a fantasy linked to the most primitive stages of the psyche, and all this with an intensity that undermines the external elements and circumstances of reality in which they will need to function.

But, at the same time, we also have to understand that we are talking about a *normal* type of psychosis because it is an experience that, while it moves us away from the external outer reality, also brings us closer to the underlying reality of who we are. Thus, rarely do we have access to experiences like falling in love that so accurately divulge our delusion and detachment from reality and, at the same time, our truth, the evidence of the underlying authenticity that is us.

In this sense, the idea expressed by Freud on more than one occasion that infatuation is only an indicator of sexual need, that once satisfied, vanishes, and that only the awareness that that need resurfaces is what leads to the phenomenon of falling in love, is highly debatable. Sexual love, then, necessitated tenderness.[6] The understanding of instinctual desire that we have established in which the genital need is only one among several factors would lead us to conclude, rather, that falling in love reflects a deeper and more essential thirst and that it corresponds to an attempt to eliminate that separation and difference that each of us experiences from birth.

It is a *normal psychosis*, which as we shall see, becomes a necessary process and a prerequisite for ensuring the stability and strength of the couple's bond. The illusory component of falling in love, which as we know makes it a

4. Sigmund Freud (1930a), *Civilization and Its Discontents*, in *Standard Edition*, 21: 108.
5. See Freud (1912–1913), *Totem and Taboo*, in *Standard Edition*, 13: 89.
6. See Freud (1921), *Group Psychology and the Analysis of the Ego*, in *Standard Edition*, 18: 111, 112.

phenomenon of blindness, eventually fades, giving way to the lovers' sense of otherness. The initial fantasy, however, will continue to matter in the relationship in some way and will also continue to nurture the relationship that develops over time. That coupled relationship, which in particular nowadays seems to be based on emotional bonds, can hardly be sustained if it has not been submitted somehow to that phenomenon of emotional overflow, the excitement, the hope, and the pain that are all felt in the process of falling in love.[7] No longer are economic and social factors the main considerations in coupled relationships. The relationship is almost entirely based on the experience of meeting and communicating. Though the phenomenon of falling in love does not imply, as we will see, any guarantee of stability, it can be said that these types of relationships do necessitate the *falling in love* period to be sustainable. In short, falling in love appears to be a phenomenon that is both insufficient and necessary in today's society. Many relationships can be maintained with a good dose of *goodwill*. The romantic couple does seem, however, to need that singular experience of falling in love, which itself can take on many forms.

THE ROOTS OF ROMANTIC LOVE

A phenomenon as unique and intense as falling in love must have important motivational factors as well. And, indeed, they exist—and they are deep and significant.

In the emergence of the process, indeed, a whole series of latent tendencies, of idealized images, of unknown expectations, of unconscious fantasies that had lain dormant for a long time, awaiting, are awakened and activated. During this time, everything may seem radically new, unexpected, and exciting. And yet a whole set of internal factors existed beforehand, as if waiting for the right moment to manifest. The infatuation thus triggers the release of a series of unconscious models, which were built alongside complex processes during childhood and adolescence. Without a doubt are those experienced through the identifications and counteridentifications based on the parental images.[8] When love is reciprocated and two people become coupled, impulses, anxieties, and desires are exchanged with the partner.

7. We saw in chapter 3 how love was not always a requirement for marriage in the past, as it is today. It was, rather, economic and social factors that influenced marriage and family. Even today, there are discussions about whether members of royalty in modern monarchical countries, such as those in Europe, may or may not enjoy the same freedom to choose a partner based on feeling, rather than public and social interests.

8. To this end, see Freud (1921), *Group Psychology and the Analysis of the Ego*, in *Standard Edition* 18: 111–16; see also *Revue Française de Psychanalyse* LX (1996) where the content (*L'amour*) addresses this issue. See also Karin Sternberg, *Psychology of Love* (New York: Springer Publishing Company, 2014); Francesco Alberoni, *Falling in Love and Loving* (New York: Random House,

Additionally, each one has a fantasy about the other but also fantasizes about how one is perceived.[9]

We already saw in chapter 4 how the parental figures were the first love objects. The aspirations and demands of instinctual desire revolved around them. What at that time we called *the law of desire*, however, restrained those first attractions. The only appropriate feelings toward parents were those of tenderness. Feelings of the erotic sort had to be subjected to a repression process. But we also saw how, in puberty, these tendencies resurfaced and forced the renunciation of the first love objects while incorporating tender feelings of an erotic sort directing them toward new love objects outside the family. But these new objects have to correspond somehow to the internal images obtained through instinctual desire's first fixations. Only in this way will an individual be able to bear the burden of affection linked to the internal representations that sprang from the parental figures. Through the process of falling in love, instinctual desire, after a long wait akin to one who has been diligently preparing an important project, finds its sought-after object and satisfies an early nostalgia. French psychologist Charles David describes a phenomenon in which the new object appears with a brightness that illuminates the self and fills one with a sudden splendorous clarity that makes one feel alight and exulted. The ideal image, the unconscious prototype of the beloved, thus merges with its representation, embodied in the lover.[10]

But it is those activated internal representations that both largely determine and cloud the real perception of the same person who awoke them. The lover somehow becomes an excuse for that whole world to resurface and reactivate. The triggering factor may remain hidden for those experiencing the phenomenon. It could have been anything, the color of someone's eyes, the tone of voice, a simple gesture, anything could innocently lead to a *crush* and invite the accumulation of internal images with their respective emotional loads.

All this brings with it that characteristic tendency of idolizing the lover. Strong surges of emotional intensity are transferred from the Ego to the love object, broadening those internal images that are activated by its presence. That infatuation thus transforms the narcissistic libido, deposited in the

---

1983); A. Balfour, "The Couple, Their Marriage, and Oedipus: Or Problems Come in Twos and Threes," in *Oedipus and the Couple*, ed. Francis Grier (London: Karnac, 2005), 49–71.

9. Along these lines, see Antoni Bobé, "Mecanismos inconsciente en la elección de la pareja," in *Conflictos de pareja. Diagnóstico y tratamiento*, comp. Antoni Bobé and Carles Pérez Testor (Barcelona: Paidós/Fundació Vidal i Barraquer, 1994), 35–40; David E. Scharff and Jill Savege Scharff, eds., *Psychoanalytic Couple Therapy* (London and New York: Karnac, 2014); Amita Sehgal, "Family and Couple Psychoanalysis: A Global Perspective," *British Journal of Psychotherapy* 35 (2019): 487–89; Molly Ludlan-Viveka Nyberg, *Couple Attachments: Theoretical and Clinical Studies* (London and New York: Routledge, 2007).

10. See Charles David, *L'état amoureux* (Paris: Payot, 1971), 245; Ayala M. Pines, *Falling in Love: Why We Choose the Lovers We Choose* (New York: Routledge, 2005).

Ego, into object libido, transferred to the beloved.[11] The Ego, says Freud, becomes less demanding and more modest, and, also, the object becomes more and more magnificent and precious, until it embodies all the love that the Ego had felt for itself.[12] The person in love, as we well know, can forget about himself, humble and lower himself as needed, surrender to the wishes of the other, and even at times neglect his habits and essential needs. His surrender to the loved one is similar to the relationship of the hypnotized toward the hypnotist.

But one could say that the idealization of the beloved[13] is very self-interested, as it attempts to mirror the desired internal representations. As a result, it unconsciously eliminates those aspects that might cast doubt on those deepest desires. Particularly, in the early stages of the relationship, there is no room for aggression, only the positive current of affection. Even more so if the love is not reciprocated. In this scenario, the idealization increases, prohibiting the other's reality to dampen the effect of the projected fantasy. The object has taken the place of the Ego Ideal.[14]

The idealization that takes place in the process of falling in love is related to the particular psychodynamics of each individual. This idealization exhibits the particular hue with which each one colors his internal world from his particular psychobiography and the type of demand that has arisen there. Everyone has his or her own unique and usually unconscious motives to fall in love in a particular way and with a certain person.

In psychoanalytic literature, Freud made a well-known distinction between two essential ways of forming a romantic relationship. The first one is essentially driven by the search for someone representing the internal image of the mother or the father. Maternal or paternal images internally spun from the dialectical relationship established and that, therefore, suggest a psyche in which external elements are mixed with one's own needs and fantasies. But, in short, it is a way of choosing the love object that somehow reflects those principal actors in our life. It could be the search for a woman who recalls that first childhood love or the search for a man who rekindles the introjected image of the father figure. The choice of women or men, therefore, is directly

11. As we will see later in the chapter dedicated to narcissism, Freud distinguished a narcissistic from an object-oriented libido, according to whether the focus was on oneself or something external. See Sigmund Freud (1914), "On Narcissism: An Introduction," in *Standard Edition*, 14: 67–100.

12. See Freud (1921), *Group Psychology and the Analysis of the Ego*, in *Standard Edition*, 18: 113.

13. Psychoanalytic theory differentiates between idealization and what we'll analyze later as sublimation. In the latter, as we shall see, instinctual desire is transformed, by transcending its primary objectives and renouncing them, and can access another objective through a process of symbolization. In idealization, however, instinctual desire does not change or alter its objective. It is only the object that is viewed differently through the process of exaltation.

14. Freud (1921), *Group Psychology and the Analysis of the Ego*, in *Standard Edition*, 18: 113. Freud compares infatuation with melancholy—there too, the ego is ruled by the object.

or indirectly related to that first childhood love, the mother who fed or the father who protected.[15]

The choice in a partner can also be influenced by the search for a maternal or paternal counterimage, that is, by someone who very much departs from those early models and, in that sense, clearly motivated by an attempt to flee the frustration felt toward the parents and by the idealized image that was internally developed in that undesirable situation. But, even in these cases, we see that sometimes in those relationships that tried so hard to avoid those negative parental traits by finding a very different type of partner, they will eventually find themselves echoing those very qualities within this relationship. These are some of the unconscious dynamics that become practically unavoidable.

But according to the models proposed by Freud, let us recall that there is another way of falling in love. It involves the search for the parallel image of oneself, that is, an object-choice in accordance to a narcissistic model in which one unconsciously intends to recover something analogous to what one is—thus, searching for something as identical as possible to one's own reality. Or, to what one used to be and which time or circumstances forced one to abandon—childishness, naivety, rebelliousness, perversity, and so on. Or to what one hoped to be or could have been—dreams that, for one reason or another, went unfulfilled. Or, still, to what was once a part of the person, for example, the case in which one intends to restore that union with the mother, projecting on to the other an object that represents oneself, to revive that old love that time forced to leave behind. To love and be loved like in those early times.

We see that this overidealization of the object that is so typical during the process of falling in love occurs either through the seeking of those deep images of the first love of the parental figures or with how the individual relates to oneself. But ultimately, they bolster the claim that every object found is not, in fact, but a rediscovered object.

These relationships, however, are complex and may very well lead to the integration and stability of a couple, or they may, on the contrary, expose a certain amount of conflict or incompatibility. The relationship that is born from these unconscious fantasies can, as in any living process, transform itself by repairing damage while broadening horizons, or it can, on the other hand, open wounds and deepen the imbalances concealed buried deeply within. All these intense emotions that arise when falling in love can, therefore, nourish the process of personal growth or launch a dangerous dynamic of destruction. Ultimately, falling in love seems to be a process

15. This type of relationship leads individuals to identify with the image of the same-sex parent, possibly perpetuating the internalized ideas of the parental couple.

without which one can hardly think of a future life as a couple, but, at the same time, due to the unconscious roots that nourish it and the emotions that feed into it, can lead both to a balanced enriched life or drag one toward a dangerous decompensation.

DANGEROUS LIAISONS

There is nothing like falling in love to show us so clearly that, rather than *having* a feeling, we are *had* by feeling. Seemingly, the phenomenon takes over the individual in such a way that it often leaves little to no room for maneuvering. Whether one likes it or not, depending on the circumstances, the experience of feeling polarized by the attraction to the love object taints everything. Hence, literature, in its various manifestations, has both praised and cursed this tidal wave of feeling that drags one and overwhelms any personal desire or will.

All of this suggests that falling in love can sometimes lead to situations that can become quite conflictive and problematic. In many ways, the awakening of romantic love can cause great difficulty for those who experience it, weakening the person or even causing his downfall. Falling in love, then, creates an experience that allows for both the best and the worst that can occur in a person's life.[16]

As we explored in chapter 2, the objects of desire may be forever ignored, split off from conscious thought through repression. The object remains in the realm of the unconscious, only occasionally revealing partial and distorted aspects. A series of complex processes intervene so that these desires remain suppressed. Our deepest aspirations can clash and become incompatible. Hence, why we all, to one degree or another, experience conflict. Through falling in love, that is, when an aspiration facilitates a relationship, the individual may very well be reduced to hosting the scene of a battle, participating only as a suffering spectator.

One of the reasons falling in love can become a trap for an individual is because that feeling of love can spring from emotions that are not in harmony with the whole person, including its conscious and unconscious aspects. In other words, the relationship was established in the realm of feeling and now imposes itself in a space that was excluded and that now rejects it. Sooner or later, a conflictive situation will develop. Freud's structuring of personality in the so-called second topic, that is, in the categorization of the *Id*, the *Ego*,

---

16. W. Colman, "The Intolerable Other: The Difficulty of Becoming a Couple," *Couple and Family Psychoanalysis* 4 (2005): 22–41.

and the *Superego*, can help us better understand the type of situations that we are trying to describe.[17]

Sometimes, the relationship between two people originates within the dark throws of passion and, due to their association to repressed elements of the *Id*, are not able to harmonize with the ideals that the *Ego* was developing. The love bond is fed by the individual's suppressed dimensions, colliding with other concerns as the relationship tries to take shape. It is as if a dark past surges up to the present, unbalancing the harmony that was attained over time. But the infatuation is so strong that it also prevents a type of discernment that would ideally be needed to have a balanced life. The dark forces of the *Id* come forward on the margins of the psyche, deviating from the Superego's established ideals. One is thus split between two opposing forces that want to tear the individual apart. It is a love that takes over and that is deeply satisfying while at the same time refuses to completely align with the goals, interests, and attitudes that one had prioritized. A thousand attempts to rebuild the relationship are bound to fail a thousand times over because those opposing internal forces cannot find balance.

On other occasions, relationships are based on ideals that were established in earlier times and deeply felt (for example, religious ideals) but where other important aspects of the individual (for example, sexual inclinations) were relegated or repressed. Once the ideals start to erode either through personal development or changing life circumstances, the subconscious becomes aware of the futility of continuing the relationship. The relationship was inspired by the needs of the *Superego* but left out the most primitive aspects related to the *Id* and that are better suited to the type of human relations that romantic partnerships require.

They are, therefore, dangerous liaisons, romantic bonds that, far from providing balance and assisting personal development, either result in conflictive situations where one loses a part of oneself or simply lead to a failed relationship. They are the *impossible loves*, or *dangerous liaisons*, like those that appear in Stephen Frears's impactful film, in his adaptation of the novel *Les liaison dangereuses*.[18] The infatuation is an expression of instinctual desire that, when it emerges without having been properly integrated, and due to its intensity, can be one of the most turbulent experiences in a person's life. It is here that we most clearly see the potential that instinctual desire has, for both plentitude and destruction.

17. See Freud (1923), *The Ego and the Id*, in *Standard Edition*, 19: 1–66.
18. Christopher Hampson's novel was brought to the big screen (*Dangerous Liaisons*) by the English director Stephen Frears in 1988.

LOVE AS THE ARROW THAT FITS THE WOUND

It is easy to go astray where desire is concerned because someone's real intentions and wishes are not always clear. Hence, in the choice of partner, so many things can go wrong, and there are so many painful examples of *impossible loves* or *dangerous liaisons*. In other situations, however, desire seems to be able to hone in on the most authentically longed for object. This, however, does not have to mean that the seekers will attain something good in the finding. The outcome may result in a pathological or regressive fixation. It might be an attainable love, even a stable love. But it will be a reality and stability that will be costly for those who partake, just as Kafka alluded to when he said that the arrow fits the wound.

We cannot forget that couples have a synergistic relationship in which both parties feed off of each other, both consciously and unconsciously. The couple thus becomes a new psychic entity, made up of something greater than its parts. From this perspective, we can see that the nature of each part of the couple is in a constant relationship with the other part. They complement each other. The individual internal impulses, anxieties, desires, needs, and frustrations and come into contact and interact with the other's corresponding internal components. In that new psychic entity that the couple represents, any intrapersonal adjustment becomes an interpersonal adjustment and vice versa. Each couple thus builds their own inner world, a unique way of interpersonal relating, as well as way of relating to the external environment.[19]

From this new dynamic that results when two individuals come together as a pair, the phenomenon known as *collusion* can result. That is, a set of unconscious and hidden emotions between the two members of the couple can interact in secret complicity and can be problematic from the mental health standpoint. Each, then, as Spanish Catholic psychologist Antoni Gomis warns, plays mental games with the other, despite not knowing exactly what type of game they are playing.[20] And the game can sometimes be very dangerous.

Sometimes, these amorous relationships can be very intense and also very toxic. The alliance between the individuals can have the effect of magnifying the most regressive and childish tendencies of both. And by feeding off of each other, they can maintain an intense relationship, maybe even a stable one. Its stability, however, is based on satisfying childhood

---

19. To this end, see the excellent study by Antoni Gomis, "La prevención," in *Conflictos de pareja. Diagnóstico y tratamiento*, ed. Antoni Bobé and Carles Pérez Testor (Barcelona: Paidós/Fundació Vidal i Barraquer, 1994).

20. Bobé, 151.

needs that were never quite met but now find a way to mutually sustain and strengthen these wants.

In this way, a man anchored in childish desires of a sadistic type can find his coupled stability in a woman eager to maintain masochistic views within the relationship. Luis Buñuel's 1967 film *Belle de jour* masterfully illustrates the intensity that can be found in these types of relationships. In another scenario, a woman with a sense of envy and rivalry toward the masculine may find her match through a man eager to *rediscover* a castrating mother to whom he can submit, attaining a reciprocal give and take. The repressed masculine and feminine components of each partner can also intervene in a type of *collusion*, appeasing the other through his or her own denied aspects. The woman, from a male position, sustains and nourishes the man's unrecognized femininity and vice versa. This all occurs in a concealed manner, feeding off of each other in a way that neither would be able to declare openly. The pathology thus becomes structural, seemingly without conflict and, therefore, preventing the possibility of questioning or changing the dynamic. This scenario echoes the idea that the arrow fits the wound.

In other scenarios, the conflict comes to light within the same relationship in which it is established. Details of psychopathological aspects of instinctual desire go beyond the scope of these pages.[21] However, it is worth touching upon some of the types of bonding in which desire becomes entangled in an unhealthy way. These patterns showcase what can often occur in romantic relationships.

Among these problematic ways of pairing up, Freud highlighted the scenario in which a man seeks out women with dubious or questionable sexual history, or far from the pure and virginal ideals that others might actively seek.[22] In these situations, we see a sensuality and eroticism that is devoid of empathy and caring, which, as we saw in chapter 5, is necessary for a mature sense of instinctual desire. Accepting that the law of desire that required tender feelings to be separated from erotic ones in relationship to one's parents had to be revisited to be able to merge with another who was no longer a mere reflection or replacement of those parental figures. With the lover, it would now be possible to merge affectionate feelings with erotic and sexual ones,

21. Regarding the pathological aspects of couples, see Jordi Font, "Psicopatología de la pareja," in Bobé, 41–78. Here we find an elucidating analysis of five types of pathology including hysteria predominance (in relationships of alternating passion and rejection), obsessive (showing both reciprocal control and ambivalence), psychotic (overdependent and dangerously detached from reality), personality disorder (characterized by its instability and superficiality), and, finally, psychosomatic predominance (marked by obliviousness to mental conflict that is then manifested physically). Also, Vickie Bhatia and Joanne Davila, *Mental Health Disorders in Couple Relationships* (New York: Routledge, 2017).

22. See Freud (1910), "A Special Type of Choice of Object Made by Men," in *Standard Edition*, 11: 163–75.

overcoming the situation described by Freud in which those whom we love could not be desired and those whom we desire could not be loved.

The man who seeks what in exaggerated terms could be termed "love of prostitutes" is unable to love a woman who stirs feelings of tenderness, analogous to those his mother herself engendered. This type of relationship suggests a desire to *save* that woman from her depravity. Other men, however, will not be able to emotionally bond with a woman who is not pure or unable to prove her virginity. Freud and subsequent psychoanalysts analyzed these scenarios that echoed with Oedipal resonances. Only an *untouched* woman could attract his desire because only in this way could he connect with his childhood Oedipal aspirations, coveting an exclusive claim on the mother. Alternatively, women could also easily fall into the trap of feeling omnipotent in their desire to *cure* their beloved, in the same fashion as an upright mother would be able to mold and bring up her children according to her wishes. It is not unheard of for a woman to have believed herself capable of transforming the homosexual leanings of a beloved or in other cases to modify the perverse tendencies of her lover. Then, there are those who, usually unconsciously, look for someone who is already in a committed partnership and try to both strip the adversary of his love object and simultaneously win over that love object. This tendency of causing jealousy or subjecting oneself to jealous feelings can be a tactic in triangular relationships that produce emotional and sexual arousal.

It is easy, then, to misread desire, and easy to go astray. Relationships become unconsciously complicit, leading to unhealthy dynamics that are mutually reinforcing and particular to these interactions. On the other hand, few human experiences outside of romantic relationships can fulfill the deepest aspirations of instinctual desire; offer a direct channel of expression; and offer a basis through which to achieve stability, an enriched life, and personal fulfillment. The awareness that this is indeed possible is what largely motivates most human beings to seek partnerships in their lives. It is essential, then, to work to make this a tangible reality.

COMING BACK TO EARTH

The process of establishing a relationship based on love has distinct stages. From the first phase where *the crush* becomes apparent, we will move on to the next step, that of falling in love, with all the previously described symptoms, which will allow one to enjoy that *love blindness*, which elevates the other person and makes them immune to any reality outside the love experience. It is a stage that is often referred to as *the honeymoon period*. We should not diminish this stage, as it establishes an important emotional connection that will serve as support structures for the future. This period, in effect, is well suited for deepening reciprocal communication and, therefore, for increasing and expanding the range of emotional ties that appear spontaneously during its course.[23]

After the honeymoon period, however, there will be a progressive descent back to earth, with all its side effects and inconveniences, which return the lovers to a reality that once seemed distant. Undoubtedly, this process will have repercussions on the couple's future, having to now convert all of those romantic feelings into something viable in this new more grounded reality.

During this time, there is some degree of mourning. Mourning for the changes that coupled life demands for the individuals and the consequent renunciation of attitudes and behaviors that each one had led individually. And, more importantly, still, grieving for the loss of the fantasy that was felt during the falling in love and honeymoon period. The other's true nature becomes evident not only in what separates them but also in what differentiates them. The attempt by instinctual desire to eliminate that separation, which was in full display during the process of infatuation, becomes unworkable.

We saw earlier how this period of infatuation led desire to attempt to eliminate any trace of separation. But now, one must recognize that the lover is not the total good object once imagined but a real person who sometimes frustrates and other times satisfies and who cannot, therefore, mend that separation that would satiate our inner lack. A process of renouncing of infantile fantasies becomes necessary, fantasies that during the process of falling in love were necessary to generate interest and attraction.

By refusing to carry out a process of mourning, we cannot open up to the other, discovering aspects and values that had been previously overlooked. The internal images projected over the other had prevented these insights. But without a *reunion* of sorts, on a new and higher level, the sexual relationship will easily end up becoming banal, falling into a kind of routine. Sexuality needs to be a joyful expression of newness, of coming to terms with having to depart from certain fantasies, of the desire to remain committed to the other. One must be willing to discover new aspects of the partner, to attend to the other as a joyful guest who is always full of surprises and ever evolving. In short, couples will forever experience a mix of successes and frustrations, joy and suffering.

The challenge of transitioning from the fantasy of falling in love to the reality of the relationship will be experienced in differing ways by both members. Thus, it will be critical that they support each other through the

23. Jean G. Lemaire insists that the prognosis is bleak for couples that do not properly take advantage of the honeymoon period. This phase is well suited for engaging in deep and meaningful communication that will set a strong foundation.

depressions that this stage can cause. They must also restrain the feelings of anger and hostility triggered by the inevitable frustrations that come from the separation and differences that exist. At the same time, the couple will also need to be creative in finding new ways of connecting that are pleasurable and rewarding, replacing the excitement that was present during the crush period and subsequent falling in love. The earth also offers pleasures that were not found on the moon, however honey sweet they might have been. To discover these pleasures, however, the couple must end their euphoric trip to the moon and descend back to earth.

FREEDOM AND COMMUNICATION

We analyzed earlier how the maturation of instinctual desire occurs through the recognition of our *lack of being* as the only way we can have a true encounter with the other, with each one's specific peculiarities as free and unique individuals. Only in this way, can the individual cease to be an object of partial satisfaction, a chest or a mouth with which to calm hunger or feel nourished. Only then can the other become an individual who, from his essential subjectivity and a unique voice, can say yes or no. In short, one can be both an object of satisfaction and a source of frustration since one can never fully match the fantasy of a *total good object* that will always satisfy all of our desires. By being open to the other, we can find delight in the continual newness of the other.

For the couple to connect and harmonize, they each must renounce the fantasy of totality while being open to the other's reality as distinctive beings. Only the acceptance of the inescapable separation that is innate in us, accepting the absence, will allow us to understand the other, to celebrate that person, to relate to his particular triumphs, to empathize with his needs and anguishes, to take on pleasures and pains, and so on. This also implies avoiding the propensity to mold the other into the idealized union that instinctual drive longs for. In some way, the relationship must be driven by a fundamental respect for the other's freedom, of respect for the intimacy of one's desire. Only in this way is true companionship achievable, being mindful of the intimacy and exclusiveness that relationships usually entail. It is a type of companionship that should never nonetheless annul the inner sense of solitude that we all have within us.

Separation is thus unconquerable, and those differences between individuals will never be eliminated. For this reason, feelings of frustration and flare-ups of conflict will almost certainly be unavoidable. Disappointment, reproach, rivalry, and envy are feelings that can arise at any time within relationships. Therefore, identifying those feelings that will inevitably arise in the clash of personalities is of extreme importance. The difference must then be addressed through honest communication that is both direct (the *loving cruelties* that Spanish poet Gabriel Celaya described) and tender, balanced with understanding and mutual support. It is about that communication that is restorative and that accommodates the other's differences. Couples should not fear arguments. Those arguments bring about solutions to the reshaped identities that spring out of the relationship.

Only from identifying the conflictive elements within a relationship and verbalizing them properly can a couple be spared from degrading into a banal and confusing relationship. Clear, lucid thinking will come only after overcoming the most infantile emotions and from the liberation from those early affections that, on their own, would lead only to a rudimentary way of acting, unaware of underlying factors that cause relationship deterioration. In this sense, as Spanish psychologist Antoni Gomis affirms, the ability to think, or to have *insight*, understood as *an aptitude and attitude of emotional sensitivity* for understanding oneself, is critical for couples to avoid falling into chaos and unconscious behavior. When there is an absence of this type of self-reflection, when one is not aware of what is happening and able to verbalize it, the couple will fall into monotony and a routine expected from the social normative at best. Trying to resolve the problems outside of the relationship will also fail.[24]

An issue that directly affects a couple's communication is facing limitations, both inner and outer, with the world at large. On the one hand, the couple needs to establish its own internal dynamism of exchange and communication to create a particular space that is uniquely their own, well defined in relation to the external world. A space that, on the other hand, should not be too rigid, enclosing it in a *world apart*, oblivious to the surrounding reality. Setting clear yet sufficiently negotiable boundaries is the right course of action, though sometimes hard to enact.[25]

The couple's intimate and exclusive space must, therefore, be shielded from the sometimes invasive influence of the respective families. It is not an easy task because, so often, neither was able to entirely *leave the house of the father and mother*. This results in a double bind with the established family and, with the one in the making, generating internal division and tensions with one's partner. Maintaining a proper distance with the family that does not result in rupture will be a continual challenge. Regardless, each member in the relationship should understand that the relationship with the significant other will always imply a relationship with that individual's family, their

24. See Antoni Gomis, "La prevención," 158–59 and 172–73.
25. Jürg Willi, *Die Zweier-Beziehung* (Hamburg: Rowohlt Verlag, 1975).

particular mythology, their *legend*, and *saga*, with its allusions, attitudes, behaviors, and specific ways of resolving difficulties and conflicts. That *legend* is incorporated into the internal dynamics of the partner and will surface again and again in future interactions.

Nor should children invade the couple's exclusive space. Despite the significant emotional charge that maternity and paternity brings, children must learn to recognize that their parents require a space that belongs only to them and from which they are barred. In short, the parent identity should not equal the spouse identity, even for the sake of those children. The differentiation, then, of the couple's own relationship from all other types of relationships that must be maintained—it is an essential step in the formation of that new identity that each partner will need to create a strong love bond.

STRENGTHENING THE BONDS OF LOVE

To ensure the healthy evolution of the couple, awareness of *separation and difference* is not enough, nor the exclusive space that allows for open and frank communication. Within each relationship, a great effort will need to be made so that the love is reinforced, nurtured, and expanded into a range of transformed feelings and emotions.

The positive experiences must prevail over the negative, frustrating, or conflicting ones. It will be important, therefore, to ensure that there is a healthy give and take at every level. Because only in this way can there be a mature interdependence, which overcomes the needy and perpetual seeking of affection that seeks to dominate the other, with a parallel need to revolt when love is not given as expected. A mature interdependence means a couple can have a relationship of cooperation and harmony with well-differentiated objects and know how to maintain the feeling of autonomy within love. It does not infringe on the respect and freedom that we referred to previously, nor does it view the separation that lies between them as insurmountable.[26]

In the process of nurturing the bonds of love, sexual relations play a role of considerable importance. They tap into the most primitive roots of relationship and, because of the pure enjoyment that can be experienced, they also help to temper life's inevitable difficulties. It is an area, therefore, that both partners have to actively work at. Only in this way will sexual relations evolve creatively and offer an outlet for the new experiences that transpire as the

26. See Henry V. Dicks, *Marital Tensions* (New York: Routledge, 1967); Kira Birditt et al., "The Development of Marital Tension: Implications for Divorce among Married Couples," *Developmental Psychology* 53 (2017): 1995–2006; Kira Birditt et al., "Beyond Destructive Conflict: Implications of Marital Tension for Marital Well-Being," *Journal for Family Psychology* 33 (2019): 597–666.

relationship deepens and intensifies. Frank conversations addressing desires, struggles, fantasies, and fears will help the relationship to expand and grow.[27]

The bonds of love, within sexual relations and outside of them, should strive to meet emotional needs, all the while avoiding a fixation with those needs. Couples can experience primitive satisfactions that are seemingly regressive but that can be nurturing when experienced with awareness and presence. From a certain vantage point, it could be seen as a partial, provisional regression for the sake of the Ego, capable of recovery, providing clarity and stability from a place of love. The relationship, then, demonstrates the ability to accept the subject's oldest and most primitive past, while also being able to preserve the sense of wholeness that has been developed throughout one's life. At certain times, for example, a man may feel that his wife is making him feel nurtured and taken care of like a son, while a woman may feel protected by her husband in a fatherly sense. What is important, however, is that both individuals acknowledge that the other cannot be reduced to a parental object and that such experiences should not turn one into the mother or father but rather a partner.

We should also be wary of mistaking an attitude of pseudo-confidence and allusions of self-sufficiency with maturity when in reality one might be avoiding being vulnerable, unable to display tenderness and affection in times of need. In all likelihood, most men have been raised to express themselves as strong and independent individuals and, therefore, released from having to express any sort of deep emotion. That role has been reserved for women, who can easily take on the role of the weak partner in need of protection.

It is evident that, in the world of romantic love (particularly in the area of sexual relations), the oldest, most archaic and primitive tendencies can surface. The oral, anal, and phallic components of instinctual desire can find the means for expressing and fulfilling themselves. But all this must happen when the individual is developed and evolved and where those deep personality traits, having been incorporated at a higher level, are experienced differently than they would be in a true regression. In this way, the couple's love can harmonize past and present and, at the same time, have a synergy that creates a vision for the future.

FAREWELL TO THE MACHO

We must recall the great strides that women have made in society and the impact this has had on the psychodynamics of today's couples. In chapter

27. There are many books written about this subject. For starters, see Helen S. Kaplan, *The New Sex Therapy* (New York: Brunner/Mazel, 1973). See also Francesco Alberoni, *Il volo nuziale* (Roma: Garzanti, 1992).

3, we looked at the changes that have occurred in the sexual sphere for women due to scientific progress and, from there, how couples are viewed in general. A life that was almost completely focused on procreation and the upbringing of children gave way to a relationship in which the emotional and relational aspects lay a claim in time and space that would have been previously inconceivable.

Other social factors have contributed to the liberation of women's conscience that, without a doubt, has been the most important social revolution in the 20th century. The impact it has had on couples is evident and has manifested in the various predicaments that have resulted in this new reality. It is a complex subject that cannot be fully addressed in these pages. We only wish to highlight the most relevant psychodynamic aspects that influence relationships nowadays.

Ultimately, the impact of the women's liberation movement is such that it casts doubt on the traditional model for couples, so often introjected into men according to their own parental ideals. This generates bewilderment, perplexity, anger, and frustration that is difficult to assimilate and overcome. Marco Fererri, the Italian film director, expressed it best in memorable films like *The Last Woman* (1976) or *Bye Bye Monkey* (1978). There are many who, like the protagonists of these films, bemoan unanimously that they have been brought up to be the patriarch of a family that no longer exists.

In short, the women's liberation phenomenon means that women have become the subject of their own desire. That is, women have ceased to be the object of masculine desire—women who wait patiently for a man to come to their rescue. As a consequence, today's woman refuses this alienating reality of absolutes that sees her only through the emotional and maternal lens, rejecting (or repressing) all of her other instinctual expressions. All of this has had a significant impact on women's emotional landscapes. Among those impacts is a desire to separate the currents of tenderness from sexuality that, as we saw earlier, is a critical part of growing up and being emotionally mature. For a long time, the woman was condemned to existing as a baby-making machine and a meal generator. For a long time, the only glory a woman could claim was to possess a fertile body and skilled hands for cooking. These were her greatest social assets. But this has all changed in unprecedented ways.[28]

Additionally, the confinement in her affective and maternal potentialities led her to a genuine narcissistic deepening—that is, to see her body as the

28. See Janine Chasseguet-Smirgel, *La sexualité féminine. Recherches psychanalytiques nouvelles* (Paris: Payot, 1964); Monique Schneider, *Le paradigme féminine* (Paris: Flamarion 2004); Judith Butler, *Gender Trouble: Feminism and the Subversion of Identity* (New York: Routledge, 1990); *Undoing Gender* (New York: Routledge, 2004); Stefan Hirschauer "Gender (In)Difference in Gender (Un)Equal Couples: Intimate Dyads between Gender Nostalgia and Post Genderism," *Human Studies* 40 (2017): 309–30.

only object worthy of love. But also, such a narcissistic investment was encouraged to turn her into an appropriate erotic object for the male, whom he needed to attract and *passively* seduce if she wanted to attain the only thing that was permitted of her—to be a wife and mother. Then, by endorsing the role of an erotic object, a woman was forced to squander a good part of her energy in maintaining herself as such—of always being that attractive erotic object, with the resulting drama of losing these qualities that she had fought so hard for.[29]

But it is also evident that this reality has engendered a great deal of unconscious aggression toward men. Aggression that has been expressed symptomatically in a variety of ways, either through alterations in sexual behavior like frigidity, asthenia, and psychosomatics symptoms (unconscious methods of punishing a man by, for example, stoking his fears of being a poor lover or lacking in sexual vigor) or in other more passive-aggressive ways, by controlling the man emotionally, an area where a woman may feel more empowered. In other circumstances too, the male takes advantage of and channels that desire to be emotionally possessed by the female (while he dominates in sexual affairs), just as he was possessed by his mother. The feminist movement itself, in some extreme cases, has failed to overcome the temptation to exercise its revenge on men. An aggressiveness that has been a diversion from its original purpose (a struggle that attempted to regain authority so long withheld by men) and instead revels in feelings of resentment, envy, and destructive desire. These are situations that, paradoxically, would seem to validate the Freudian theory of penis envy, which, as we know, was met with so much hostility by feminist groups. The expression *feminism is the theory, lesbianism is the practice* that came out of the American women's lib movement, displayed a retaliatory attitude that rejected the male. It is a type of reaction to a just cause.

THE SUSPECT IDEALIZATION OF WOMEN

The factors that contribute to the marginalization of women are undoubtedly varied and complex—economic, political, ideological, and so on. But here we are interested in investigating the psychodynamic motivations that lead to such exclusion. They shed light on the changing role that today's woman is expected to display in relationships.

Undoubtedly, one of the main reasons women have been and continue to be socially marginalized and belittled is due to the involvement of a series of unconscious ghosts. As we saw when exploring the development of instinc-

29. See Carlos Castilla del Pino, *Cuatro ensayos sobre la mujer* (Madrid: Alianza, 1971).

tual desire, the female genitals often invoke powerful and menacing castration ghosts in men. When women are seen as mutilated beings, they must be dismissed and confined. The situation is distressing, and an effective way to mitigate that fear is precisely by weakening her position. The desired and imaginary phallic supremacy (we spoke earlier of the need for both men and women to renounce the symbolic phallus) is threatened by the differences perceived, and men try to gain the upper hand by relegating women to a lower position. Because of this type of unconscious motivation, the concept of menstruation and blood permeates society at the collective and individual level with powerful taboos that perpetuate these distressing ghosts.[30] This leads to the separation of women in certain areas of life, while simultaneously idealizing the feminine, which, as we shall see, correlates to very infantile desires.

Indeed, for some time now the song of "eternal feminine," romanticized and passionate, is viewed suspiciously as having hidden motives. The idealization of women, the eulogistic way of viewing their maternal functions, the exaltation of their unique worth, and the insistence on their irreplaceable role in the family have been thoroughly exposed and criticized during this last century. We will not insist on this then. Suffice it to say those very deep unconscious motivations have provoked an ideology that from the analytical point of view serve only to rationalize certain attitudes. That is to say, of intentional theorizations, that as unconscious defense mechanisms, aim to hide unspeakable truths.

We would have to ask ourselves, then, what man's real intention is in exalting the feminine. We must start by questioning and exploring the deepest desires that make up the affective structure of masculinity. As we have already seen, the individual, physically separated from the mother since birth, will not be able to psychologically integrate that until much later, and only through a complex and painful process undertaken by the psyche. There, the Oedipus complex has a culminating role, where that separation and difference with the original maternal matrix needs to be cemented. Only then, will subjectivity itself be truly independent, limited and distinct evermore, based on the lack that such separation entails.

We have previously reflected that it is not uncommon for individuals to struggle with acknowledging and integrating that separation, limitation, and difference. The complex interaction of maternal and paternal functions will affect the structuring of each individual and how each one relates to others. Also, in a very particular way, how the male relates to the female. The desire to maintain the ghost of a complete mother-object, a good object that is always available. In this way the man can perpetuate the ideal of being the sole

30. See Freud, "The Taboo of Virginity," in *Standard Edition*, 11: 193–208.

and total object of the mother's desire, to be what satiates his lack, to become the phallus that makes up for his deficiency.

But we must highlight an important point. We cannot forget that the marginalization of women in society is not a simple case of rivalry, envy, or aggression toward men, to gain power for themselves. It is a matter of love. So entrenched and primitive that it becomes much more relevant than other yearnings for authority or dominance, despite how influential the latter influences might be.

It is a matter of love that, indeed, is of such a regressive and childish nature that it immediately results in alienating the male and entrapping the female. A love, therefore, that we must battle against tirelessly. Because as popular wisdom affirms, and, as we have described in other contexts, *there are loves that kill.* With the best of intentions, although these good intentions spread a hidden poison. It is important, however, to understand and take charge of these dynamics because, otherwise, we could greatly misunderstand the changes that seem to transpire between men and women during the course of a relationship.

Perhaps the most fundamental change that must take place is for the woman to refuse to play along as the man's support system, maintaining the fantasy of his mother. Something that a man, especially an open-minded one, can comprehend, even when he feels resistance within himself. His own introjected parental models, together with his difficulties in maturing, impede the evolution of the relationship, which the woman, newly adapted to her new roles and social responsibilities, demands of him. In many cases, that woman no longer seems willing to reduce herself to a passive object of masculine desire nor therefore to deny her own desires, including sexual ones, nor be reduced to someone passive, silent, and accommodating to male needs. Something deep within her has changed that propels her to be a partner in life, not the idealized object that reactivates the fantasy of the imaginary mother.

Both men and women will need to find a sense of balance within their relationship. In every partnership, the individuals involved will have to define their roles and functions, such as who does what household chores, who raises and educates the children, and so on—all the while maintaining a respectful sense of fairness and equality within the relationship.

HAVING CHILDREN

Becoming a parent means subjecting oneself to a whole new range of desires, which, as in romantic relationships, is influenced by biological strata of personality. However, the human experience of parenthood widens and extends far beyond what instinct could arouse and sustain. And it is likely an area in which human beings are indebted to culture far more than what we might think. In any case, children have a big impact on the parent's relationship, with significant repercussions. Let us look at the factors that have the greatest effect on the world of desire.

The couple's love relationship is significantly transformed by the arrival of children. The identity of each individual is altered and radically reconfigured—the woman becomes a mother and the man a father. When this occurs, all previous associations held with one's own parents become complemented in noteworthy ways.[31] They have come to embody those formative roles from their respective childhoods. Once that primitive identification has been revived, there will be many elements from that past that now come into play in their respective relationships with their children. Many fantasies, anxieties, and ambivalences from those early parental relationships will frequently influence the emerging relationship with their kids. But, also, both members of the *dyad* will contemplate each other in a new light, reflecting the images held of the older generation of parents. The wife turned into mother will herald back to images of the mother figure, and the husband, perceived as a father, will also reflect that personage.

The arrival of children will influence the love relationship in numerous and varied ways. For many women, giving birth to a boy is a kind of guarantee that provides security to the marriage. In other scenarios, the boy's arrival will cause a disturbance and a crisis in the relationship. For example, it is not uncommon for men to experience feelings of jealousy and rivalry with the newcomer who monopolizes his wife's affection. The baby is not only a passive recipient of affection, but he also becomes an active agent that influences and shapes the mother's affective world.[32] The father can perceive the child as a rival who appropriates his wife's attention and intimacy. Certainly, the experience of motherhood often results in female desire being sublimated, which often has a significant impact on the specifically erotic and sexual dimensions of the relationship with her partner. In any case, the idealization of parenthood should not blind us to the fact that this human relationship will also be impacted in one way or another by the ambivalence that naturally characterizes all interpersonal communication. Ambivalence that is not always conscious, but that permeates the relationship with feelings that can range from jealousy to rivalry, to envy, to overt hostility. The positive feelings and emotions will need to be more substantial than the negative

---

31. Freud (1931), "Female Sexuality," in *Standard Edition*, 22: 133–34. On the repercussions of paternity for men, see Bernard This, *Le Père: acte de naissance* (Paris: Seuil, 1980); Cristopher Clulow, ed., *Partners Becoming Parents* (London: Sheldon, 1996).

32. See Andrew Balfour, Mary Morgan, and Christopher Vincent, *How Couple Relationships Shape Our World: Clinical Practice, Research and Policy Perspectives* (London: Karnac, 2014).

ones, and the ability of the former to articulate and contain the latter will be essential for that relationship to become a healthy expression of desire and a means for personal growth.

An important aspect of the relationship between parents and newly arrived children is the advent of an emotional dynamic in which the narcissistic dimensions of personality play a prime role. The child is seen (especially for women) as a part of oneself, as an extension of one's being. For that reason, loving a child is akin to loving something within oneself. All the giving, the pampering, and the tenderness that the little ones awaken is linked in good measure to that hope of providing that limitless love that every human being wants for oneself and that life progressively frustrates and limits. That child, therefore, offers a way to represent oneself in an important identification process. Freud highlighted this narcissistic dimension of love for children as an essentially feminine trademark since we are well aware of his tendency to view women as having a more narcissistic predisposition than men. This is an example of Freudian prejudices toward the feminine.

But at the same time, the separation that begins at birth also leads to a dynamic in which narcissism creates object love. That child appears to be a separate being, detached, seeking personal autonomy and independence. And that is precisely where parents face one of the biggest challenges in regard to their relationship with their children. It will be an ongoing challenge to accept the differences and separation that become more evident with time. In other words, it will be difficult to accept that the child, endowed with the family name, turns the parent into yet another link in the chain of generations.

Sometimes, parents will be tempted to channel their narcissism through their children, forcing them to identify with their own reality or, even more so, with ideals that they failed to live up to. This is what French psychoanalyst Serge Lebovici termed *unconscious transgenerational mandate*, which is a way to induce the child, sometimes even before birth, to identify with a model that correlates to a root desire.[33] It is an attempt, therefore, to turn the child into a kind of clone aligned with an ideal reality since the child's differences are seen as a threat against the self.

While the differences affect the narcissistic image of the parents, the distance that widens as children grow can also prove to be challenging. Resistance to the possibility of losing the love object usually drives parents to have Oedipal fixations with their children—in general, the mother toward her sons and the father toward his daughters. The unresolved Oedipal scenario drives a kind of counter-Oedipus in the relationship of complic-

---

33. The concept of *unconscious transgenerational mandate* is described by Bernard Golse in *Hommage à Serge Lebovici, Le Carnet Psy* 58 (2000): 18.

ity with their respective children. The situation becomes more intense and problematic for their development when the parent's counter-Oedipal fixations derive from the shortcomings that each perceives in their relationship. The children then become the object of substitute love for what the couple fails to provide.

Thus, given the enormous intensity of parental ties that manifest simultaneously as narcissism and object love, the ability to accept that separation and difference is a clear indicator of acknowledging that we are *separate beings*. In turn, it is here that we will be able to gauge the amount of growth and maturation that is possible within a couple as well as the possibility of growth for their descendants.

BIBLIOGRAPHY

Alberoni, Francesco. *Falling in Love and Loving.* New York, NY: Random House, 1983.

———. *Il volo nuziale.* Roma: Garzanti, 1992.

Aron, Arthur, and Elaine Aron. *Love and the Expansion of Self: Understanding Attraction and Satisfaction.* New York: Hemisphere Publishing Corp/Harper & Row, 1986.

Balfour, Andrew, Mary Morgan, and Christopher Vincent. *How Couple Relationships Shape Our World.* London: Karnac, 2014.

Bergman, Martin S. *The Anatomy of Loving.* New York: Columbia University Press, 1987.

———. "On the Intrapsychic Function of Falling in Love." *Psychoanalytic Quarterly* 49 (1980): 56–77.

Bhatia, Vickie, and Joanne Davila. *Mental Health Disorders in Couple Relationships.* New York: Routledge, 2017.

Bobé, Antoni. *Conflictos de pareja. Diagnóstico y tratamiento.* Compiled by Antoni Bobé and Carles Pérez Testor. Barcelona: Paidós/Fundació Vidal i Barraquer, 1994.

Burguière, André, dir. *Histoire de la famille.* Paris: Armand Colin, 1986.

Buss, David M. *The Evolution of Desire.* New York: Basic Books, 1994.

Butler, Judith. *Gender Trouble: Feminism and the Subversion of Identity.* New York: Routledge, 1990.

———. *Undoing Gender.* New York, NY: Routledge, 2004.

Castilla del Pino, Carlos. *Cuatro ensayos sobre la mujer.* Madrid: Alianza, 1971.

Chasseguet-Smirgel, Janine. *La sexualité feminine. Recherches psychanalytiques nouvelles.* Paris: Payot, 1964.

Clulow, Christopher, ed. *Partners Becoming Parents.* London: Sheldon, 1996.

———. *Sex, Attachment and Couple Psychotherapy: Psychoanalytic Perspectives.* London: Karnac, 2009.

David, Charles. *L'état amoureux.* Paris: Payot, 1971.

Dicks, Henry. *Marital Tensions.* New York: Routledge, 1967.

Freud, Sigmund (1910). "A Special Type of Choice of Object Made by Men." In *The Standard Edition of the Complete Psychological Works of Sigmund Freud*, edited and translated by James Strachey, 11: 163–75. London: Hogarth, 1966.
——— (1914c). "On Narcissism: An Introduction." In *Standard Edition*, 14: 67–100.
——— (1921c). *Group Psychology and the Analysis of the Ego*. In *Standard Edition*, 18: 111, 112.
——— (1931b). *Female Sexuality* in *Standard Edition*, 21: 223–44.
Grier, Francis, ed. *Brief Encounters with Couples: Some Analytic Perspectives*. London and New York: Karnac, 2001.
———. *Oedipus and the Couple*. London: Karnac, 2005.
Kaplan, Helen S. *The New Sex Therapy*. New York: Brunner/Mazel, 1973.
Lemaire, Jean G. *Les thérapies du couple*. Paris: Payot, 1971.
Ludlan, Molly, and Viveka Nyberg. *Couple Attachments: Theoretical and Clinical Studies*. New York: Routledge, 2007.
Meltzer, Donald, and Martha Harris. *The Educational Role of the Family: A Psychoanalytical Model*. London: Karnac, 2013.
Novakovic, Aleksandra. *Couple Dynamics: Psychoanalytic Perspectives in Work with the Individual, the Couple, and the Group*. London: Routledge, 2016.
Person, Ethel E. *Dreams of Love and Fateful Encounters*. New York: Norton, 1988.
Pines, Ayala M. *Falling in Love: Why We Choose the Lovers We Choose*. New York: Routledge, 2005.
Ruszczynski, Stanley, ed. *Psychotherapy with Couples: Theory and Practice at the Tavistock Institute*. London: Karnac, 1993.
Scharff, David E., and Jill Savege Scharff, eds. *Psychoanalytic Couple Therapy: Foundations of Theory and Practice*. London: Karnac, 2014.
Schneider, Monique. *Le paradigme féminine*. Paris: Flamarion, 2004.
Sternberg, Karin. *Psychology of Love*. New York: Springer Publishing Co., 2014.
Welldon, Estela V. *Mother, Madonna, Whore: The Idealization and Denigration of Motherhood*. London: Free Association Books, 1998.
Willi, Jürg. *Die Zweier-Beziehung*. Hamburg: Rowohlt Verlag, 1975.

[illegible] (1919) [illegible]. In [illegible], translated by [illegible] Strachey, [illegible]. London: [illegible], 1955.
[illegible]. "Introduction." In [illegible], [illegible]
[illegible]
[illegible] In [illegible]
[illegible] and New York: [illegible], [illegible]
[illegible] Paris: [illegible]
Kaplan, Helen S. *The New Sex Therapy*. New York: Brunner/Mazel, 1974.
[illegible] Paris: [illegible], 1973.
[illegible] and [illegible]. [illegible] New York: Routledge, [illegible]
[illegible] and [illegible] Harris. [illegible]
[illegible] London: [illegible], 2012.
[illegible]
[illegible] and the Camera. London: Routledge, 2016.
[illegible] New York: [illegible], 1988.
[illegible]. New York: Routledge, 2005.
[illegible]
[illegible], 1971.
[illegible] and [illegible]
[illegible] London: [illegible], 2014.
[illegible] Press [illegible], 2004.
[illegible]
[illegible]
[illegible] Books, 1993.
[illegible] Hamburg: Rowohlt Verlag, 1977.

Chapter Seven

A Different Type of Love: Homosexuality

Homosexuality is a challenging expression of desire. It is a dimension that is present, in one way or another, in all human beings and that is neither easy to navigate nor conflict free. Those who satisfy their erotic aspirations through homosexuality will find that this way of life will require confronting sociocultural schemes that, in one way or another, are also internally introjected. An inner battle of sorts will be practically inescapable. Even those who identify as heterosexual will find themselves confronted with the issue of homosexuality in some way. The homosexual dimension is also present as a reflection of desire that, although not necessarily dominant, must be sublimated, or, in the worst case, repressed. Either way, the task of negotiating these tendencies is unavoidable and the results are unpredictable. Homophobia is proof that homosexuality also affects those who theoretically have nothing to do with it. Therefore, it can be rightly said that no one is oblivious or fully objective toward homosexuality. Somehow, it's as if we are all at risk.

In effect, the issue of homosexuality gives rise to a whole series of individual and collective ghosts. It seems to harbor something destructive. On a personal level, it seems to endanger the psychosexual image of men or women that we have been so laboriously fostering and defending throughout time. On a social level, it seems as though there is a fear that this sexual lifestyle could completely dismantle the coveted family institution.

Without a doubt, there has been a significant shift in recent times in how homosexuality is perceived. This new awareness questions preconceptions and prejudices from both the ethical and scientific fields. Particularly, the psychosocial research that has gone beyond the narrow clinical framework has cast doubt over the many existing social stereotypes regarding homosexuality and of which we all have to some degree participated. The famous Kinsey Reports, despite their flaws, were the first of these types of studies to break with the established image of homosexuals. After these studies came other psychosocial investigations from the likes of Alan Bell and Martin Weinberg, and Colin Williams, who improved on the deficiencies of the Kinsey Reports and forced us to deeply rethink many of the traditional approaches. All this has also led media like film, television, and press, to present homosexuality as a perfectly acceptable orientation that individuals should not be ashamed of. And, yet, it would be naive to think that homosexuality has ceased to be a problem. This attitude is even more suspect in environments where people are constantly affirming one's freedom to choose their own sexual orientation. In spite of these assurances, there is an undercurrent of fear, anxiety, and rejection veiled under the pretense of keeping up with the times. Reflecting on a subject that ultimately involves us all is a task worth undertaking, both for homosexuals and heterosexuals.

BROADENING OUR OUTLOOK

Homosexuality has almost always been addressed from the perspective of psychiatry and clinical psychology. Hence, despite the undeniable value of the many studies that have come out of these fields, these approaches have been biased and have caused confusion.[1] Above all, they have caused homosexuality to be viewed as a pathological phenomenon of nature. As on so many other occasions (like those early medical trials looking at masturbation), unconscious ghosts stemming from the world of desire have cloaked themselves as *official science*. Nor can it be forgotten that most psychotherapists come from the psychiatric tradition, which has relied on society's standards of desired behavior as a reference point, extrapolating the deviances from there.

In fact, the methodological deficiencies of many of these allegedly *scientific* studies have been quite common and sometimes grotesque. The samples that clinical and psychotherapeutic studies have used have generally been very small and usually not representative of the general population. The absence of control groups, overlooking relevant variables, and the frequent lack of conceptual precision has led to significant oversights when drawing conclusions.

It is generally well known that sex researchers in the field of sociology have accused psychologists and psychiatrists of focusing on the most conflictive and neurotic sector of the homosexual population and that they unfairly extended their conclusions to the entire homosexual population.[2]

---

1. See Vernon A. Rosario, "The Triumph and Decline of Psychiatric Models," in *Homosexuality and Science: A Guide to the Debates*, 127–47 (Santa Barbara, CA: ABC-CLIO, 2002).
2. Martin S. Weinberg and Colin J. Williams, *Male Homosexuals* (New York: Oxford University Press, 1974), 17–33.

In fact, the first major sociological investigation carried out by the Kinsey team created controversy between sociologists and clinical psychologists that, among other things, demonstrated the psychiatric discomfort resulting from the evident collapse of their own narrative. While the Kinsey Reports were methodologically flawed, Kinsey's own team went on to carry out new investigations over a ten-year period. The updated report was first released in 1978, and it demonstrated the value of approaching the homosexual phenomenon in a broader and more objective way for society.[3] We will extract the most significant findings from this report because either they broke from conventional social stereotypes or they conformed to them in some way. We will focus specifically on the findings that address the clinical diagnosis of homosexuality and whether there is a pathological component. We will also look at the contributions of another important report carried out by Martin S. Weinberg and Colin J. Williams that looked beyond the US population[4] as well as a very interesting study done by José L. Trechera with Spanish subjects.[5] Only in this way will we be able to approach this continually contested issue in a broad and nuanced way.

RETHINKING SOME FINDINGS

The 1978 Bell and Weinberg study aimed to classify different types of homosexuality. Such an attempt was certainly appreciated given the prevalent nonobjective clustering of homosexuality in clinical studies, not to mention how homosexuals were already seen in society. Homosexuality was referred to as a uniform reality, reduced to a caricature and focusing on only the most problematic dimensions.

The authors categorized individuals according to different aspects of sexual experience and developed a typology composed of five groups. The first was named *Closed-coupled* and corresponded to homosexuals living in pairs with marriage-like relationships. The second was called *Open-coupled* and was characterized primarily by individuals who were dissatisfied in coupled life. The third group was called *Functional*, named so due to the number of sexual partners and the apparent ease with the homosexual identity. The fourth was the so-called *Dysfunctional* group; these individuals also had many sexual partners but, unlike the former group, they struggled with being gay and

3. Allan P. Bell and Martin S. Weinberg, *Homosexualities* (New York: Simon & Schuster, 1978).

4. Bell and Weinberg, *Homosexualities*. The study compares samples from the United States, Holland, and Denmark.

5. José L. Trechera, "Los homosexuales vistos por sí mismos. Datos y conclusiones de una muestra española," in *La homosexualidad: un debate abierto*, ed. Javier Gafo (Bilbao: Desclée de Brouwer, 1997), 223–67.

exhibited sexual problems. Finally was the *Asexual* group, who scored very low in the area of sexual activity, exhibited sexual problems, and were anxious about being gay. These five types of homosexual expressions involve diverse psychological and social complexities.[6]

An even more interesting finding that first appeared in the original Kinsey Reports is what the authors describe as the *Homosexual-Heterosexual Rating Scale*. Apparently, no one is purely homosexual or heterosexual—everyone is on a continuum. In fact, such psychosociological data is nothing but the expression of psychological bisexuality that was already suggested in earlier psychoanalytic thought. Freud was firmly convinced that in every homosexual there are traces of heterosexual orientation, just as in every heterosexual there is always the possibility of choosing a homosexual object. Moreover, every individual experiences through their lives—whether a man or a woman—a swing of the libido between the male and the female object. "Generally speaking," Freud says, "every human being oscillates all through his life between heterosexual and homosexual feelings, and any frustration or disappointment in the one direction is apt to drive him over to the other."[7] We will revisit this idea further on.

It is worth noting that on the Kinsey scale's 0 to 6 score, which correlates to the degree of homosexuality, there are subjects who score a 3, which would fall under the bisexual category. Masters and Johnson prefer to call it ambisexual, thus underscoring the idea that the individual feels as comfortable in a homosexual as a heterosexual relationship, as opposed to bisexuality, which usually demonstrates a greater preference for a particular sex.

The psychosociological investigations were useful in helping to question the stereotype of homosexuals as sex-obsessed beings.[8] The findings do not uphold this. Perhaps the popular belief and the affirmation of many clinical psychiatrists derives from an undue generalization, derived from the study of a specific group of homosexuals that might coincide with the *Functional* and *Dysfunctional* subgroups described in the 1978 Kinsey Reports and who probably are the ones seeking out psychotherapeutic help more frequently. In such cases, there seems to be an attempt to turn sexuality into absolutes. Nevertheless, Bell and Weinberg are forced to conclude that, for most homosexuals, sex is not the overriding concern.[9] Nor is the level of sexual activity higher than for heterosexuals.[10]

6. Bell and Weinberg, *Homosexualities*, 129–38.

7. Sigmund Freud (1911c), *Psychoanalytic Notes on an Autobiographical Account of a Case of Paranoia*, in *Standard Edition*, 12: 46.

8. For example, French psychologist Marcel Eck stated that heterosexuals could detach from their sexuality, while for homosexuals, their sexuality defined them and everything in their life is judged according to this sexuality. Marcel Eck, *Ensayo sobre la homosexualidad* (Barcelona: Herder, 1968), 243.

9. Bell and Weinberg, *Homosexualities*, 115.

10. Bell and Weinberg, *Homosexualities*, 72.

Additionally, the percentage of people with sexual problems seems to be the same for homosexuals and heterosexuals. The authors point out that these problems for homosexuals were generally not adequately focused at the clinical level until recently. As Bell and Weinberg affirm, when homosexuality was seen as the problem itself, the therapist believed the individual was complicit in something pathological if he tried to address the specific sexual problems therein.

A PROBLEMATIC ASPECT: PROMISCUITY

Promiscuity in the homosexual population is a subject that deserves special attention. There seems to be some truth to this claim—that there is, indeed, a propensity among homosexuals to have a high number of sexual partners. Half of the men surveyed by Bell and Weinberg confess to having had an average of five hundred partners.[11] These numbers may no longer be the case, as a lot has changed since the AIDS epidemic, which apparently had a big impact on how homosexual men contact each other and meet up. Nonetheless, promiscuity seems to characterize homosexuality. Thus, we stumble upon some findings that seem to provide sufficient grounds for reflecting on a pathological dimension of homosexuality. This psychodynamic would seem to suggest challenges in emotional and personal bonding. But these findings do not result in a consensus of interpretation nor concurrent psychodiagnostic valuation.

These findings must take another factor into account before being assessed. All the studies seem to demonstrate that homosexual women have relationships in remarkably different ways than their male counterparts. Women have far fewer partners, and their relationships are longer term and usually come about from known acquaintances rather than chance encounters. Female homosexual environments are not marked by promiscuity.

Undoubtedly, there are many factors that shape male homosexual promiscuity that need to be unraveled before jumping to conclusions. For Clarence Tripp, it is not surprising, for example, that promiscuous desire is somewhat specific to the male sex, based partially on biological tendencies: a high sexual impulse, an easily triggered response capacity, and a predisposition within the species for the sexual hunt.[12] According to the author, heterosexual men are limited by the shortage of mates who are readily available and by the fact that women frequently get into a relationship with men for reasons other than sexual desire. Other authors also point out men's propensity, whether

11. Similar results are found in the research conducted by José L. Trechera in Spain. José L. Trechera, *Los homosexuales vistos por sí mismos. Datos y conclusiones de una muestra española*, en: Javier Gafo, *La homosexualidad: un debate abierto* (Bilbao: Desclée de Brouwer, 1997), 248–50.

12. Clarence A. Tripp, "The Social Shape of Homosexuality," in *The Homosexual Matrix* (New York: McGraw-Hill, 1975), 119–40.

homo- or heterosexual, to base their sexual worth on the number of sexual experiences they have and to regard fidelity as a restriction on freedom. But we will put a hold on these findings and return to them later when analyzing the possible psychopathology within homosexuality.

In regard to the long-term viability of homosexual couples, they are usually known to be unstable. The problem is closely tied to the whole issue of promiscuity. To this, however, we should consider the absence of legal marriage options in many places, the absence of children, and the significant social and cultural differences that occur frequently in homosexual relationships—these are all contributors to the instability of the relationship. While heterosexual couples have the support and sometimes even the pressure of the entire social body to ensure its continuance, it is evident that homosexual couples do not. It is rather the opposite. It should not be forgotten, on the other hand, that stability does not equal quality. We know this well from the multitude of seemingly "stable" marriages.

HOMOSEXUAL PSYCHOLOGICAL ADAPTATION

In order for homosexuals to achieve mental stability, the most important thing they can do is to learn to accept themselves. So far, both the social investigations carried out and the results obtained in clinical psychology studies are conclusive. Of particular relevance in this regard is the work of W. J. Sengers—*Se reconnaître homosexuel*.[13] The more negative the homosexual's self-perception, the greater the psychological problems are likely to be. For Martin Weinberg and Colin Williams, accepting one's homosexuality and carrying on in life without abandoning one's orientation are very positive psychological signs.[14]

Homosexuals are often accused of seeing themselves as normal or even better than others. Perhaps it is true that a minority have acted out and in a sometimes zealous and overactive way. Heterosexuality has been looked at as a type of fascist sexual status quo; the concept of homosexuality has been professed to be the exclusive fruit of bourgeois ideology, homosexuality being associated with the highest human values and aptitudes. Thus, in some homosexual circles, individuals have lashed out against the heterosexual majority. It should not be forgotten, however, that these attitudes are in the minority and that the vast majority of homosexuals seem to have chosen rather the path of fear and repression. It is not fair, as Marcel Eck does, to as-

13. W. J. Sengers, *Se reconnaître homosexuel* (Paris: Name, 1970).
14. Weinberg and Williams, *Male Homosexuals*, 253. Similar data can be found in José L. Trechera's previously cited research on page 231.

sociate all homosexuals who dissent from established psychiatric views with that recalcitrant and aggressive sodomy that in fact can only be found in some minority sectors of "militant gays."[15]

Numerous investigations have tried to delve into the possible differences between the psychological adaptation of homo- and heterosexuals. The results have not always been in alignment. Nonetheless, the resulting data leads us to conclude that it is currently impossible to distinguish between homosexuals and heterosexuals. The study conducted in Spain by José Trechera concludes that no substantial differences can be perceived between homosexuals and heterosexuals. The differences that do appear have less to do with sexual orientation and more to do with the differences between the sexes.[16] For now, we will not delve into the clinical results, but instead we will summarize the results of the psychosociological investigation of the 1978 Kinsey Reports on the psychological adaptation of homosexuals.

For Bell and Weinberg, it was clear that one couldn't speak of psychological adaptation in general terms. One had to distinguish between the various homosexual subgroups. Only those falling under the *Dysfunctional* or *Asexual* categories had higher levels of psychological distress than heterosexuals. "It would appear that homosexual adults who have come to terms with their homosexuality, who do not regret their orientation, and who can function effectively sexually and socially, are no more distressed psychologically than are heterosexual men and women. Clearly, the therapist who continues to believe that it is by fiat his or her job to change a homosexual client's sexual orientation is ignorant of the true issues involved."[17] In the epilogue of the work, Bell and Weinberg concluded that relatively few homosexual men and women correspond to the dreadful stereotype that society had of them. Perhaps the most salient point of this research was that homosexuality and pathology were not necessarily correlated.[18]

It remains to be seen, however, whether at a deeper level there is a background story that gives rise to the homosexual orientation with an underlying series of unconscious traumas, fixations, or deviations that would imply a pathology that these psychosocial investigations overlook. We will come back to this later. But there is no question that the results from psychosocial research, while inconclusive, broaden our outlook and require us to reconsider findings based on a small number of yet thorough clinical research studies. An approach to the problem of the origins and diagnosis of homosexual

15. Eck, *Ensayo sobre la homosexualidad*, 346–47.
16. Trechera, *Los homosexuales vistos por sí mismos. Datos y conclusiones de una muestra española*, 234.
17. Bell and Weinberg, *Homosexualities*, 216.
18. In José L. Trechera's study, 87 percent were satisfied with their sexual orientation. Trechera, *Los homosexuales vistos por sí mismos. Datos y conclusiones de una muestra española*, 231.

orientation will require carrying out some important considerations about biological aspects of sexuality.

WITH THE PERMISSION OF BIOLOGY

Frank Beach has been one of the leading researchers in the field of sexual behavior and what motivates sexual attraction. His suggestion is that sexual arousal becomes much more varied and complex as it ascends the phylogenetic tree and that the variety of sexual behaviors in which higher animals engage is related to the development of their cerebral cortices. Hormonal regulation in lower animals gives way to neurological control in higher animals. In this sense, Beach affirms that, through evolution, the degree to which sex hormones control sexual behavior lessens, causing human behavior to become relatively independent of this influence. Experiments conducted by this and other researchers on artificial castration illustrate this progressive sexual complexity. In lower animals, castration involves the practical annulment of sexual functions. As the animal becomes more complex, hormones lose their power, until we reach the human being, where castration does not result in any loss of sexual interest or a reduction in the frequency of coupling and resulting pleasure. Sexual behavior begins to be influenced largely by the environment. As the evolution of sexual patterns progresses, they are no longer defined or guided by specific signals—individual learning becomes largely responsible. It is true that, as brains become more complex, there is a progressive loosening of the physiological control over sexuality.[19] In this sense, human sexuality displays the ultimate advancement—the ability to envision an opportunity and ready for its arrival. Renowned Spanish doctor Gregorio Marañón said it well when he stated that the brain is the human's largest sexual organ.

Although our analysis focuses largely on the psychological aspects, we must not overlook the possible biological roots of homosexuality so that these considerations do not skew the data obtained. The psychological dimensions will be evaluated differently, depending on whether biological data was taken into consideration.

One of the consequences of the loosening of specific biological controls as we branch out on the phylogenetic tree is the appearance of homosexuality in certain species. In these species, hormones continue to play an important role in sexuality, but less so for orientation. Two same-sex animals can be

---

19. See Frank A. Beach and Clellan S. Ford, *Patterns of Sexual Behavior* (New York: Harper & Row, 1969), 266; Aldo Poiani, *Animal Homosexuality: A Biosocial Perspective* (Cambridge: Cambridge University Press, 2010).

attracted to each other, leading to arousal and sexual intercourse.[20] Such behavior has been observed among lions, butterflies, porcupines, monkeys, and a wide variety of animals. This happens even in the presence of available heterosexual relationships. Such homosexual behaviors in different animal species often seem to have the aim of preservation—when cornered and attacked by another member of the same sex, a male will adopt a feminine posture.[21] However, in other cases, homosexual behaviors have been observed that could be described as primitive, or, as Jacques Corraze indicates, not something that can be explained away as a dominant-submissive relationship, or written off as a substitution for something better: "We cannot unequivocally state that homosexual relationships are due to conformity by omission. As it happens, males spontaneously partake in such behaviors even in the presence of females. Aside from the use of such behavior as a defense mechanism, one must recall the existence of primitive homosexual behavior."[22] The only possible explanation is that the more evolved the species is, the more indebted to the environment and what is acquired through it. As Jacques Corraze concludes, sexual behavior is not specific to one sex or another: "There is an ongoing possibility of sexual manifestations outside of biological sex, therefore, unrelated to the reproduction of the species. . . . In summary, the observation of animal behavior points us to a psychological bisexuality, an expression with only relative dependence on the structures of this order in relation to the genotype."[23] Thus, homosexuality emerges, like other types of behavior, with biology's permission.

The sum total of this data is not, of course, a justification for the phenomenon of homosexuality. Rather, it brings into question the voices who want to see human sexuality as something purely instinctual and involuntary. Thus, we must consider that, beyond the biological factors that may influence or condition homosexuality, it is challenging to assign psychological masculinity or femininity to purely chromosomal, gonadic, or hormonal causes or to morphological sexual differences. As Spanish bioethicist Javier Gafo asserted some time ago in a study looking at the biological factors of homosexuality, "the virility or femininity of an individual depends not so much on biological imperatives, but rather on socio-cultural or psychological conditioning."[24]

20. Along these lines, James D. Weinrich, "Is Homosexuality Biologically Natural?" in William Paul et al., *Homosexuality: Social, Psychological, and Biological Issues* (Beverly Hills, CA: Sage, 1982), 13–31.

21. G. V. Hamilton, "Incest and Homosexuality," in *The Homosexuals (As Seen by Themselves and Thirty Authorities)*, ed. Aron M. Krich, 308–13 (New York: Citadel Press, 1964).

22. Jacques Corraze, *La homosexualidad y sus dimensiones* (Madrid: Fax, 1972), 190. See also by the same author, *La homosexualité* (Paris: PUF, 2005).

23. Corraze, *La homosexualidad y sus dimensiones*, 193–94.

24. Javier Gafo, "Los factores biológicos en el problema de la homosexualidad," *Sal Terrae* 65 (1979): 630. See also John P. De Cecco and David Allen Parker, eds., *Sex, Cells, and Same-Sex Desire: The Biology of Sexual Preference* (New York and London: Routledge, 2014).

BORN VERSUS MADE HOMOSEXUALITY

However, although biology can no longer be considered the best and most obvious explanation for homosexual or heterosexual orientation, the debate is ongoing. The press, as we know, occasionally releases sensationalist news about certain discoveries that reveal biological or anatomical differences between homosexuals and heterosexuals.[25] And, indeed, the matter is far from decided. There are in fact a series of genetic and endocrine factors that also seem to play an important role in sexual orientation. Let us explore some recent findings on this topic.

There are findings from the field of biology that seem to be related, although not clearly, to the homosexual phenomenon. The male or female sex is determined, as we all know, by the XX chromosomes in women and XY in men. In fact, there seems to be a series of variations that give rise to certain anomalies. Among them, it is worth mentioning the chromosome variation seen in XXY subjects that sometimes leads to a series of psychological issues related to sexual identity.

Certain influences during the development of the human embryo, such as prenatal stress, can also lead to alterations in sexual differentiation. Gender ascertainment does not occur until the seventh week of pregnancy, and, sometimes, resistance to androgens or excessive production thereof results in apparent female genitals in men or genital masculinization in a genetically female person. It is, however, revealing that the gender identity with which one is brought up will mold that person's future psychosexual identity. The perception of the genital organs results in the masculine or feminine cultural discourse that will be imposed on the upbringing that will mold the individual as a man or woman beyond their chromosomes, gonads, or sexual organs. The works of Money, Hampson, and Hampson reassess the opposition of biological sex and gender construct with which the subjects were raised.[26]

The hormones seem to have an influence on the sexualization of the brain's primitive bisexual structure.[27] In particular, the research carried out by Gunter Dörner in Germany and continued in the United States by Simon LeVay, has once again generated controversy about the biological origin of homosexual

25. There are certain enzymes (particularly 21-hydroxylase) that may signal a genetic predisposition to homosexuality. A splendid assessment and explanation of this theory can be found in the work of Juan Ramón Lacadena, "Biología del comportamiento sexual humano: genética y homosexualidad," in *La homosexualidad: un debate abierto*, ed. Javier Gafo, 97–135.

26. See John Money, *Hermaphroditism: An Inquiry into the Nature of a Human Paradox* (Cambridge, MA: Harvard University, 1952).

27. William H. Masters and Virginia E. Johnson approach the discussion on hormonal influence by stating that it interacts with the environmental, merely offering a predisposition: "The Fetal Hormonal Environment May Predispose Individuals Towards Particular Patterns of Sexual Behavior," in *Homosexuality in Perspective* (Boston: Little Brown and Co., 1979), 409.

orientation. This research insists that both homosexuality and heterosexuality are functions of the hypothalamus, including the amount of androgens present thereof between the fourth and fifth months of fetal development.[28]

Thus, based on the data offered to us in this field of biological research today, it would seem that although biological factors do not explain everything, they are to an extent contributors. As Spanish geneticist Juan Ramón Lacadena assures, genes can predispose, rather than determine, homosexual behavior and that, even if the genetic and neuroanatomic features appear to be correlated with sexual orientation, the causal relationship is not clear.[29]

Many facets of homosexuality remain hazy, both within this biological field and in the psychological determinations that we will analyze later. With the research data we have at the moment, it seems reasonable to conclude that homosexual orientation derives from a combination of biological, psychic, and social factors with varying degrees of interaction. The existing potentials in each of these areas would be activated only to the extent that the remaining others provided it. Thus, a strong biological predisposition for homosexuality could dwindle if the environmental factors did not facilitate the psychosexual identification that would lead one in that direction. However, a minimally favorable environment would suffice for homosexuality to flourish. Similarly, a minimal biological predisposition could be enough to direct sexual orientation toward homosexuality if psychosocial factors contribute basically along these lines.

FREUD: THE PSYCHODYNAMIC ORIGIN OF HOMOSEXUALITY

Freud is often framed as the greatest exponent of the psychogenetic theory of homosexuality. His interpretations are almost unanimously seen as foundations for the current medical discourses. This is also the reason Freud is often blamed for the unjustified negative image of homosexuals that have developed in scientific circles. For others, Freud laid the foundation for the pathological view of homosexuality. For yet others, however, his views

28. See Günter Dörner et al., "Stressful Events in Prenatal Life of Bi and Homosexual Men," *Experimental and Clinical Endocrinology* 81 (1983): 83–87; Günter Dörner's investigations were surrounded by controversy from the outset. He was accused of improperly tainting the data with value judgments and that, under the cloak of science, he hid with his prejudices and discrimination. However, Döner said in 1991 in Madrid that both bisexuality and homosexuality were natural variants of sexuality and that we should avoid their criminalization, discrimination, or pathologization. See Günter Döner, "Gene and Environment-Dependent Neuroendocrine Etiogenesis of Homosexuality and Transexualism," Lecture, Universidad Complutense, Madrid, 1991.

29. See Lacadena, "Biología del comportamiento sexual humano: genética y homosexualidad," 131.

represented the breakdown of social prejudices, as homosexuality was seen as an essential dimension of human sexuality.[30]

It is possible that Freudian discourse gives rise to all these interpretations; it is possible that he revolutionized how homosexuality is viewed, while conforming to the social convictions of his time and, in this way, unconsciously cherry-picked his discourses for or against one's views. The fact is that Freudian discourse, with its gaps and contradictions, is offered with a rigor and coherence that, certainly, is lacking in the subsequent psychoanalytic literature on homosexuality. Humble Freudian theories have turned into dogmatic doctrines, critical information is suspiciously cast aside or biasedly distorted, and ideas open to debate are closed.

Freud's reflection on the origin of homosexuality is based on the affirmation of its fundamentally psychogenetic nature, at odds with the theories of his time that saw it as the result of congenital nerve degeneration. In his *Three Essays for a Sexual Theory*, Freud takes a stand regarding the "degenerative" or "innate" positions. The acquired, therefore, prevails over the congenital.[31] Hence, Freud's disagreement with homosexuals of his time who, like Magnus Hirschfeld, wanted to be seen as a biological "third sex."[32]

This Freudian insistence on the acquired character of homosexuality was never a complete denial of constitutional factors. Freud was aware of the biological presence of bisexuality, although he did not equate this to psychological bisexuality. There is no direct relation between the physical and psychological intersex expression. Regardless, Freud was fully aware that, among the various factors giving rise to homosexuality, there would be some that were intrinsic to the individual, even when these were not completely understood.

But, without a doubt, the most revolutionary aspect of Freud's understanding of homosexuality was his affirmation of its *universality*, that is to say, by the affirmation that everyone's sexuality has within it a homosexual dimension. Homosexuality is therefore not an oddity but could even be a part of what is considered normal.[33] Because of this, everyone has to confront a certain degree of homosexuality in his or her biology and psyche that will determine, in large part, future sexual orientation as well as the degree of psychological stability. Depending on the nature of the person and the environment, the various influences that affect the homosexual dimension will result

---

30. Paul Robinson, "Freud and Homosexuality," *Constellations* 6 (1999): 80–84; S. Flanders and F. Ladame et al., "On the Subject of Homosexuality: What Freud Said," *International Journal of Psychoanalysis* 97 (2016): 933–50.
31. See Freud (1905d), *Three Essays on the Theory of Sexuality*, in *Standard Edition*, 7: 136–44.
32. See Freud (1910c), "Leonardo da Vinci and a Memory of This Childhood," in *Standard Edition*, 11: 98–101.
33. Freud (1905d), *Three Essays on the Theory of Sexuality*, in *Standard Edition*, 7: 172.

in the condition of manifest homosexuality, of neurosis, or of "normality" (understood here as heterosexuality).

But let's focus in on what interests most of us about the origin of discernible homosexuality. Homosexual forces within every individual can, as we have seen, lead to different outcomes, depending on the individual and the environment. What then are the critical factors for Freud that determine a person's definitive homosexual orientation?

The first mention on the origins of homosexuality can be found in the 1905 first edition of the *Three Essays on the Theory of Sexuality*. By focusing on a level of influence that is merely external, Freud merely points out that, in puberty, homosexuality is more likely when the child's early care is entrusted to people of the same sex. Such a situation could hinder what Freud sees as the cause of heterosexuality—the childhood memory of a mother's tenderness and the rivalry with the father. We are, then, at a psychopedagogical, rather than scientific level, and with a blind spot for the origins of female homosexuality. This will not be the first time we encounter such an omission.

Three years later, while doing research for *On the Sexual Theories of Children*, Freud came up with a theory on the origins of homosexuality that would become one of his hallmarks—that boys, overlooking sexual differences, imagined everyone to have male genitals, even females. That fantasy of a "phallic mother" could become engraved in the child's mind so that, subsequently, it would become impossible to give up the penis in his subsequent choice of sexual object. Under this scenario, the individual "would become homosexual."[34] The female genitals would be seen as a product of mutilation that would produce an anguished feeling of castration and, therefore, would result in fright rather than pleasure. The transition from autoerotism to object love is thus hindered and only partially fulfilled.[35] Thus, in 1908, Freud outlined for us his most significant and repeated theories on homosexuality. However, he neglected to address women.

In 1910, with the second edition of the *Three Essays on the Theory of Sexuality*, he delineates his theories more firmly. For the first time in Freud's work, we see the concept of narcissism as well as the idea of fixation and identification with the mother, which are all seen as the roots of homosexuality. After confessing that psychoanalysis had not gotten to the bottom of homosexual transformation, Freud stated that "the future inverts, in the earliest years of their childhood, pass through a phase of very intense but short-lived fixation to a woman (usually their mother), and that, after leaving this behind, they identify themselves with a woman and take themselves as their

34. Freud (1908c), "On the Sexual Theories of Children," in *Standard Edition*, 9: 216.

35. Freud (1908d), "'Civilized' Sexual Morality and Modern Nervous Illness," in *Standard Edition*, 9: 189.

sexual object. That is to say, they proceed from a narcissistic basis, and look for a young man who resembles themselves and whom *they* may love as their mother loved them."[36] At this point in his thinking, Freud saw homosexuality through a singular lens—the one exalted by Greek civilization: love is transactional; it is a compromise or a pact between the masculine and the feminine, as in the figure of Efebus. Thus far, attachment to the mother, narcissism, and the threat of castration were the three main hallmarks of homosexuality. Freud's theories continued to expand without any references to women.

In the 1915 third edition of the *Three Essays*, Freud adds a long note that could be regarded as one of the great texts on homosexuality. Here, we are merely interested in highlighting that in terms of its origin. Freud finds the "narcissistic object-choice and a retention of the erotic significance of the anal zone"[37] to be key, without elaborating on what such an anal connotation means.

In the case of *The Wolfman*, we find another theory for the cause of homosexuality—the incestuous relationship with the same-sex parent from the negative dimension of the Oedipus complex, or the so-called inverted Oedipus complex. According to the bisexual disposition, the Oedipal situation has both an active and a passive phase[38] so that, during this stage, every individual goes through a homosexual period. Hence, in the 1919 paper "A Child Is Being Beaten," Oedipal bisexuality is seen explicitly as a factor that can determine sexual aberration, both in infancy and adult life.[39]

From 1920, the impact of the death drive, which arose as a concept in *Beyond the Pleasure Principle*, is felt throughout Freud's work. The view of homosexuality is also impacted by it. Thus, the transformation of hostile impulses into affectionate ones appears in a 1922 text as a new motive for homosexual orientation. Frequently, Freud tells us, it is a rivalry with an older brother toward whom death was once wished upon, is subsequently repressed and transmuted so that "the hated rivals are transformed into love-objects."[40] Likewise, in *The Ego and the Id* (1923), homosexuality is seen as a way to transform hostile drives into erotic ones—"The hostile attitude has no prospect of satisfaction; consequently—for economic reasons, that is—it is replaced by a loving attitude for which there is more prospect of satisfaction."[41]

---

36. Freud, *Three Essays on the Theory of Sexuality*, 7: 145.
37. Freud (1905d), *Three Essays on the Theory of Sexuality*, 7: 146.
38. Freud (1925h), "Some Psychological Consequences of the Anatomical Distinction between the Sexes," in *Standard Edition*, 19: 249–50. See Whitney Davis, *Drawing the Dream of the Wolves: Homosexuality, Interpretation, and Freud's "Wolf Man"* (Bloomington: Indiana University Press, 1995).
39. Freud (1919), "'A Child Is Being Beaten': A Contribution to the Study of the Origin of Sexual Perversions," in *Standard Edition*, 17: 199.
40. Freud (1923a), "On Some Neurotic Mechanisms in Jealousy, Paranoia, and Homosexuality," in *Standard Edition*, 18: 231.
41. Freud (1923b), "The Ego and the Id," in *Standard Edition*, 19: 44.

Parallel to the affirmation of the death drive, castration anxiety becomes one of the final Freudian elements that is seen to create psychic conflict in general and also in relation to homosexual orientation. The threat of castration is closely linked to the phallic period, during which boys and girls recognize only one genital organ, the male one. The idea of castration as an influencer in homosexuality was already present, as we saw, in 1908. It now takes on a new and progressive importance against the background of the death drives. In the 1925 *An Autobiographical Study*, Freud synthesizes the origin of homosexuality as "traced back to the constitutional bisexuality of all human beings and to the after-effects of the phallic primacy."[42] In the brief and dense 1927 paper titled "Fetishism," castration anxiety is also pointed out as a possible trigger for homosexuality. Freud confesses that it remains a mystery why, when "probably no male human being is spared the fright of castration at the sight of the female genital. . . . some people become homosexual as a consequence of that impression," while others deny such an impression by creating a fetish and others overcome it by becoming heterosexual without suffering any aberration.[43]

The threat of castration is also the key piece in the explanation of female homosexuality. Until 1931, Freud does not give any specific explanation about the homosexual choice in women. It is, in Freud's expression, *a dark continent*. But in the paper "Female Sexuality," we see the two paths that women can take when faced with the castration complex: to walk away altogether from sexuality, turning the father into an object and transitioning to the feminine form of the Oedipus complex with the consequent acceptance of her femininity, or remaining in a stubborn affirmation of the threatening masculinity while holding on to the hope of someday having a penis. To this end, Freud asserts—"The extreme achievement of such a masculinity complex would appear to be the influencing of the choice of an object in the sense of manifest homosexuality."[44] The same motivation appears in the unfinished text dated July 1938 and published posthumously in 1940, *An Outline of Psycho-Analysis*—the insistence in wanting to be male is a critical component in the psychogenesis of female homosexuality.[45]

Thus far, we have taken a look at Freud's most significant mentions in relation to the origin of homosexuality. To summarize the main motivations for homosexual orientation, we have, firstly, *the adherence to the mother* that leads to identification with her and, from there, a *narcissistic choice of an object* by which the subject seeks himself in the image of another while avoiding

42. Freud (1925d), "An Autobiographical Study," in *Standard Edition*, 20: 38.
43. Freud (1927e), "Fetishism," in *Standard Edition*, 21: 154.
44. Freud (1933a), "Feminity": "New Introductory Lectures on Psycho-Analysis," in *Standard Edition*, 22: 194.
45. Freud (1940a), *An Outline of Psycho-Analysis*, in *Standard Edition*, 23: 194.

the anguish of castration. Secondly, there is the *inverted Oedipus complex* by which the father becomes the primary object of desire. Finally, according to Freud, there is another type of motivation linked to the problem of aggression, either *bypassing the rivalry of a third party* or by *transforming hostile impulses into affectionate ones toward a same-sex person*. As for women, the *masculinity complex* and the consequent *penis envy* are also influencers.

NARCISSISTIC AND PERVERSE?

Freud always saw a relationship between homosexuality and narcissism.[46] Homosexuality seemed closer to something autoerotic than object oriented.[47] This relationship was particularly lucid in *The Schreber Case* published in 1911, which introduces the narcissistic stage as an intermediate period of libidinal evolution between the first autoerotism and object love. Homosexuality is then seen as a necessary stepping-stone between narcissism and the eventual choice of heterosexual object. It is not pure narcissism since there is an object-choice involved, but, at the same time, it does not result in what should be the final objective, which would be heterosexuality.[48] Hence, it follows that homosexuality is "perverse"—it has failed to achieve what is considered to be a normal sexual object.

However, all of this seems to be symptomatic of Freud's growing difficulty in seeing homosexuality as a perversion. Particularly, from 1909, this struggle was becoming increasingly more evident—Freud draws attention to the difference between homosexuality and the rest of the perversions[49] and analogies that are better suited to heterosexual relationships. On the other hand,[50] he points out that "this class of perverts at any rate behave to their sexual objects in approximately the same way as normal people do to theirs"[51] and, later, concludes that "we are compelled, however, to regard choice of an object of one's own sex as a divergence in erotic life (*regelmässige Abzweigung*) which is of positively habitual occurrence."[52] A case dealing with

46. Freud (1900a), *The Interpretation of Dreams*, in *Standard Edition*, 391; See David Greven, "Rereading Narcissism: Freud's Theory of Male Homosexuality and Hawthorne's Gentle Boy," *Modern Psychoanalysis* 34 (2009): 48–78.

47. Freud (1908d), "'Civilized' Sexual Morality and Modern Nervous Illness," 9: 189–90 and 9: 109; (1909b), "Analysis of a Phobia in a Five-Year-Old Boy"; (1905d), *Three Essays on the Theory of Sexuality*, 7: 145.

48. Freud (1911c), *Psycho-Analytic Notes on an Autobiographical Account of a Case of Paranoia*, in *Standard Edition*, 12: 61.

49. Freud (1909b), "Analysis of a Phobia in a Five-Year-Old Boy," in *Standard Edition*, 10: 109.

50. Freud (1910a), *Five Lectures on Psycho-Analysis*, in *Standard Edition*, 45–46.

51. Freud, "Introductory Lectures on Psycho-Analysis," in *Standard Edition*, 16: 308.

52. Freud, 307 (original German text: G. W., XI, 318).

female homosexuality is expressed in similar terms. Freud refuses to see the girl as sick simply because she is gay. "Further unfavorable features in the present case were the facts that the girl was not in any way ill (she did not suffer from anything in herself, nor did she complain of her condition) and that the task to be carried out did not consist in resolving a neurotic conflict but in converting one variety of the genital organization of sexuality into the other (*eine Variant of the genitalem Sexual organization in die andere überzuführen*)."[53] Nor can we forget the contents of a letter (from April 9, 1935) to an American mother, who sought out Freud's help in curing her son's homosexuality. The text reveals the extent to which Freud had evolved over the years in how he viewed homosexuality—"I gather from your letter that your son is a homosexual. I am most impressed by the fact, that you do not mention this term yourself in your information about him. May I question you why you avoid it? Homosexuality is assuredly no advantage, but it is nothing to be ashamed of, no vice, no degradation, it cannot be classified as an illness." Later, in considering the futility of converting this gentleman into a heterosexual, he states—"What analysis can do for your son runs in a different line. If he is unhappy, neurotic, torn by conflicts, inhibited in his social life, analysis may bring him harmony, peace of mind, full efficiency, whether he remains a homosexual or gets changed."[54] The contrast between Freud's later views on homosexuality and the opinions of his contemporaries and later psychoanalysts is quite surprising.

Because, indeed, homosexuality after Freud's time is going to continue to be looked upon as a perversion, following the earlier Freudian formula. In this way, many analysts, forgetting Freud's own evolution, preferred to stick to their earlier views, instead of evolving alongside the new understanding of instinctual desire that had surfaced.[55] The progressive evolution, then, which we see so clearly in Freud's theories about homosexuality, will practically vanish altogether, falling into a regressive dynamic that even precedes Freud's early thinking.

The extreme scientific prudence with which Freud progressed on the issue of homosexuality contrasts with most of the subsequent psychoanalytic literature around the issue. There have been too many arbitrary, dogmatic, and, often, passionate statements that have been made about the homosexual phenomenon. So much so, that it has led experimental psychologists,

53. Freud (1920a), "The Psychogenesis of a Case of Female Homosexuality," in *Standard Edition*, 18: 151–52.

54. Freud, "Letter to an American Mother," *American Journal of Psychiatry*, 107 (1951), 787; also in Ernest Jones, *The Life and Work of Sigmund Freud*, vol. 3 (New York: Basic Books), 195–96.

55. Guy Hocquenghem, *Homosexual Desire* (Durham, NC: Duke University Press 1993), 77; H. J. Beattie, "W. R. D. Fairbairn and the Problem of Homosexuality: A Study in Psychoanalytic Prejudice," *The Psychoanalytic Quarterly* 85 (2016): 889–928.

psychosocial researchers, and anthropologists to discredit psychotherapists at times. Certainly, many of the explanations offered made for easy ridicule of psychoanalytic technique and interpretation. It seems as if the ghosts of homosexuality had set traps for those who were theoretically best prepared to circumvent them.

And thus, it seems that the revolution that led to the affirmation of the homosexual dimension in all human sexuality would also have been intolerable for many psychoanalysts. The entire American faction that endorsed the idea of homosexuality as a reactive adaptation attempting to escape the opposite sex found a way to defend their theory through the denial of the concept of bisexuality. A key pillar, if not *the* key pillar, of Freudian theory was thus eliminated.

The truth is that the post-Freudian discourse on homosexuality has covered over these confusions, contradictions, lack of scientific rigor, impregnation of prejudices, and defensive attitudes, suggesting an underlying theoretical impossibility, fruit of the falsification of some preconceptions, or an insufficient clarification upon them. In fact, the field of psychoanalysis is still far off from offering a consistent, unified, and holistic theory on homosexuality. In few other areas do the contradictions build up so quickly. Therefore, a string of omissions, oversights, and post-Freudian deformations force us to rethink some fundamental issues. Among them, we must highlight the relationship between the drive and the object as well as narcissism and castration.

Perhaps one of the most overlooked details, one that has led to a progressive dumbing down of the homosexual phenomenon is the original separation of the drive and the object established by Freud from the beginning and which we have referred to in chapter 2. Hence, the continued belief in the libido's intrinsic and necessary heterosexual orientation. But that would mean disregarding one of the basic pillars of how psychoanalysis views sexuality.

CHOOSING A HOMOSEXUAL RELATIONSHIP

Psychoanalysts make another mistake related to the belief of the drive's indisputable heterosexuality. It is a rather overt conviction that only the homosexual object choice is related to narcissism. There is a willful blindness in this regard.

As we saw in the previous chapter in reference to Freud's "On Narcissism," there are two types of object choices: one referred to as *support* (or anaclitic) and another of a narcissistic type. The *support* choice is one in which the object of love is chosen based on the model of parental figures; the narcissistic one is based on the model of the subject's relationship with his own person. We will explore the choice of *support* object later on. For now, we will mention that the second type of object choice, the narcissistic one, is not exclusive to homosexuality according to Freud.

Childhood narcissism is present in all types of object choice (even the anaclitic one), without being limited to the homosexual object. On the other hand, we should not assume that *supportive* or *narcissistic* object choices are mutually exclusive. To a certain degree, all kinds of object choices are made with both anaclitic and narcissistic dimensions. Freud states, "We have, however, not concluded that human beings are divided into two sharply differentiated groups, according to their object-choice conforms to the anaclitic or to the narcissistic type; we assume rather that both kinds of object-choice are open to each individual, although he may show a preference for one or the other."[56] As a result, it seems that to a certain extent, we love what has been a reflection of us, reflects us still, or corresponds to a certain ideal about ourselves that has not come to fruition in this life (our feminine or masculine part).

The tendency of psychoanalysts, psychiatrists, and moralists to see narcissism as an innate part of homosexuality implies a misrepresentation of the facts and Freudian texts on which they intend to rely. They forget that the narcissistic object choice is equally likely for homosexuals as heterosexuals and that, in every type of object choice, there is always a narcissistic dimension present.

In Freud's work "On Narcissism: An Introduction," he dove deeper into the theses articulated shortly before in *The Schreber Case*. Like in the latter text, we saw the expansion on the idea of the evolution of libido—the introduction of a narcissistic stage between the autoerotic and the object choice. One would have to ask, then, in the light of the new formulations expressed in "On Narcissism: An Introduction," whether *The Schreber Case*, which seemed to suggest the sequence of autoerotism to narcissism to election of homosexual object to heterosexual object choice, should not be modified as follows:

autoerotism-narcissism-object choice → *homosexual* / *heterosexual*

Additionally, we shouldn't overlook the way in which Freudian thought was conditioned to adhere to a rigid and, sometimes, forced evolutionism. It is understood that Freud's way of thinking was influenced by the Darwinian approach so prevalent during his time. The need to define successive steps and stages sometimes became a real obsession that, on more than one occasion, led to skewing of the data. The fact that heterosexuality was seen as the ultimate goal in the process of libidinal evolution seemed influenced by the field of biology, where heterosexual relationships were seen as superior.

56. Freud (1914c), "On Narcissism: An Introduction," in *Standard Edition*, 14: 88.

Much of the research on homosexuality and data from lab experiments should, additionally, correct, or at least clarify, many of the psychoanalytic statements made about the impossibility of homosexuals having meaningful relationships. Thus, for example, the research by Masters and Johnson highlights the fact that (the most revealing finding, according to the authors' own statement), heterosexual couples can learn a lot from the way homosexuals relate to each other sexually. Among homosexuals, according to these researchers, there is greater subjective involvement, which the authors attribute to better communication. There is, in general, a greater concern for the satisfaction of the other, as compared to heterosexual relationships, where real injustices are committed due to lack of information, communication, and, undoubtedly, the sexist mentality prevailing in our culture.[57]

In short, the propensity to imagine a homosexual inclination toward a narcissistic object choice (we will touch upon this later) is a misrepresentation and an exaggerated tendency, forgetting that homosexuals do not have a monopoly on narcissism and its choice of object. There is a tendency to enclose homosexuals in a hall of mirrors, where they are unable to stop seeking themselves.

Many times, when homosexuals are seen as choosing a narcissistic object, it is deduced by suppressing other data that he has made a wrong choice, that the correct choice would have been to see an object reflecting not the self but another, that is, according to anaclitic object choice. Reference points are easily exchanged, by which narcissism is seen as selfish and the anaclitic choice as surrender and love. One cannot extrapolate because, as we saw in the previous chapter, the choice of the object that heterosexual couples make according to the anaclitic object-choice does not guarantee maturity. Within the context of the Oedipus complex, the individual can get trapped in a ghostly form or grow beyond the stereotype of a nourishing woman or protective man. Something similar can happen within homosexual relationships, neither conforming to the "homosexuality to narcissism to lack of connection" pattern, nor the "heterosexuality to search for the other to love" configuration, when, in reality, the six elements can be combined in myriads of ways.

Because data analyses also seem to suggest that many homosexual object choices are based on a dynamic that is more in line with the support object choice than with the narcissistic one. The choice of a partner, therefore, could be one where a homosexual man searches for a protective father and a woman searches for a nourishing mother, without this choice guaranteeing maturity, contrary to narcissistic choice. Both homosexuals and heterosexuals can be imprisoned in the meshes of Oedipal ghosts or of narcissism, or they can,

57. See Masters and Johnson, "The Fetal Hormonal Environment May Predispose Individuals Towards Particular Patterns of Sexual Behavior," 210–25.

from the Oedipal models and narcissism, approach an authentic encounter with another, having come to accept one's own lack derived from the castration complex.

THE GHOST OF CASTRATION

We thus enter into one of the most heated areas of debate regarding research opinions on homosexuality. Many thinkers consider the *threat of castration* to be the indicator of something that was never overcome in one's personal dynamics. Homosexuals are frightened beings threatened by castration. Women arouse a phantom of mutilation that is impossible to bear, and, hence, their search for the penis that comforts in the face of the continuing threat. The fear of heterosexuality explains, thus, the origin and dynamics of homosexuality. But these generalizations regarding homosexuality reveal that there are many pieces that are without a clear explanation.

Because, as French psychiatrist Jacques Corraze rightly insists, being reactive toward women is one thing, but homosexuality is another. Avoiding women can lead to various inhibitions, neurotic structures, or perverse practices that, in turn, do not necessarily mean accepting a homosexuality that one was not inclined toward.[58] It seems, then, that not every attempt to avoid castration necessarily leads to homosexuality or even that homosexual orientation implies a flight from castration. The fear of heterosexuality may imply, of course, a key to the origin of a homosexual orientation, but it seems, at the very least, reckless to suggest that homosexuality derives from a fear of heterosexuality.

In short, it seems that there are various paths that lead to homosexuality and that the threat of castration is perhaps only one of these paths. Extending this to all types of homosexuality is an unjustified generalization. Not every gay man runs to another man because he is fleeing from a woman, nor does a woman choose another woman because she is fleeing from men. These dynamics, based on the individual biographical vicissitudes, respond to a search for something specific in the other. It should also be noted that a lack of attraction to the genitals of the opposite sex does not always have to mean that the individual is fleeing from the fear of castration; rather, it is based on a specific dynamic, that sexuality has not become the object of desire (we know how tenuous the link between preference and object is), similar to why heterosexuals are not interested, based on their own particular dynamics, in the genitals of another same-sex individual. Sometimes, it is similarity and other times difference that softens masculinity or femininity.

58. See Jacques Corraze, *La homosexualidad y sus dimensiones*, 253.

Aside from the aforementioned reasons for rejecting the notion that homosexuality stems from a perverse character, we should question something else. The fact that homosexuality may not involve any other type of neurotic symptom (which Freud and many other psychoanalysts have admitted to) combined with the claim that homosexuals have not overcome the Oedipus complex and have not assimilated the threat of castration. Acknowledging this possibility would mean rejecting a critical idea within psychoanalytic theory—the significance of the Oedipus and castration in the formation of personality and the etiology of neurosis. To address homosexuality as if it were a monosymptomatic pathology (that is, exhibiting a sole symptom that is keeping an individual from leading a normal life) would be incoherent, reflecting the clinical psychologist's last redoubt in his or her effort to hold onto this idea of homosexuality as a pathology. The only symptom is the deviation from the sexual object that is considered normal. Having said that, "normal" could only then be understood in a statistical sense, which evidently, is not solid ground for clinical conclusions.

Homosexuals are not necessarily negating the differences between the genders, nor are they attempting to identify themselves with a kind of gender neutrality (neither masculine nor feminine, that is, representing an absolute essential narcissism), a phallic expression of totality. A homosexual individual can understand the differences between sexes and accept them, as an internal acknowledgment of limitation, lack, recognition of death, and origin of desire. That acceptance of difference means censorship, a castration of the potentialities of enjoyment. It is thus possible for both homosexuals and heterosexuals to choose and, therefore, to give up, give in, to accept that loss. One does not have to be fatally indebted to the ghost of gender neutrality in the way in which French psychologist André Green makes reference to.[59]

Clinical research shows that, generally, homosexuals display a predominant male or female identification that is both complementary and contradictory with what is masked and subjugated. Desire, through castration, has been channeled in one direction. Because, as Pontalis rightly affirms, the difference is felt not so much *between* the sexes as it is *within* the specific gender. He explains that the envy and the fear of the other sex is secondary; it helps to define and reinforce; it is a signpost of sorts, to everything that seeks to disrupt the object of desire, to everything that separates the individual from himself.[60]

---

59. André Green, "The Neuter Gender," in *Psychic Bisexuality: A British-French Dialogue*, ed. Rosine Jozef Perelberg (London: Routledge, 2018).

60. See Jean Bertrand Pontalis, "L'insaisissable entre-deux," *Nouvelle Revue de Psychanalyse* 7 (1973): 13–26.

What, then, does it mean ultimately to accept castration? The findings so far seem to require us to go beyond the assumption that homosexuality stems from a heterosexuality blocked by men's fear of a woman's missing penis or a woman's denial of her missing organ. Along these lines, it should be noted that accepting castration means more than approaching an inexorable heterosexuality. According to everything we have said, we should view it as a potentiality for enjoying one another without the erroneous belief that one can become the other's everything or that the other can become everything for oneself. In short, like we have said previously, of displaying the capacity to accept the separation and the absence that is in our constitution, of accepting the uncertainties of life and human limitations in the face of the desire's omnipotence, and, ultimately, of accepting death. This, we are convinced, is both challenging yet doable for both homosexuals and heterosexuals. Because, as Spanish homosexual poet Luis Cernuda articulated, "desire is a question without an answer."[61]

HOMOSEXUALITY AS A SEXUAL VARIANT

Now that we have explored the most significant psychosociological, biological, and psychoanalytical findings on homosexuality, all that remains is to draw conclusions about whatever psychopathological characteristics may be present. The data that came from the psychosociological studies seems to discard any type of inherent pathology. The biological angle informed us about certain factors that can predispose an individual toward homosexuality, absent a pathological label. In psychoanalysis, as we have seen, the tendency to frame it as a type of perversion has prevailed. It is time, then, to synthesize the findings available to us thus far.

If we go through the clinical literature on homosexuality, we find that there is no type of neurosis or psychosis that has not been associated with homosexuality at some point nor a psychopathological trait that has not been attributed to it. For some there is an intimate relationship between homosexuality and obsessive neurosis; for others, homosexuality is related to hysteria, for others to phobic neurosis. There are those who think that homosexuality is rather close to psychosis, for some manic-depressive, for others paranoid, and for others, schizophrenic.[62] Homosexuals, we are told, suffer from a profound type of masochism, an intense sadism, an autistic background, a vivid depression, a type of exhibitionism, an inexorable pathological loneliness,

61. Luis Cernuda, "No decía palabras," in *Los placeres prohibidos* (1931): *Poesía Completa* (Barcelona: Barral, 1977), 123.
62. See Charles W. Socarides, *The Overt Homosexual* (New York: J. Aronson, 1968), 35–102.

a swelling anguish, an inability to experience deep emotions, to fulfill the intellectual potential, to hold a normal job, living for the fantasy of revenge, aiming to dehumanize relationships and hurt others. And, of course, a severe narcissism that makes it absolutely impossible to accept differences and, therefore, the other.[63]

Not all psychoanalysts, of course, have veered so far from the Freudian perspectives. There have also been voices within the psychoanalytic and psychiatric communities that have ideas that are the opposite of the aforementioned. There are many who have understood and accepted without issue that, in fact, homosexuality and heterosexuality are as equally as likely to present neurotic or psychotic symptoms. But as the social and psychoanalyst philosopher Ernest van den Haag states: "There is nothing to prove that a homosexuality results in a type of character that it is necessarily linked to it (regardless of cultural factors)."

Not all psychoanalysts, of course, have been shown to defend positions so far from what Freudian approaches were. There have also been voices within the psychoanalytic and psychiatric settings that have made statements that are very much contrary to those indicated. There are many who have understood and accepted readily that, in fact, homosexuality can present neurotic or psychotic symptoms of all kinds as in heterosexuality. Social philosopher and psychoanalyst Ernest van den Haag argued that there was no proof that homosexuality led to any specific type of personality.[64]

When psychoanalysis meets its own objectives of providing health and relieving disease, it will not see homosexuality as an illness or something that must be fixed in some way. To the extent that homosexuals are able to live a harmonious, creative, and satisfying life, to the extent that they can work and love, execute personal projects, and relate lovingly to others from a place of freedom and uniqueness, the field of psychoanalysis must stop seeing them as a psychic conflict to be solved. As French psychoanalyst Gerard Bonnet points out, the field of psychoanalysis does not see homosexuality as a fault or a handicap from which the individual should be severed from at all costs. And not for lack of ambition, or a certain laxness, or outright rejection of all normality, but as a result of a series of conclusions. "It is part of our perverse game," Bonnet tells us, "to believe that every homosexual is perverse."[65]

---

63. All these psychopathological features are compiled from among various psychoanalytic authors by Franco Giunched, "La Chiesa e L'omosessualità," *La Civiltà Cattolica* 130, no. 4 (1979): 468–78.

64. Ernest van den Haag, "Notes on Homosexuality and Its Cultural Setting," in *The Problem of Homosexuality in Modern Society*, ed. Hendrick Ruitenbeek (New York: Dutton 1963), 361.

65. Gerard Bonnet, "Une forme méconnu du désir," *Lumière et Vie* XXIX (1980): 51–65. Perversion in homosexuality occurs when there is a predominance of destructive personality dimensions. See Antonio Pérez Sánchez, "Perverse Structure of Personality and Additive Components," *Revista de Psiconálisis de Madrid* 14 (1996): 35–59.

Beyond psychoanalysis, psychodiagnostic research related to homosexuality is also quite interesting. This type of research looks at the degree to which homosexuals adapt to their environment through a series of personality tests. Briefly stated, the research concludes that, firstly, there are no apparent differences between homosexuals or heterosexuals based on tests like the Rorschach, TAT, or MMPI. And, secondly, that it is has been impossible to distinguish a pathology that characterizes the homosexual population. The conclusions from one of the more interesting studies that have been carried out is that homosexuality is not a medical diagnosis, since its forms are as varied as within heterosexuality and that it must be considered, therefore, as a deviation from traditional sexual norms, psychologically within the range of normalcy.[66]

HOMOPHILIA AND HOMOPHOBIA CHALLENGES

No longer seeing homosexuality as a disease should not, however, lead to other misconceptions. This should not be a justification for the participation of indiscriminate sexual behavior. As within heterosexuality, there are many perverse and neurotic ways of behaving. It would not be fair to the homosexual population if it were to be understood that the homosexual experience lends itself to whatever expressions are desired. Perhaps certain homosexual groups, reacting to the various vexations suffered throughout history, are now unwilling to accept the problematic dimensions that can be seen in their own way of living out their sexual-emotional experience. Understanding the causes and recognizing the consequences of less healthy behaviors would, however, help homosexuals to be accepted in the homophobic society that now excludes them.

The reality of promiscuity, for example, which we touched upon at the beginning of this chapter, remains a problem worthy of consideration as well as the probable cause of much of the conflict and neuroticism within the gay population. Analysis and investigation into the roots of this problem should be undertaken, once the sexual orientation is discarded as the cause of promiscuity (as earlier stated, the seeming absence of promiscuity in the female homosexual population lends itself to this idea).

---

66. See Evelyn Hooker, "The Adjustment of the Male Overt Homosexual," in *The Problem of Homosexuality in Modern Society*, ed. Hendrick Ruitenbeek, 181–204. Similar results were obtained in other investigations by applying the MMPI. See Marvin Siegelman, "Psychological Adjustment of Homosexual and Heterosexual Men: A Cross-National Replication," *Archives of Sexual Behaviour* 7 (1978): 1–11; and "Adjustment of Homosexual and Heterosexual Women: A Cross-National Replication," *Archives of Sexual Behaviour* 8 (1979): 121–25. Due to social science findings, in 1974 the American Psychiatric Association removed homosexuality from the list of mental disorders. See Jack Drescher, "Out of DSM: Depathologizing Homosexuality," *Behavioral Sciences*, 4 (2015): 565–75. The World Health Organization also withdrew homosexuality from its list of diseases.

Undoubtedly, introjected social rejection seems to be one of the major factors in explaining this promiscuous pathology. Such internalized rejection, from even early childhood, becomes a source of internal division and intense repression as well as a generalized inhibition about giving away any sign, however minimal, that could raise suspicion about one's homosexuality. In short, internalized rejection undoubtedly leads to a deep anxiety that, many times, finds no other release aside from compulsive and self-destructive promiscuity. Behind the scenes, there is probably a deep desire to break the rules and to attack a society that eroded one's most intimate aspirations. As the society is deeply internalized, outward destruction inevitably also becomes self-destruction. To understand what the introjected social rejection entails, we would have to imagine the effect of the deep repression homosexuals experience from childhood. We know that self-acceptance toward one's homosexual orientation generally results in a significant decrease in anxiety and, with it, the promiscuous tendency. This is a fundamental reason (together with the above-mentioned reasoning) that today there is less and less talk about treating homosexuality itself and more focus on the treatment of conflicts that derive from it.

Another important factor to consider regarding the phenomenon of promiscuity among male homosexuals, especially given its relative rarity in female homosexuals, would be the difference between men's and women's roles in sexual attainment. In a heterosexual relationship, the male is predisposed to play the role of conquistador, which beyond cultural factors, also points to men's and women's differing sexual response times. When the sexual object belongs to the same gender, the response time can be as slow or as quick as that gender's predisposition allows.

Regardless of these factors, individual aspects should also be taken into account, such as one's own perverse or neurotic tendencies, the kind that sometimes surface in homosexual relationships. The perverse homosexual (obviously in the psychoanalytic, not ethical sense) shows a severe difficulty in integrating impulsivity as well as in establishing meaningful long-lasting relationships that respect the other as a free and unique individual. Homosexuality, then, as Bonnet accurately analyzes it, becomes an absolute imperative, carried out with precise requirements and according to a ritual and conditions specific to the individual in question.[67] The perverse homosexual is tied to his practice; he is one with it. He is perverted, that is, condemned to walk along a certain path, without knowing why. He cannot find meaning in life but on the basis of a sexuality that becomes a whirlwind of self-destruction. This is the place where psychoanalysis could come in to change the perverse dynamics of the subject. It would not be, then, to *cure* homosexuality but, as stated

67. Bonnet, "Une forme méconnu du désir," 52–61.

earlier, to facilitate a symbolic castration, that is, to acknowledge the impossibility of being or finding a total Other, one without separation or difference that would totally satiate all desire. Only in this way could the homosexual individual be able to experience, within his same affective orientation, an empowering and creative desire.

As we noted previously, homosexuality does not correlate to neurosis or psychosis, yet it is equally as vulnerable to these tendencies as heterosexuals. Without contradicting this general principle, we can say that there do seem to be certain types of conflict that are more frequently associated with homosexual affectivity. The controversy over their eventual pathological condition seems to have left little room to investigate these possibilities. It would seem incumbent, however, to explore the relationship between homosexuality and certain identity disorders, indicative of an emotional confusion not dissimilar from hysteria. Attention should also be paid to the appearance of (particularly in male homosexuals) certain forms of narcissism that could be magnified within homosexuality.[68] These would be based on assumptions of identifying with what we might call the "cultural-feminine." In these particular cases, it would be an identification with the socioculturally role assigned to women, who, as objects for men, are driven to cultivate their own image in order to carry out the assigned role of becoming an attractive object. On the other hand, the macho culture can also create identifications with the pure male model, which further another narcissistic dynamic. We can see this in homosexuals who orbit the worlds of body worship and bodybuilding.

A psychoanalytical look at how homosexual groups sometimes organize is also warranted. Gay groups sometimes fulfill unhealthy functions in the inevitable ghetto dimension to which they are driven. No one with a certain awareness of the homosexual dilemma will deny the critical role that homosexual groups have played for their members and also for the betterment of a homophobic and heterosexist society. But also those groups, paradoxically, have become too often complicit in the social tenure to marginalize and exclude themselves in their own spheres. Society pushes them beyond their limits, and they are thus forced to see themselves almost exclusively through their sexual orientation. As if this were the only defining quality and there were no other predominant elements to someone's life. In this way, homosexual groups, if they are not careful, fall prey to the dynamics that every closed minority group does.

But the homosexual conflict is not only a matter for homosexuals. It concerns us all in some way. We also know that working through this dimension in our sexual and emotional world is not always easy. The repercussions,

68. This is what emerges from a study by Moukhtar-Baczako titled *Homosexuality in the Mirror of Narcissus*, presented at the First Congress on Psychotherapy in Vienna, 1996.

however, can be significant. All of our relationships to some degree, whether with men or women, are affected to a certain degree by how we resolve internally the relationship with the homosexual components that, either in our makeup or through our experiences, form part of our emotional dynamics. We should not forget that nobody reaches a definitive sexual orientation and that there is a whole oscillation between the masculine and the feminine in human erotic life. "In all of us," says Freud, "throughout life, the libido normally oscillates between male and female objects."[69] Films and novels have often picked up on this oscillation better than many psychology treatises. But our culture, marked by a macho mentality and by a certain heterosexism, poses a challenge in this regard. Impoverished personal development, when not resulting in outright conflict, is the most common outcome.

That homosexual dimension can hinder many types of relationships (for example, with friendships), and as we will later see, it can also lead to confusion in the heterosexual identity similar to homosexuals; it can also significantly condition, and not always in a positive way, the choice of a romantic partner. It can also be used as self-punishment in the form of a ghost that essentially seeks to self-destruct and can, of course, be channeled via a homophobic projection. In this case, it becomes a ghost representing either the concept or the reality of homosexuality that must be conjured and aggressively annihilated. The speculations that have been made, for example, of Hitler's latent homosexuality would seem to explain why he was driven to massacre thousands of homosexuals.

It is with good reason that George Weinberg never considered a patient to be recovered unless he had overcome his prejudice toward homosexuality. Indeed, we must conclude that this prejudice is also harmful to heterosexuals, to the degree to which it is an expression of this homophobic disease. It is this homophobia that has produced all manner of theories concerning the origin and diagnosis of homosexuality, not to mention the social, political, and religious marginalization and the persecutions that have taken place throughout history.

BIBLIOGRAPHY

Beach, Frank A., and Clellan S. Ford. *Patterns of Sexual Behaviour*. New York: Harper & Row, 1969.

Bell, Allan P., and Martin S. Weinberg. *Homosexualities*. New York: Simon & Schuster, 1978.

Bieber, Irving, ed. *Homosexuality. A Psychoanalytic Study*. New York: Basic Books 1967.

69. Freud (1920a), "The Psychogenesis of a Case of Female Homosexuality," 158. See also Freud (1937), *Analysis Terminable and Interminable*, in *Standard Edition*, 244.

Bonnet, Gerard. "Une forme méconnu du désir." *Lumière et Vie* XXIX (1980): 51–65.
Bullough V. L., and B. E. Bullough. *Human Sexuality: An Encyclopedia*. New York and London: Routledge, 2014.
Byne, William, and Bruce Parsons. "Human Sexual Orientation." *Archives of General Psychiatry* 50 (1993): 228–39.
Carlin, Nathan, and Donald Capps. *The Gift of Sublimation: A Psychoanalytic Study of Multiple Masculinities*. Eugene, OR: Cascade Books, 2015.
Corraze, Jacques. *La homosexualité*. Paris: PUF, 2005.
———. *Les dimensions de la homosexualité*. Paris: Privat, 1968.
D'Angelo, Lucía. *La homosexualidad masculina. Ensayos freudianos sobre la sexualidad.* Madrid: Síntesis, 2004.
Dean, Tim, and Christopher Lane, eds. *Homosexuality and Psychoanalysis.* Chicago, IL: University of Chicago Press, 2001.
De Cecco, John P. and David Allen Parker, eds. *Sex, Cells and Same-Sex Desire: The Biology of Sexual Preference.* New York and London: Routledge, 2014.
Domínguez-Morano, Carlos. "El debate psicológico sobre la homosexualidad." In *La homosexualidad: un debate abierto*, edited by Javier Gafo, 13–95. Desclée de Brouwer: Bilbao, 1997.
Döner, Günter. "Gene- and Environment-Dependent Neuroendocrine Etiogenesis of Homosexuality and Transsexualism." Lecture at Universidad Complutense, Madrid 1991.
———. "Neuro-Endocrine Response to Estrogens and Brain Differentiation in Heterosexuals, Homosexuals, and Transsexuals." *Archives of Sexual Behavior* 17 (1988): 57–76.
Flanders, Sara, Francois Ladame, Anders Carlsberg, Petra Heymanns, Despina Naziri, and Denny Panitz. "On the Subject of Homosexuality: What Freud Said." *International Journal of Psychoanalysis* 97 (2016): 933–50.
Freud, Sigmund (1922b). "Some Neurotic Mechanisms in Jealousy, Paranoia, and Homosexuality." In *The Standard Edition of the Complete Psychological Works of Sigmund Freud*, edited and translated by James Strachey, 18: 223–32. London: Hogarth, 1966.
——— (1905d). *Three Essays on the Sexual Theory*. In *Standard Edition*, 7: 125–245.
——— (1908c). "On the Sexual Theories of Children." In *Standard Edition*, 9: 207–26.
——— (1911c). *Psychoanalytic Notes on an Autobiographical Account of a Case of Paranoia* (Dementia paranoides). In *Standard Edition*: 12: 3–82.
——— (1920a). "The Psychogenesis of a Case of Female Homosexuality." In *Standard Edition*, 18: 147–72.
——— (1927e). "Fetishism." In *Standard Edition*, 21: 149–57.
Gafo, Javier. *La homosexualidad: un debate abierto.* Bilbao: Desclée de Brouwer, 1997.
Greven, David. "Rereading Narcissism: Freud's Theory of Male Homosexuality and Hawthorne's *Gentle Boy.*" *Modern Psychoanalysis* 34 (2009): 48–78.
Hocquenghem, Guy. *Homosexual Desire.* Durham, NC: Duke University Press, 1993.

Kinsey, Alfred, Pomeroy Wardell, and Clyde Martin. *Sexual Behavior in the Human Male*. Philadelphia and London: W. B. Saunders Company, 1948.

Krich, Aron M., ed. *The Homosexuals: As Seen by Themselves and Thirty Authorities.* New York: Citadel, 1964.

Marmor, Judd., ed. *Homosexuality Behavior: A Modern Reappraisal*. New York and London: Basic Books, 1980.

———. *Homosexuality Inversión: The Multiple Roots of Homosexuality*. New York and London: Basic Books, 1965.

Masters, William H., and Virginia E. Johnson. *Homosexuality in Perspective.* Boston: Little, Brown and Co., 1979.

Mirabet, I., and A. Mullol. *Homosexualidad, hoy*. Barcelona: Herder, 1985.

Money, John. *Hermaphroditism: An Inquiry into the Nature of a Human Paradox*. Cambridge, MA: Harvard University Press, 1952.

Omoto, Allen M., and Howard S. Kurtzman, eds. *Sexual Orientation and Mental Health: Examining Identity and Development in Lesbian, Gay, and Bisexual People.* Washington, DC: American Psychological Association, 2006.

Paul, William, James D. Weinrich, John C. Gonsiorek, and Mary E. Hotvedt. *Homosexuality: Social, Psychological and Biological Issues.* Beverly Hills, CA: Sage, 1982.

Perelberg, Rosine Jozef, ed. *Psychic Bisexuality: A British-French Dialogue.* London: Routledge, 2018.

Plummer, Ken, ed. *Modern Homosexualities: Fragments of Lesbian and Gay Experiences.* London and New York: Routledge, 1992.

Poiani, Aldo. *Animal Homosexuality: A Biosocial Perspective*. Cambridge: Cambridge University Press, 2010.

Robinson, Paul. "Freud and Homosexuality." *Constellations* 6 (1999): 80–84.

Ruitenbeek, Hendrick. *The Problem of Homosexuality in Modern Society.* New York: Dutton 1963.

Ruse, Michael. *Homosexuality: A Philosophical Inquiry.* Oxford: Basil Blackwell, 1988.

Sandford, Theo, Judith Schuyf, Jan Willen Duyvendak, and Jeffrey Weeks, eds. *Lesbian and Gay Studies: An Introductory, Interdisciplinary Approach*. London: Sage, 2000.

Sengers, W. J. *Se reconnaître homosexual.* Paris: MAME, 1970.

Siegelman, Marvin. "Adjustment of Homosexual and Heterosexual Women: A Cross-National Replication." *Archives of Sexual Behaviour* 8 (1979): 121–25.

———. "Psychological Adjustment of Homosexual and Heterosexual Men: A Cross-National Replication." *Archives of Sexual Behaviour* 7 (1978): 1–11.

Socarides, Charles W. *The Overt Homosexual.* New York and London: Grüne & Stratton, 1988.

Tripp, Clarence A. *The Homosexual Matrix.* New York: McGraw-Hill, 1975.

Weinberg, Martin S., and Colin J. Williams. *Male Homosexuals.* New York: Oxford University Press, 1974.

Chapter Eight

Life and Death of Narcissus

Instinctual desire thrives and grows within our own personal reality. In truth, there is nowhere else where it can seed itself. It is our reality that becomes its primary object. Eventually, it will detach itself as it finds other objects that provide satisfaction and continuity. But desire will always spring back and forth from objects, to love objects, to one's own coveted reality. Narcissus, therefore, will be one of the names that desire will sometimes adopt. It is a part of life but, more than that, a necessity for thriving in this world. But Narcissus must allow an opening for the Eros that can facilitate connection to others and to life itself. Otherwise, Narcissus leads to sterility, madness, and death itself. As Freud pointed out, without love, we fall ill.

But today we live in an era in which Narcissus takes on particular relevance. It is a subject that is forever relevant because the ability to love oneself is a basic requirement for mental health and personal development. Understood this way, self-esteem has risen in prominence and become a central concept within certain psychological currents. Let us start this chapter then by closely analyzing this phenomenon.

THE CONCEPT OF SELF-ESTEEM AND ITS ORIGINS

Self-esteem has become a ubiquitous term. There are few other concepts derived from the field of psychology that have gone on to be so commonly used in everyday speech. Just about any conversation can inadvertently lead to remarks about an individual's self-esteem and its significant consequences. Having high self-esteem is seen as essential for functioning well in life since its presence appears to affect innumerable aspects of relationships with self and others. It affects how individuals function both in the private and public spheres.[1] It is not surprising then that whole sections of self-help books fill the shelves in bookstores and that the various publishers are eager to publish works on this theme. Internet web pages on the subject multiply exponentially. Success is assured.

We find, then, that this concept has acquired mythical status. Explanations and methods are used to cast a light upon a variety of situations, and it is self-esteem that is seen as the solution for curing the most confounding behavioral enigmas. Even politicians are eager to incorporate this concept into their talking points. For many, it has become a magic wand that can lead to good mental functioning. Others, however, are less sure, feeling uncertain about this concept. Obviously, the self-esteem boom could not happen without an overlay of other factors converging from elsewhere. Some of these critical factors should be reviewed, albeit briefly.

Self-esteem truly burst forth on the scene and took shape in the humanist psychological movement involving figures from various technical-theoretical backgrounds,[2] unanimous in their portrayal of the negative image that both American behaviorism and psychoanalysis had created around the individual. Humanistic psychology thus proclaimed itself to be the third branch of the general field of psychology via a 1962 manifesto, addressing those human capacities and potentials often overlooked by psychoanalysis and behavioral psychology: "love, creativity, self, growth, organism, basic need-gratification, self-actualization, higher values, being, becoming, spontaneity, play, humor, affection, naturalness, warmth, ego-transcendence, objectivity, autonomy, responsibility, meaning, fair-play, transcendental experience, peak experience, courage, and related concepts."[3] The hopeful and optimistic terrain that self-esteem requires was well suited for this new humanist psychological conception where the conscious becomes more prevalent than the unconscious, the normal over the abnormal, and the spiritual over the instinctual.

---

1. See Jude H. Borders, ed., *Handbook of the Psychology of Self-Esteem* (New York: Nova Publishers, 2014); David A. Levy, "The 'Self-Esteem' Enigma: A Critical Analysis," *North America Journal of Psychology* 21 (2019): 305–308.

2. Figures from the other movements were also influential, such as from the Gestalt school (like Kurt Goldstein, who was an early influencer of this type of therapy), phenomenological psychology, existentialism, or even of certain psychoanalysis (such as Erich Fromm with his theory of humanistic psychoanalysis). The most representative figures have been (apart from Kurt Goldstein), Abraham Maslow, Carl Rogers, and Fritz Perls. The most recent cognitive psychology has also tuned in in large part with important aspects of humanistic psychology, as can be seen in the work of Albert Ellis, *Reason and Emotion in Psychotherapy* (New York: Lyle Stuart, 1994). See Kirk Schneider, J. Fraser Pierson, and James Bugental, *The Handbook of Humanistic Psychology* (Los Angeles: SAGE, 2015).

3. Stansfeld Sargent, "The Humanistic Approach to Personality," in *Handbook of General Psychology*, ed. Benjamin B. Wolman (New York: Prentice Hall, 1973), 818; H. Quitmann, *Humanistische Psychologie* (Göttingen: Hogrefe, 1996).

But it is also evident that each area of psychology takes shape in certain sociocultural, economic, and even political environments. Although many of the figures from humanistic psychology came from Nazi Europe (Kurt Goldstein, Fritz Perls, Charlotte Bühler, and Erich Fromm), it was in America where the movement truly flourished and where we encounter the field's most representative figures (Abraham Maslow and Carl Rogers). The enthusiastic and youthful spirit of American culture thus merged with the phenomenological and existentialist currents prevalent in European thinkers. The optimistic spirit of the New Deal that was Roosevelt's political centerpiece, meant to lift a nation that had experienced the strong economic crisis of the 1920s, was also influential. Humanistic psychology was brought forth in a culture that had not directly savored Greek tragedies or the European Theater of the Absurd but, rather, one that was raised on an impulsive, youthful, and creative spirit (Walt Whitman being a prime example) together with economic well-being. The concept of self-esteem thus found an ideal environment in which to flourish.

More importantly, it should be noted that the concept of self-esteem and self-love stems from an awareness that a person has value, an idea that flourished in Western culture through the development of individual rights. The exultation of the individual is, without a doubt, the great achievement of modernity. It is an ethic that, like an illustration of egoism and a passionate interest in well-being, is espoused through a theoretical framework by some[4] and understood implicitly by others. Individualism, says Fernando Savater, could be seen as the conquest of the postindustrial and postmodern subject, free of collectivism and totalitarianism.[5] But as Savater himself points out that the same process of individuation resulting from social change also has risks.[6] We will revisit this later.

We should also not overlook the influence of guilt and the superego ingrained in Judeo-Christian culture and thus in the rise and interest toward the concept of self-esteem. It has helped to relieve the weight of deeply introjected culpability stemming from pedagogical or spiritual approaches that centered on self-denial and blame. It is not surprising, therefore, that, in very religious environments, the concept of self-esteem gained adherents quickly. Among them, we find some of the most troubled individuals. Self-esteem has allowed individuals to administer a self-love that was once stigmatized. It has become permissible to think well of oneself and to be treated with consideration and care without the feelings of guilt. "Treat yourself to the good life" is the tongue-in-cheek title that Spanish philosopher Fernando Savater gave to

4. There are works that were influential in Spain, such as Fernando Savater, *Ética como amor propio* (Madrid: Mondadori, 1988) and *Ética para Amador* (Barcelona: Ariel, 1992).
5. Savater, *Ética como amor propio*, 146.
6. Savater, *Ética como amor propio*, 146–59.

one of the chapters of a book titled *Ética para Amador* [*Ethics for Amador*],[7] designed to teach ethics to high school students.

As previously mentioned, the concept of self-esteem has not always been well-received. Many have expressed misgivings about this concept. Undoubtedly, the biggest concern is how self-esteem could become complicit with the more narcissistic and individualistic dimensions of personality. In general, the same authors who study and analyze the concept of self-esteem take care to scrupulously point out how this differs from problematic modes of childish egocentrism. Self-esteem is not opposed to *hetero-esteem*, or esteem for others, but to lack of self-respect. However, a more detailed analysis of literature addressing self-esteem seems to indicate that the boundaries and implications between self-esteem and narcissism are not sufficiently delimited. All too often, a certain exaltation of otherwise beneficial self-esteem turns into superficial practices that greatly diverge from the original ideal. Let us, then, explore this topic further.

RETHINKING NARCISSISM

Indeed, the psychological concept that self-esteem most resonates with is that of narcissism. But the fields of psychology and psychoanalysis have treated this concept with an enormous degree of ambiguity.[8] The terms have never been clearly defined. Hence, the boundaries between the two fluctuate and are depicted differently, depending on the context. Some exhibit a narcissism that is not accompanied by self-esteem and even a narcissism that seriously hinders the attainment of self-esteem. Others might believe that someone can have an inborn sense of self-esteem without traces of narcissism. In short, whether self-esteem and narcissism are interrelated or not will depend on the way each concept is interpreted. We should, therefore, dive into their particular meanings. In order to do this, we must return to the concept of narcissism, a recurrent theme in today's psychoanalytic theorizations.

7. Savater, *Ética como amor propio*, 67–81.

8. See Avi Besser, ed., *Handbook of the Psychology of Narcissism: Diverse Perspective* (New York: Nova Publishers, 2014); P. Guillem, J. A. Loren, and E. Orozco, "Introduction: Le narcissisme dans le processus de structuration et de déstructuration psychiques," *Revue Française de Psychanalyse* LV (1991): 39–100. In this wonderful study, the authors point out that Freud's concept of narcissism appears simultaneously as a perversion; a libidinal stage (between autoerotism and object choice); a regressive state similar to sleep, an organic disease, hypochondria, psychosis, and a state of love; a type of object choice and something that thwarts the supportive choice; a type of self-identification; a destination for the libidinal drive that withdraws from external objects; a libidinal complement of selfishness; an original, primordial state of the Ego; and, finally, a narcissism that brings out the "small differences."

We should recall the origin of the term from the Greek mythological character known as Narcissus, who, condemned by the goddess Nemesis to fall in love with himself, drowns in a pool of water after attempting to embrace his reflection. Misguided affection, detachment from reality, and a devastating conclusion—all these are indicative of the nature of the concept known as narcissism.

The term was introduced into the psychiatric field by Havelock Ellis in 1898 and used by criminologist Paul Näcke in 1899 to describe a type of sexual perversion.[9] Elisabeth Roudinesco and Michel Plon, however, inform us that it was the Frenchman Alfred Binet who first used it in 1887 to describe a form of fetishism, consisting of taking oneself as a sexual object.[10] In any case, it was Freud who normalized it within the field of psychoanalysis, making it a common term within the fields of psychopathology and psychiatry, and eventually everyday speech.[11]

The field of psychoanalysis introduces narcissism as a mechanism for understanding a series of phenomena within the psyche in which there is an apparent difficulty in accessing a reality outside of one's own. The subject seems to be trapped in his own mind, incapable of recognizing that which, however close, is different or contradictory to his own world of desires. Like the mythological character, an individual intoxicated by an inner reality,[12] characterized by the self-image that is powerfully captivating.

As we saw, it was with the concept of homosexuality, seen as a difficulty in accepting the differences between the sexes, where Freud first made an association with narcissism.[13] We also saw in the chapter on homosexuality that eventually Freud began to look at it as a particular stage of affective (libidinal) development that served as a type of bridge between a primitive autoerotism and the possible choice of an external object, that is, the ability

9. This is what Freud pointed out in his *Three Essays on the Theory of Sexuality* in a 1915 note, confessing his error in attributing this concept to Näcke. See *Standard Edition*, 7: 218, and *Standard* Edition, 14: 73.

10. See Elisabeth Roudinesco and Michel Plon, *Dictionnaire de la psychanalyse* (Paris: Fayard, 1997), s.v. "narcissisme."

11. Joseph Sandler, Ethel Person, and Peter Fonagy, *Freud's "On Narcissism: An Introduction"* (London: Routledge, 2012).

12. The term *Narcissus* etymologically stems from *narcosis*, which means something like stupefied. It has the same root as *narcotic*.

13. The first appearance of the term seems to be in a 1915 note in Freud, *Three Essays on the Theory of Sexuality*, 7: 145, which sees the homosexual object choice as choosing someone that reflects oneself. According to Freud, attachment to the mother leads to an identification with her and, from there, a narcissistic object-choice in which one tries to find someone in whom to see his reflection while avoiding the anguish of castration. We see the same line of thought in (1910c) "Leonardo da Vinci and a Memory of His Childhood," in *Standard Edition*, 11: 99–100. Since then, the relationship between homosexuality and narcissism has been widely discussed. I addressed this in "El debate psicológico sobre la homosexualidad" [The psychological debate over homosexuality], in Javier Gafo Fernández, *La homosexualidad: un debate abierto* (Bilbao: Desclée de Brouwer, 1997), 13–95.

to care for people or things externally.[14] Thus, in self-eroticism, the subject would be in a primitive situation in which, without even having formed a unified image, he would obtain an erotic satisfaction from his reality, without any interference from the outside world. Narcissism would then be an intermediate step in which the subject, without yet becoming interested in any external love object, fixates on that new unifying structure of personality that is the self. That narcissistic phase that Freud considered indispensable could, however, become undesirable, lingering in the later stages of evolution or even reestablishing itself during a behavioral regression.[15] We would thus encounter personalities whose essential affective dynamics would be marked by that particular affection of self, with a subsequent difficulty in recognizing and accessing an external reality. The inner world, the activity of thinking itself, the particular individual's affections, would be favored over the possibilities and demands of the outside world.

Expressions of Narcissism

From this early perspective, where narcissism is understood as a stage in the process of libidinal evolution, Freud goes on to see it as a component of emotional development, a critical component in understanding both pathological and normal life situations. It is not so much a stage in the evolution of the libido but, rather, a reality that has particular intensity during the infant period but should also be deemed a vital part of emotional development since it always presents in a variety of forms. There will always be an oscillation between the individual's narcissistic focus, which repeatedly refers back to one's own reality, and the interest, attention, and attraction to the world of external objects, personal or not. Thus, when seeking to understand an individual's relationship with himself and with external objects, the narcissistic aspects must be taken into account. This is how narcissism is presented in the most relevant work on this topic within this area of psychoanalytic theory—Freud's 1914 essay "On Narcissism."[16]

From this new perspective, narcissism becomes the key to understanding the dynamics of personality and its conflicts. Neurosis, from this perspective, is understood as having a loose connection with reality, while madness is seen in more radical terms as a break with the external world along with

14. Sigmund Freud (1911c), *Psychoanalytic Notes on an Autobiographical Account of a Case of Paranoia*, in *Standard Edition*, 12: 59–60; Freud (1913), *Totem and Taboo*, in *Standard Edition*, 13, 89–90.

15. "Thus narcissistic libido is constantly being transformed into object-libido, and vice-versa," affirms Freud (1925d), *An Autobiographical Study*, in *Standard Edition*, 20: 56.

16. In this work, Freud focuses primarily on the double current of sexual drive, one object-libido and the other narcissistic. The Ego now seems to be the great reservoir for libido—it is the one that handles the libidinal flows, being also an object for the libido.

a totally self-absorbed psyche.[17] Indeed, in a state of psychosis, the subject loses interest in the world and withdraws into a private sphere at the whim of the deepest desires or fears. For example, if in a state of delirium a psychotic individual is convinced that he is Napoleon, no sensible justifications to the contrary will make a difference. He will only worry about finding his Josephine in an extreme refusal of reality. It is this type of extreme narcissism where it becomes impossible to project libido onto the external world. All of it is tragically suppressed inwardly.

To some degree, neurotic individuals will also perceive that inner excess of libido. Hence, the severe difficulty in adapting to external challenges. "Neurotics," Freud expressed in *Totem and Taboo*, "are only affected by what is thought with intensity and pictured with emotion, whereas agreement with external reality is a matter of no importance."[18] The emphasis on the mental processes overrides judgment, creating a kind of malicious and perilous disregard of reality, which gives rise to all that additional suffering that characterizes neurosis. They say that the psychotic individual is the one who after breaking with reality insists that two plus two equals five. While the neurotic knows and recognizes that two plus two equals four, he experiences discomfort with this reality. The neurotic individual thus relates to people and things through personal ghosts, mixing them with the relationship objects and, therefore, blurring those boundaries. The psychotic individual simply casts an object aside, dispenses with it, preferring his own desires.

But narcissism also plays an important role in everyday life. We somehow cannot help revisiting, as a kind of maternal womb, the oldest and most primitive aspects of our psyche, where there is no reality other than our own. This happens daily, when we sleep and dream, for example. Like with psychosis, during that period of time, there is nothing other than our inner experience. Like psychosis, when we dream, we have imaginary experiences created by the world of more primitive desires and needs. We believe what we see and hear in those fantastical imaginings, which in reality are only a by-product of the mind. And we believe it with fervency. Like with psychosis, we cloister ourselves in an inner world of radical narcissism, resembling a silkworm that sees its cocoon as the entire world.[19] To understand ourselves better we

17. Already in the aforementioned work, (1911c) *Psychoanalytic Notes on an Autobiographical Account of a Case of Paranoia*, in *Standard Edition*, 12: 59; 72; 75–77, Freud posits that in a state of repression the withdrawn libido is in suspension, producing somatizations via hysteria and an accumulation of the Ego itself through paranoia, resulting in delusions of grandeur. In the case of schizophrenia, the regression is even greater, reaching the stage of primitive autoerotism. Along these lines, see *Introductory Lectures on Psycho-Analysis*, in *Standard Edition*, 428–30.

18. Freud, *Totem and Taboo*, in *Standard Edition*, 13: 86.

19. See Sigmund Freud (1914c), "On Narcissism: An Introduction," in *Standard Edition*, 14: 82–83; (1916–1917) *Introductory Lectures on Psycho-Analysis*, in *Standard Edition*, 16: 427.

should remember that much of our life, which is spent sleeping, occurs in a state of profound narcissism.

In a less intense form, narcissism also materializes like continuous waves throughout our life in various ways. Through illness, for example, we often see a normal narcissistic retraction prototype. A toothache tends to make individuals lose interest in life while they focus their attention on that which is experiencing pain.[20] A dose of narcissism will likely be necessary to implement remedies that alleviate our discomfort. Moreover, if that dose of narcissism were missing, we would have to suspect that something was wrong with us.[21]

We should not forget that, as we saw in chapter 4 in the analysis of the evolution and development of instinctual desire, we all start from a place of profound narcissism,[22] in which the only reality is our own, and which persists as a tendency to go back to that primitive state in which the inner and outer were blurred. From there, begins a complicated and difficult process of opening to the external reality. But that necessary renunciation of the centripetal tendency that forever wants to place us at the center of our universe while ignoring that hazy outer reality is never easy, and it rarely occurs without complications. We can all fall prey to regressions of primitive and previously overcome narcissistic positions. A love disappointment, a failure in social relations, or a general intensification of the libido without a proper outlet can all cause a regression to take place.[23]

The fascination for our own reality resembles that of Narcissus confronting his mirror image. And there are many ways in which it is revived in us without realization in most cases. Often, even others appear to hold up the mirror that fills us with complacency. They operate as an excuse for camouflaged self-contemplation. Or is it not something like what happens, as we analyzed when talking about the relationship with children, when we are fascinated by the baby that lives in a world of absolute complacency and in total indif-

20. Freud (1914c), "On Narcissism: An Introduction," in *Standard Edition*, 14: 82–83; (1926d), "Inhibitions, Symptoms and Anxiety," in *Standard Edition*, 20: 171–72.

21. See Heinz Kohut, *The Kohut Seminars: On Self Psychology and Psychotherapy with Adolescents and Young Adults*, ed. Miriam Elson (New York and London: Norton, 1987); Mario Jacoby, "Reflection on Heinz Kohut's Concept of Narcissism," *Journal of Analytical Psychology* 28 (1981): 19–32.

22. Without delving into Freud's theories in "On Narcissism: An Introduction," where he distinguishes between a *primary narcissism*, in which no object load has yet taken place, and a *secondary narcissism*, which would occur with the return to the ego after an object has been targeted. From the psychoanalytic theorizations on the object relations carried out by Melanie Klein, W. Ronald D. Fairbairn, and others, the idea of a primary narcissism was questioned in the sense that a search for an object is essential and natural for the drive. Libido, as Fairbairn pointed out, is not primarily aimed at the pursuit of pleasure but rather at the pursuit of an object. See *Psychoanalytical Studies of the Personality* (London: Routledge, 1952).

23. See Freud (1911c) *Psycho-Analytic Notes on an Autobiographical Account of a Case of Paranoia*, in *Standard Edition*, 12: 60–61; (1914c) "On Narcissism: An Introduction," in *Standard Edition*, 14: 99–100.

ference to everything that happens around it? The baby is the remembrance of a lost paradise, that of an existence without the otherness that disturbs us. Something similar also happens when we relate to characters from cinema or literature that flagrantly live for themselves, in a state of selfishness and indifference, or even as psychopaths. As Freud says along these lines, "It is as if we envied them for maintaining a blissful state of mind—an unassailable libidinal position which we ourselves have since abandoned."[24] The degree of adulation that the great cultural narcissists of our day are able to attract is curious indeed and very telling.

NARCISSISM AND CULTURE

Society seems to understand our deep narcissistic needs and provides us whatever is needed to alleviate our nostalgia by various means. Among them some are better for us than others, some are more productive, and some are more dangerous. We all experience a healthy dose of narcissism through a developed sense of humor, which we can use to laugh at, with a certain childish omnipotence, those realities that we are subjected to. We have the example of dancers who channel a personal experience through body movement as well as artists who eloquently convey a most subjective reality into the elaboration of an aesthetic creation.[25] However, if the narcissism was so strong that it eliminated communicative intentionality, our humor, our dance, or our art would drown us, like the water did to Narcissus.

If art, humor, and professional work are methods for alleviating our narcissistic demands, religion is also indisputably a social institution that can broadly establish complicities with narcissism, both healthy and pathological. Often, it offers a feeling of safety, evoking infantile feelings of omnipotence that buffer the onslaught of life challenges. *Everything is possible for those who have faith.* With all of its ambiguity, religion can, on the one hand, empower the human being to the highest potential with an optimistic view of life or, on the other hand, be destructive, by intensifying suppressed infantile feelings of omnipotence or in negating reality. Indeed, *anything is possible* from that fervent faith, from the best to the worst.[26]

Similar to religion, we see that morality is ripe for the development of narcissistic attitudes. Fulfilling ethical ideals and defeating those lower inclinations can be a healthy reinforcement for the Ego's feeling of achievement and success, but it can also turn into a narcissistic pride that is extremely

24. Freud, "On Narcissism: An Introduction," in *Standard Edition*, 89.
25. See Freud (1927c), "The Future of an Illusion," in *Standard Edition*, 21: 13–14.
26. I have referred to this complicity between childhood feelings of omnipotence and religiosity in *Belief after Freud* (London and New York: Routledge, 2018), 39–61.

dangerous for individuals and those who surround them.[27] We cannot forget that childhood narcissism evolves but also remains as the Ego Ideal, which, by identification with social representations, becomes the personality aspect that is most intimately associated with moral life.[28]

Social groups also offer themselves to us, allowing our image to be reflected in whatever they intend to represent. We feel ourselves a part of something greater when we belong to this or that prestigious institution; when we become members or fans of a successful soccer team; when we ascribe to this or that region, nation, or ethnic group that intends to set itself apart and somehow feel superior to what surrounds it. The *narcissism of small differences* was a term coined by Freud to refer to groups hostile to other groups that, despite similarities, find fault with some small details that set them apart, using this as a springboard for feelings of superiority. Today's rise in nationalism should give us pause and encourage us to reflect on Freud's provocative insights. Furthermore, we should remember that group narcissism is exploited by political powers, exacerbating injustice and disempowering marginalized members of society. It is as if belonging to an esteemed group could diminish the pain inflicted and somehow compensate for the resulting oppression.

NARCISSISM, LOVE, AND DEATH

Thus, narcissism percolates continually within our personal and collective dynamics. And often in a surreptitious way, even camouflaging itself in what would appear to be a triumph over narcissism itself—that is, under the guise of love. This may be its greatest triumph. To mask itself in a selfless loving devotion to obtain a most refined fulfillment. There is much turbidity that can be hidden in love. Because, in essence, not every interpersonal relationship is necessarily an object relationship between self and other. There are loves where the other represents but a part of himself (object-self, we could call it). From there, we get the hysterical dynamics where, with a seemingly generous sacrificial attitude, one yields to the other but only to satisfy a selfish experi-

27. Freud analyzes this idea as it pertains to the Jewish feeling of superiority: Sigmund Freud (1939a), *Moses and Monotheism*, in *Standard Edition*, 23: 111–22.

28. See Freud (1914c), "On Narcissism: An Introduction," in *Standard Edition*, 14: 102 and 93–96. The concept of the Ego Ideal, the basis of the future Superego, is perhaps the most relevant contribution in the aforementioned work. A very important differentiation will be between the Ego Ideal (which energizes the Ego and helps it to achieve certain value ideals) and the ego's ideal, which is nothing other than the amplification of the Ego, without any other reference than its own reality. A key work on this subject is that of Janine Chasseguet-Smirgel, *The Ego Ideal: A Psychoanalytic Essay on the Malady of the Ideal* (New York: W.W. Norton, 1985).

ence of love. The hysterical person, it has been said, loves Love[29]: that is, there is only love for self, not the other; rather, one basks in the experience of love. That is why the lover can harass, overprotect, and invade the other justifying it through love. In reality, the lover ignores the needs of the other because that person cannot relate to the differences implied by otherness.

It is not always easy to offer love and care to another in an effortless, straightforward, selfless way. We should not forget that it is primarily narcissistic gratifications that jump-start the journey toward love for another. And that the other is not recognized as such but through complex and difficult emotional processes, which allows one to overcome the primitive resistance to anything outside of one's own reality. The impulse to possess the object, incorporating it into one's reality, is the first step in the process of opening oneself to a love encounter. But so is the desire to control and dominate (in an ambivalence that stains the relationship with desire and rejection, love, and hate). Later, we will see the difficulty we all experience in accepting the other as both a free and unique entity. And when the other's reality, mostly (but never totally) stripped of selfish interests, is finally revealed, the narcissistic dynamic will persist, waiting to project the image of self onto others. Narcissus never stops in his efforts to reduce the world to his own reality.[30]

If Freud started out seeing narcissism as a stage of libidinal development and, subsequently, as an oscillating state for all affectivity, in his final reflections, narcissism was essentially related to the death drive and destructiveness. Narcissus seeks to go back to where he can be alone in his totality. Narcissus tries to recreate himself in the image that is reflected. And it is this repetitive tendency that Freud assigned to the concept of the death drive and annihilation.[31] The death instinct is "accompanied by an extraordinarily high degree of narcissistic enjoyment, owing to its presenting the ego with a fulfillment of the latter's old wishes for omnipotence."[32] The post-Freudian

---

29. See Fritz Riemann, *Grundformen der Angst* (München: Ernst Reinhardt Verlag, 1975). Additionally, we should not forget that there are no love relationships, even healthy ones, that do not involve some degree of narcissism. As Heinz Kohut points out, narcissism is not the opposite of object relations; it is the opposite of object love. Some of the most intense object relations, as in the aforementioned case of hysterics, are essentially narcissistic. See Heinz Kohut, *The Kohut Seminars: On Self Psychology and Psychotherapy with Adolescents and Young Adults*, ed. Miriam Elson (New York and London: Norton, 1987).

30. This dynamic is brilliantly explained in (1915c), "Instincts and Their Vicissitudes," in *Standard Edition*, 14, 209–32.

31. The magnificent study by P. Guillem, J. A. Loren, and E. Orozco, "Le narcissisme dans le processus de structuration et de déstructuration psychiques," *Revue Française de Psychanalyse* LV (1991): 39–100, the authors clarify the four stages in Freud's thinking about narcissism. Until 1910, it was a precursory state where he spoke about auto-eroticism. In a second stage, between 1910 and 1914, he introduced the concept of narcissism. From 1914 to 1920 was a third stage where he expanded on some fundamental ideas about narcissism. Finally, from 1920 onward, we see a critical reformulation that takes into account new theories about the drives (1920) and the second topic (1923).

32. Sigmund Freud (1930a), "Civilization and Its Discontents," in *Standard Edition*, 21, 121.

field of psychoanalysis strengthened that close relationship between narcissism and death. Relationship that in a paradigmatic way is illustrated in the Greek myth—Narcissus leads us to a dead end. Mesmerized, in his watery reflection, he finds nothing but his own demise.

THE GOOD NARCISSUS

Within the polysemic concept of narcissism that we find in Freudian literature, it should be noted that Freud also explored the more positive dimensions of this concept. An important note was added in 1931 to the 1930 *Society and Its Discontents*,[33] where Freud clarifies that a healthy articulation of object libido and narcissistic libido is possible on the road to happiness. The primitive narcissism of the child is critical for the development of character, also noted in the 1914 work *Totem and Taboo*.[34] It is in fact narcissism that from a place of self-love drives that fear of castration that puts a brake on incestuous tendencies during the Oedipus complex stage. In this way, narcissism directs the subject to a necessary resignation, an essential step in overcoming the Oedipus complex.

Narcissism is also responsible for the development of strong and independent figures, sometimes as a result of narcissistic dynamics that prefer loving to being loved (we have already seen that narcissism sometimes manifests as apparent surrender) and that because of this they are particularly apt to be supportive of others, take the lead, and stimulate cultural development. Narcissism thus leads to what we call *big personalities*, individuals who, although imperfect in some ways, nevertheless shine and become positive influences in social and cultural development.

But, despite these clear Freudian indications, the ensuing field of psychoanalysis was able to build upon and elaborate on this subject, more clearly differentiating between a healthy narcissism versus pathological narcissism. The former is essentially understood as a necessary element in the development of personality (which is tied to the concept of healthy self-esteem[35]), and the latter translates to emotional fixations and regressions leading to a clinical diagnosis much studied nowadays and that is generally known as *narcissistic personality disorder*.[36]

33. Ibid., 85.

34. Sigmund Freud (1912–1913), *Totem and Taboo*, in *Standard Edition*, 13, 89–90.

35. Michael Kernis, "Toward a Conceptualization of Optimal Self-Esteem," *Psychological Inquiry* 14 (2003): 1–26.

36. See Zlatan Krizan and Anne D. Herlache, "The Narcissism Spectrum Model: A Synthetic Review of Narcissistic Personality," *Personality and Social Psychology Review* 22 (2018): 3–31.

Heinz Kohut is likely the most prominent figure to draw attention to narcissism's positive aspects, that of molding and supercharging personality.[37] His criticisms of the generally accepted understanding of narcissism have been controversial.[38] The correct development of *Self*[39] must experience the important moments that narcissistic aspects of personality acquire. A series of positive experiences result from what Heinz Kohut calls empathic mirroring with the maternal object. Through an adequate relationship with the mother in which she is the sustainer (that *holding* that Winnicott refers to), the child can move from a primitive position of autoerotism (in which the *Self* is still in a state of fragmentation) to the narcissism that empowers and fulfills, rather than weakens. The time will come when that early grandiose feeling will be subjugated, shaped, and transformed into a healthy narcissism, which will mean having a cohesive and integrated *Self.* This narcissism, according to Kohut, is a phenomenon that occurs in the interpersonal relationship domain, particularly between the mother and child. It is motherly care that infuses her offspring with that essential self-love, critical for acquiring confidence later in life. From the psychoanalytic perspective, this is where emotional support turns into self-esteem.

The way in which narcissism can shape a person is also what contributes to the identification process, which is progressively embodied in the Ego and confers its particularities and solidity. It is the interest in oneself, that self-love, that effectively leads us to that appropriation-incorporation of the other or an aspect of the other that appeals to us and influences the identification process. Our potential for creativity and sublimation, our ability to lovingly engage or be in solitude, all of this is owed to that narcissism that nudged us to form those personally meaningful identifications. Narcissism has thus been seen as foundational in the process of personality building.[40] Other structural

---

37. There are other relevant figures within the psychoanalytic field that have also highlighted the constructive and influential dimensions of narcissism. Among them are Jean Laplanche, Bela Grunberger, Francis Pache, Wilfred R. Bion, and Andres Green.

38. This author's views on narcissism (1913–1981) grew progressively until he came to fully replace Freud's theory of drives with his own analysis of narcissism, which became the centerpiece of his vision of psychoanalytic theory. See Heinz Kohut, *The Analysis of the Self: A Systematic Approach to the Psychoanalytic Treatment of Narcissistic Personality Disorders* (New York: International Universities Press, 1971) and the previously cited *Kohut Seminars: On Self Psychology and Psychotherapy with Adolescents and Young Adults*; "Forms and Transformations of Narcissism," *Journal of the American Psychoanalytic Association* 14 (1966): 243–72.

39. This concept from recent psychoanalysis refers to affective-cognitive structures that reflect the way in which an individual perceives himself in real interactions with others and fantasized interactions with internal representations of other significant people.

40. See Guillem, Loren, and Orozco, "Introduction: Le narcissisme dans le processus de structuration et de déstructuration psychiques," 73. The authors rightly insist on the progressive and not only regressive side of narcissistic identifications. The same sublimatory processes, these authors point out, are also closely related to narcissism, to the extent that sublimation is guided by the Ego Ideal, which we know is something essentially narcissistic. Ibid., 84–92.

elements will be added, perhaps partitions or beams, that serve as the good and bad objects that get incorporated into our relationships with others. But narcissism is what gives coherence, or lack thereof, to all those subsequent elements that become adjoined to our individual structure.

Thus, we see that narcissism plays a critical role in the formation of personality and that its failures can easily lead to serious damage.

NARCISSUS THE DESTROYER

It now becomes even clearer that narcissism is one of the most ambiguous and polysemic concepts of all of psychoanalytic theory. Present in our very own being, resurfacing intermittently over and over again in our lives, enabling our progress and our hindrances, Narcissus is an ambiguous force that befuddles both those who experience it and those who ponder it. While the strength of Narcissus is needed to forge ahead in our lives, it can also overtake us, becoming an impediment in connecting to others and possibly isolating us in a very problematic way.

Wilhelm Reich, who continued to advocate for the positive aspects that narcissism has on our development, described what is now referred to as phallic-narcissistic character, individuals that display a high degree of arrogance, ambition, high impulsiveness, exhibitionism, sadism, and so on.[41] But it was undoubtedly Kohut, that well-known apologist for a beneficial narcissism, who in 1968 introduced the concept of narcissistic personality disorder, which has acquired enormous relevance within the current psychopathological landscape. It was, however, Otto Kernberg who offered perhaps the most consistent description of this clinical diagnosis that he referred to as the structure of the narcissistic personality.[42] There have been several clinical descriptions of narcissistic pathology since then, although there are some common features that are collected under the term of narcissistic personality disorder by the DSM-V of the American Psychiatric Association. Therefore, people with this condition are thought to:

- have an exaggerated sense of self-importance;
- have a sense of entitlement and require constant, excessive admiration;
- expect to be recognized as superior even without achievements that warrant it;
- exaggerate achievements and talents;

41. This is described in detail in Wilhelm Reich's work *Analysis of Character* (New York: Farrar, Straus and Giroux, 1990), 217–23.

42. See Otto Kernberg, *Borderline Conditions and Pathological Narcissism* (Dallas, TX: Jason Aronson, 1995). See also Marie Claire Durrieux, *Otto Kernberg* (Paris: PUF, 2003).

- be preoccupied with fantasies about success, power, brilliance, beauty, or the perfect mate;
- believe they are superior and can only associate with equally special people;
- monopolize conversations and belittle or look down on people they perceive as inferior;
- expect special favors and unquestioning compliance with their expectations;
- take advantage of others to get what they want;
- have an inability or unwillingness to recognize the needs and feelings of others;
- be envious of others and believe others envy them;
- behave in an arrogant or haughty manner, coming across as conceited, boastful, and pretentious;
- insist on having the best of everything, for instance, the best car or office.[43]

We see how many guises narcissism can take on. From the one that shapes the Ego and produces an integrated individual, inheritor of the Eros that seeks to merge with all of life, to the one that becomes lethal, not so much a masochism that longs for pain but something more dangerous that seeks nonexistence, amnesia—total emptiness. No longer representing the Eros that seeks oneness, but becoming the Thanatos who intends to absorb and obliterate everything it comes across.[44]

SELF-ESTEEM AND NARCISSISM

Let us now return to this chapter's initial look at self-esteem. We are now probably in a better position to understand the deeper psychodynamic significance of the phenomenon of self-esteem as well as the possible links to narcissism.

The term *self-esteem*, although not an emblematic psychoanalytic concept (it is rare to see it in psychoanalytic dictionaries[45]), appears in Freudian works as *Selbstgefühls*. And, yes, always in relation to narcissism. In the work "On Narcissism: An Introduction," Freud seeks to undertake a study

43. American Psychiatric Association, *Diagnostic and Statistical Manual of Mental Disorders* (Washington DC: APA, 2013) Cluster B Personality Disorders. "Narcissistic Personality Disorder."

44. The aforementioned study by Guillem, Loren, and Orozco, makes a splendid synthesis of the authors who have highlighted the most destructive side of narcissism. Ibid., 70–72.

45. No mention is made in the well-known work by Jean Laplanche and Jean-Baptiste Pontalis, *The Language of Psychanalysis* (London: Karnac, 2006), ni en el más actual de Elisabeth Roudinesco - Michel Plon, *Dictionnaire de la psychanalyse*, Fayard, Paris 1997.

of self-esteem in both normal and neurotic individuals. In either case, Freud explains that "self-regard appears to us to be an expression of the size of the ego (*Ichgrösse*) . . . everything a person possesses or achieves, every remnant of the primitive feeling of omnipotence which his experience has confirmed, helps to increase his self-regard."[46] He goes on to explain that there is a close relationship between self-esteem and narcissistic libido. Hence, self-esteem can be an expression of deeply pathological situations or, conversely, like with narcissism, express normal and positive dimensions of normal life.

Without going so far as to say that self-esteem is the opposite of *hetero-esteem*, it is possible, like in the relationship established between narcissistic and object libido, that *hetero-esteem* could lessen self-esteem. In certain love scenarios, for example, the reverence for the beloved object will simultaneously lessen one's self-worth—*the lover is humble*, Freud says in this regard. He who loves loses a part of his narcissism, which can only be compensated by being loved by another. It is the wisdom with which self-esteem recovers from its loss. It also follows that the difficulty in loving others can make it difficult to love ourselves, greatly weakening the feeling of self-esteem.

To recap, Freud considers self-esteem to be a residue of childhood narcissism, an expression of satisfaction that provides the fulfillment of an ideal and is also the beneficial result of the satisfaction experienced after bonding with objects.[47]

It could, therefore, reasonably be concluded that self-esteem is a form of *satisfaction of the narcissistic libido in the adult*[48] without this automatically being correlated with any insane, regressive, or infantilizing characteristics. A correct perception of narcissism would have us understand that it is a basic aspect of emotion and that a narcissistic remnant is an essential component in relationships with oneself and also with others. The either beneficial or pathological aspect will, therefore, derive from the type of narcissism to which it is linked and of which it is an expression. It is clear that the type of self-esteem

46. Sigmund Freud (1914c), "On Narcissism: An Introduction," in *Standard Edition*, 14, 98.

47. The concept of self-esteem reappears in Freud's works on the subject of the fulfillment of an ideal, as in the case of Moses and the Jewish people: accomplishing a great feat and renouncing the most primitive dimensions of personality and strengthening self-esteem. See Sigmund Freud (1939a), "Moses and Monotheism," in *Standard Edition*, 23, 116–17. We also find valuable insights regarding the relationship between love, the loss of love, and self-esteem in (1917e) "Mourning and Melancholia," in *Standard Edition*, 14, 247.

48. This is the definition found in *Diccionario Freudiano* [Freudian Dictionary] by José Luis Valls (Madrid: Juan Yébenes, 1995). This author explains that self-esteem produces a feeling of indefinite well-being, not directly related to drive discharges. *It is rather a basic state*. Self-esteem is closely related to self-confidence, temperament, or mood, with self-worth. In this sense, it is a basic pillar of health and of the Ego strength. Hanna Segal, meanwhile, defines it as a feeling based on a good relationship between the self and internal objects, not idealized. See "Some Clinical Implications of Melanie Klein's Work: Emergence from Narcissism," *International Journal of Psychoanalysis*, 46 (1983): 269–76.

that is displayed by a paranoid or manic individual blurs the edges of personality and makes it difficult to relate to others. On the other hand, the self-esteem that arises from a well-done job or the feeling of being a suitable lover is an example of healthy self-love. Thus, narcissism can be of the paranoid type and also a positive type and take on many shades and colors.

For all these reasons, it could be rightly said that narcissism is not always as negative as it is generally understood, nor is self-esteem as positive as we tend to think nowadays. Nor are they, in fact, easily distinguished. Rather, it is conceivable that there could be a narcissism devoid of self-esteem, though one can hardly imagine self-esteem without some type of narcissism, whether positive or not.

Narcissism can, in fact, sometimes inhibit the development of adequate self-esteem. This is the case of the Ego Ideal that has very high aspirations but a reality that does not match the ideals. This can only lead to a terrible sense of self-esteem. Like Narcissus, who does not truly love himself but rather the imaginary and idealized representation he sees reflected in the water. The reality could be detestable. We saw that, paradoxically, those with narcissistic personality disorder suffer from fragile self-esteem and are vulnerable to critique. Self-esteem, then, needs narcissism to blossom, but the situation can turn sour, however, when narcissism crosses certain thresholds.

AFFECTION AND COGNITION IN SELF-ESTEEM

There is an aspect of self-esteem that is given little consideration and leads to striking contradictions in how the phenomenon is interpreted. The question has to do with the degree to which self-esteem shapes cognitive processes alongside the merely affective ones. We find that the best definitions of self-esteem include a self-critical, evaluative element that would guarantee its healthy development. "Self-esteem," affirmed the Spanish Jesuit thinker José Vicente Bonet, "is how one evaluates and perceives oneself, or in other words, what one thinks and feels towards oneself."[49] According to Burns, it is the set of attitudes toward oneself, *attitude* being understood as a sufficiently stable pattern of sensory perception, thought, assessment, feeling, and action in relation to an object, an institution, or a person. It is, then, a way of seeing reality that is founded on a correct self-perception. In defining the concept of self-esteem, there are always reminders about the need to focus that positive regard toward oneself in such a way that it does not turn into egocentrism or

49. See José Vicente Bonet, *Sé amigo de ti mismo* (Santander: Sal Terrae, 1994), 18, and *Aprender a quererse* (Valencia: Manantial, Valencia, 1998), 35.

infantilizing narcissism. Self-esteem is therefore accompanied by the critical work of self-analysis that involves cognitive functions.

It does not seem, however, that there is consensus about how to see self-esteem function simultaneously as a vehicle for expressing emotion and cognitive processes. Rather, it is the love dimension that receives the most attention, pushing aside, when not totally overlooking, those other reflective or inward-looking aspects. Sometimes, we even speak directly about *self-love* in such a way that it coincides with how we understand the term *self-esteem*.

We should not be surprised then at how the term *esteem* is used in the English language. The *Merriam-Webster Dictionary* defines it as "the regard in which one is held, especially: high regard."[50] The *Collins Dictionary* defines it as "the admiration and respect that you feel towards another person."[51] The *Longman Dictionary* defines it as "a feeling of respect for someone."[52] The term clearly has a positive connotation. It could have derived from a process of reason and critical thought. But esteem seems to be the end result of the process of appreciating and thinking well of someone.

We most often hear about self-esteem in the context of loving, pampering, encouraging, rewarding, thinking well, and feeling good about oneself.[53] All of which can be, indeed, very positive and significant for personal development and maturing at certain times. But the overemphasis in this regard, the quasi-allergy and misgivings to practically any type of self-criticism or feeling of guilt (which is so often essential in the process of individual transformation) or, even worse, adapting all efforts of maturation through the lens of self-esteem could have negative side effects for the desired process of growth.

In this regard, Otto Kernberg's reflections on self-esteem are very enlightening. This should not be a simple reflection on instinctive cathexis. That is, it should not be the result of a blind self-love but should be tempered by emotional and cognitive components that serve as adaptive regulation. Therefore, Kernberg distinguishes primitive self-esteem involving diffuse affective components with a more advanced self-esteem in which there are more subtle differentiated cognitive components and the emotional repercussions are tempered. This author points out, moreover, that mood swings related to self-esteem would indicate a lack of evolution, insofar as they would be highlighting a key role of feeling in self-perception. When self-esteem is

50. Merriam-Webster, s.v. "esteem," accessed March 22, 2020, https://merriam-webster.com/dictionary/esteem.

51. Collins Dictionary, s.v. "esteem," accessed March 22, 2020, https://www.collinsdictionary.com/us/dictionary/english/esteem.

52. Longman Dictionary, s.v. "esteem," accessed March 22, 2020, https://ldoceonline.com/dictionary/esteem.

53. Along these lines, Louise Hay's publications fill bookstore shelves, including diaries and calendars filled with inspirational messages and slogans. For example, *Love Yourself, Heal Your Life Workbook* (UK: Hay House Inc., 1990).

regulated by the more advanced functions of the superego, that is, through critical assessment, self-evaluation is more precise and allows for heightened reasoning capacities.[54]

SELF-ESTEEM AS A WAY STATION

It is uncertain whether the kind of self-esteem that facilitates feeling and reasoning is the same as that one widely touted nowadays, pressured by a culture that shrugs off responsibility and encourages the cult of individualism. In recent decades there has been a displacement from a commitment to social change to widespread disillusionment. Our postmodern culture has heavy individualistic leanings, which is the reason, despite the efforts to understand self-esteem as a tool for introspection and evolution, self-esteem is instead reduced to a mere love for one's own person, naive and infantilizing.

Today's culture abandons collective emancipations and raises the ego as the departure point and the destination. From there, one thirsts for the self, finds excitement in inner explorations, and consecrates self-realization as the ultimate goal. We find a scenario in which there is no religion other than the self, no liturgy aside from self-discovery. It is not surprising that historians, sociologists, and psychologists agree that we are experiencing the height of narcissism in our culture. Meanwhile, psychopathologists add, and not without reason, that the neurotic tension of other times seems to give way to the narcissistic rise of our day.[55]

It is worth highlighting how this phenomenon proliferates in social media nowadays.[56] Significantly, the relationship established with others happens in their physical absence (especially through the popular medium of chatting), which encourages every type of fantasy regarding the virtual participant, to the point that, in many cases, it becomes uncertain whether a relationship has actually been established between two people or it is only a vehicle for satisfying unfulfilled fantasies. Frequently, we see how a real postvirtual encounter undoes within minutes whatever fantasies had been fabricated via chats or emails over a period of time. The individual, just like with a *selfie*,[57] is only relating to him or herself.

---

54. Kernberg, *Borderline Conditions and Pathological Narcissism.*

55. Gilles Lipovetsky, *L'ère du vide: Essais sur l'individualisme contemporain* (Paris: Gallimard, 1983); Pinsky Drew, *The Mirror Effect: How Celebrity Narcissism Is Seducing America* (New York: HarperCollins, 2009).

56. See Annmarie Bennet, *Social Media: Global Perspectives, Applications and Benefits and Dangers* (New York: Nova Science Publishers, 2014).

57. Jessica L. McCain and W. Keith Campbell, "'Let Me Take Another Selfie': Further Examination of the Relation between Narcissism, Self-Perception, and Instagram Posts," *Psychology of Popular Media Culture* 8 (2019): 22–33.

On the other hand, those aspects of anonymity, immediacy, and atemporal experience that typify social media offer a pseudo-reality that amplifies a basic desire for contact, which by suppressing distance and difference gives the impression of connecting to the primary object in a dangerous narcissistic loop.[58] This then leads to the growing phenomenon of addiction that these environments foment. A type of addiction and dependence that ends up imprisoning these individuals in essentially imaginary relationships, progressively marginalizing them from any encounters and connections outside the web.[59] The replacement of traditional hangouts in bars and cafes by cyber-cafes, in which we find a large number of individuals sitting next to each other but each one engaged with "myworld.com," illustrates this new state of affairs.[60]

In addition, insisting on making self-esteem the crux of one's personal development journey or behavioral guideline can be catastrophic. What should be a mere foundation becomes an entire edifice. What should be but a point of departure becomes the ultimate purpose. This produces a narcissistic overdose that drowns the subject in an infectious reality. It can be fascinating and promising, as Narcissus found when he saw his image reflected in the water, but extremely dangerous and destructive. We are reminded of Federico García Lorca, who expressed that he would like to become the wine in order to drink himself.

With this understanding, it seems unreasonable to cluster such a disparate variety of processes of the psyche under the umbrella of self-esteem, considering that some are not even relevant, while others, although related, are paradoxically intended to move the subject beyond the said concept. Compassion for others, a healthy awareness of guilt, and assertiveness are examples of traits that are associated with a good sense of self-esteem. While this is true, and while self-esteem is related to certain dynamics, these processes spring from and are identified with a much broader structure different from what self-esteem is and represents. On the other hand, there is also an effort to detach it from other dimensions, such as narcissism, which, according to our previous analysis, should be seen as a phenomenon that is intertwined. We thus come to a theoretical explanation of self-esteem in which everything that is considered a positive contribution to personal growth is attributed to its essence. In this way, the concept becomes too much of the focus, erroneously

58. This concept is illustrated in a study by Martine Vautherin-Estrade, "Courriers cybernétiques: un jeu ambigu?" *Revue Française de Psychanalyse* LXVIII (2004): 581–89.

59. See Tonino Cantelmi et al., *La mente in Internet. Psicopatologia delle condotte on-line* (Padova: Piccin, 2000).

60. See Carlos Domínguez-Morano, "La alteridad difuminada. Reflexiones en los tiempos de los 'vínculos.com,'" *Proyección* LI (2004): 347–67; Christina Frederick and Tianxin Zang, "Narcissism and Social Media Usage: Is There No Longer a Relationship?" *Journal of Articles in Support of the Null Hypothesis* 16 (2019): 23–32.

making it the cornerstone for life, which would be questionable in the larger scheme of personal growth and maturity.

Self-esteem is a way station. As Kohut pointed out, a significant dose of narcissism is necessary in early childhood in order to acquire sufficient self-confidence. When this is lacking, narcissistic chaos ensues, manifested in an acute need to be recognized by others in an attempt to heal past wounds. It would, therefore, be very dangerous for self-esteem to cover up and legitimize an urgent irrational need to retake a throne that was never fully enjoyed in infancy. This would mean losing sight of the fact that the ultimate goal will always be to leave oneself behind to enjoy the fruitful encounter with otherness. In Freud's eloquent words, "A strong egoism is a protection against falling ill, but in the last resort we must begin to love in order not to fall ill."[61] Maybe in childhood it made sense to be the king or the queen of the house. But without dethroning the royalty in question, that individual will remain in a state of stupidity, intoxicated with narcissism and childish self-esteem.

A PINCH OF SELF-ESTEEM

It is certainly the case that many individuals have suffered a certain upbringing or type of religious indoctrination that brought out the most negative dimensions of themselves and that emphasized guilt and self-loathing. It is true that this upbringing has looked down upon positive self-confidence and that this has been terribly harmful to those same individuals. Raising awareness regarding the problem of low self-esteem can in many instances be a key aspect of personal healing. Examining and criticizing irrational opinions and ideas that contribute to a negative self-image (according to the theories put forth by the likes of Albert Ellis or Aaron T. Beck) can sometimes be very beneficial. What seems to be more problematic is to focus the entire process of personal growth and maturation on that tendency to look inward with nothing but positivity. It can also become a strategic error when reestablishing a normal sense of self-esteem to overanalyze and focus on the damaged image itself. Those past wounds are unlikely to heal by continually licking them or demanding that others do so as well. One will most likely have to learn to journey onward, experiencing the pain of that wound that has not yet healed and finding relief in the effort of work and love, those important pillars on the road to maturity. That may be the best way to acquire true self-esteem.

Some spend life "navel-gazing." From the standpoint of psychoanalysis, Denis Vasse has viewed the navel, that peculiar physical formation, as a symbolic representation of what encloses us and confines us in a world bound

61. Freud, "On Narcissism: An Introduction," in *Standard Edition*, 14: 85.

by our skin. Through the umbilical closure, there is a desire for the child to live. The umbilical cord must be cut and sutured so that the child can become an independent being through that closure. Confronted by this closure, the individual voice will arise to provide an opening for another whose separation is also innate.[62] That inner voice implies that we are called and driven to uniqueness from our innate separation.

But the navel seems to hold a kind of terrible fascination. It is a trace of something lost—a place in which there was no distance or difference and in which everything was exclusively our own reality, that is, the primary and extreme narcissism of the intrauterine reality. Therefore, the idea of a life spent naval-gazing has a much deeper meaning that hints at an inclination within us all. Certain ideas concerning self-love and self-esteem may become unconsciously entangled in a dangerous complicity with that tendency.

Psychoanalysis rightly invites us to conclude that what is important for self-esteem is to give ourselves to efforts driven by external objects, without being overly obsessed with contemplating ourselves. As Otto Kernberg points out, the increase in the capacity to love, to feel and express gratitude, to care for others, as well as in the capacity for sexual love, sublimation, and creativity, those are the things that truly uplift a person.

Therefore, navel-gazing does not seem like the best way to develop self-esteem. Nor should one lick and demand that others lick the narcissistic wounds that were inflicted upon him. Rather, by looking beyond one's self-esteem and in approaching life with a loving attitude, by embarking on a collective project of liberation, this is how self-esteem would be best served. There will likely be times when we need to consider the impediments that stem from a negative and undesirable self-image. But it is important that this effort not get derailed. From the moment that this endeavor loses its functional and provisional nature, we will be going awry by perverting its usefulness. Today, under significant sociocultural pressure, the danger of overdosing on self-esteem is all too real. The consequences can be serious. As it was for Narcissus—drunk on his image, indifferent to his true nature, bewitched by his own reflection—this is what led to his fateful end.

BIBLIOGRAPHY

American Psychiatric Association. *Diagnostic and Statistical Manual of Mental Disorders, 5.* Washington DC: American Psychiatric Association, 2013.

Bennet, Annmarie. *Social Media: Global Perspectives, Applications, Benefits, and Dangers*. New York: Nova Science Publishers, 2014.

---

62. Denis Vasse, *L'Ombilic et la voix: Deux enfants en analyse* (Paris: Editions du Seuil, 1974), 21.

Besser, Avi, ed. *Handbook of the Psychology of Narcissism: Diverse Perspectives*. New York: Nova Publishers, 2014.

Borders, Jude H., ed. *Handbook of the Psychology of Self-Esteem*. New York: Nova Publishers, 2014.

Cantelmit, Tonino, Carlamaria Del Miglio, Massimo Talli, and Alessia D'Andrea, eds. *La mente in Internet. Psicopatologia delle condotte on-line.* Padova: Piccin, 2000.

Chasseguet-Smirgel, Janine. *The Ego Ideal: A Psychoanalytic Essay on the Malady of the Ideal*. New York: W.W. Norton, 1985.

Domínguez-Morano, Carlos. "La alteridad difuminada. Reflexiones en los tiempos de los 'vínculos.com.'" *Proyección* LI (2004): 347–67.

Drew, Pinsky. *The Mirror Effect: How Celebrity Narcissism Is Seducing America*. New York: HarperCollins, 2009.

Eagle, Morris N. *Recent Developments in Psychoanalysis: A Critical Evaluation.* Cambridge, MA: Harvard University Press, 1987.

Fairbairn, W. R. D. *Psychoanalytical Studies of the Personality*. London: Routledge, 1952.

Frederick, Christina, and Tianxin Zang. "Narcissism and Social Media Usage: Is There No Longer a Relationship?" *Journal of Articles in Support of the Null Hypothesis* 16 (2019), 23–32.

Freud, Sigmund (1905d). *Three Essays on the Theory of Sexuality*. In *The Standard Edition of the Complete Psychological Works of Sigmund Freud*, edited and translated by James Strachey, 7: 125–245. London: Hogarth, 1966.

——— (1914c). "On Narcissism: An Introduction." In *Standard Edition*, 14: 69–102.

——— (1912–1913). *Totem and Taboo*. In *Standard Edition*, 13: 7–161.

——— (1911c). "Psychoanalytic Notes on an Autobiographical Account of a Case of Paranoia (Dementia paranoides)." In *Standard Edition*, 12: 223–32.

——— (1916–1917). *Introductory Lectures on Psycho-Analysis.* In *Standard Edition*, 15.

Gubern, Ramón. *El Eros electronic.* Barcelona: Taurus, 2000.

Guillem, Pedro, Jose Antonio Loren, and Eduardo Orozco. "Le narcissisme dans le processus de structuration et de déstructuration psychiques. Introduction." *Revue Française de Psychanalyse* 55 (1991): 39–100.

Jacoby, Mario. "Reflection on Heinz Kohut's Concept of Narcissism." *Journal of Analytical Psychology* 28 (1981): 19–32.

Kernberg, Otto. *Borderline Conditions and Pathological Narcissism (Classical Psychoanalysis and Its Applications).* New York: Jason Aronson, 1995.

Kohut, Heinz. *The Analysis of the Self: A Systematic Approach to the Psychoanalytic Treatment of Narcissistic Personality Disorders.* New York: International Universities Press, 1971.

———. "Forms and Transformations of Narcissism." *Journal of the American Psychoanalytic Association* 14 (1966): 243–72.

———. *The Kohut Seminars: On Self Psychology and Psychotherapy with Adolescents and Young Adults.* Edited by Miriam Elson. New York and London: Norton, 1987.

Krizan, Zlatan, and Anne D. Herlache. "The Narcissism Spectrum Model: A Synthetic Review of Narcissistic Personality." *Personality and Social Psychology Review* 22 (2018): 3–31.

Lipovetsky, Gilles. *L'ère du vide: Essais sur l'individualisme contemporain*. Paris: Gallimard, 1983.

Rosenberg, Morris. *Society and the Adolescent Self-Image*. Princeton, NJ: Princeton University Press, 1965.

Sandler, Joseph, Ethel Person, and Peter Fonagy. *Freud's "On Narcissism: An Introduction."* London: Routledge, 2012.

Savater, Fernando. *Ética como amor propio.* Madrid: Mondadori, 1988.

Schneider, Kirk, J. Fraser Pierson, and James F. T. Bugental, eds. *The Handbook of Humanistic Psychology*. Los Angeles: SAGE, 2015.

Trechera, José Luis. *¿Qué es el narcisismo?* Bilbao: Desclée de Brouwer, 1999.

Vasse, Denis. *L'Ombilic et la voix: Deux enfants en analyse*. Paris: Seuil, 1974.

Vautherin-Estrade, Martine. "Courriers cybernétiques: un jeu ambigu?" *Revue Française de Psychanalyse* 68 (2004) 581–89.

Chapter Nine

The Bonds of Friendship

It is the most universal kind of relationship, where anyone, independent of age, culture, or condition, can partake. The place where, unlike romance or other types of relationships, we find ourselves bound and accompanied throughout life. Children, teenagers, adults, and the elderly can be friends. Men and women are friends.[1] Individuals of the same sex are friends, as are those of the opposite sex. These bonds of friendship can overcome differences in age, culture, or beliefs. Friendship can exist between lovers and between parents and children, even when that friendship was not necessary for the relationship to exist. Thus, neither age, nor sex, nor culture seems to be a barrier to this manifestation of human bonding. Like a blessing from the sky, and like the sun and the rain, neither does it discriminate between the good and the bad or the just and the unjust. It makes itself available regardless of gender, age, or condition and creates connections both within and without societal institutions. It both precedes other types of relationships and lives on afterward, and the law does not bind it. It is the most liberating type of relationship. Therefore, as Aristotle believed, friendship is one of the most essential life requirements and something that nobody would wish to be deprived of, even if everything else were to be taken.[2]

1. Though studies on friendship have focused primarily on the friendship between men, today there are also specific studies on the friendship between women. See Luise Bauchenbaum and Susie Orbach, *Between Women: Love, Envy, and Competition in Women's Friendships* (New York: Penguin Books, 1989); Pat O'Connor, "Women's Friendships in a Post Modern World," in *Placing Friendships in Context*, ed. R. Adams and G. Allan (Cambridge, UK: Cambridge University Press), 117–35.
2. Aristotle, *Nicomachean Ethics* (New York: Oxford University Press, 2009). A wonderful overview of friendship throughout time can be found in Barbara Caine, ed., *Friendship: A History* (London and New York: Routledge, 2014).

And, yet, it is surprising that friendship, being such an important human bond, should appear so rarely in writings, seemingly overlooked in most human sciences. And strangely, there appears to be a discomfort nowadays in approaching and talking about friendship, this vital human bond that touches us all to some degree.

The great treatises and reflections on friendship are found mostly among the classics. Aristotle appears to have been one of the first to focus on this type of relationship (known as *philia*), as Plato did on love (*eros*). Cicero, another great orator and philosopher, also devoted one of his best-known works to friendship.[3] Saint Thomas Aquinas, reviving the Aristotelian tradition and articulating it through Christian theology, looked at friendship as a relationship founded on benevolent love and characterized by reciprocity. Previously, within Christian thought, it was Saint Augustine, who picking up where Cicero left off, wrote beautifully on this topic without actually developing a comprehensive theory about it. He also introduced a particular theological perspective that revealed a darker side of friendship. Like, for example, when he expressed that he would rather have a dead friend than a corrupt one. The English Cistercian monk, Aelred of Rievaulx, deserves special mention. He wrote one of the most beautiful spiritual treatises on the subject, titled *Spiritual Friendship*.[4] Finally, we have Immanuel Kant, the great modernist classic, with interesting insights on friendship. He distinguished between the bonds based on aesthetics, characterized by the sharing of pleasurable experiences (the gratification of a shared meal would be an example), and those based on morality in which there is complete trust between two people who have similar ideals and share intimate feelings while maintaining reciprocal respect. Accepting the friend for who he is generates trust and prevents that individual from being used as a means to an end. For Kant, the perfect friendship is hard to achieve insofar as the love and respect for the other cannot be fully realized.[5] Between Saint Thomas and Kant, one of the most frequently cited authors on the subject of friendship is Montaigne, with his pain-tinged reflections after the death of his friend. In those pages, we find the famous expression. "If you press me to say why I loved him, I can say no more than because he was he, and I was I,"[6] which aligns with today's concept of friendship. Montaigne sees friendship as the height of perfection in human relationships.

3. Marcus Tullius Ciceronis, *De Re Publica, De Legibus, Cato Maior de Senectute, Laelius de Amicitia* (Oxford: Oxford University Press, 2006).

4. *L'amitié spirituelle* (Bruges/Paris: Charles Beyaert, 1948).

5. See Immanuel Kant, *Groundwork for the Metaphysics of Morals*, trans. ed. Allen Wood (London: Yale University Press, 2002), 24, 164–67.

6. See Michel de Montaigne, *On Friendships* (New York: Penguin Books, 1991). On the narcissistic dimension of friendship, as expressed by Montaigne's famous phrase "because he was he, and I was I," see Sharon M. Hymer, "Narcissistic Friendships," *The Psychoanalytic Review* 71 (1984): 423–39.

We should reflect on why friendship so rarely comes up as a subject after the Enlightenment. For the great Spanish thinker Pedro Laín Entralgo, it has something to do with the dilution of the notion of *person* throughout the 19th century (dissolved in Hegelian idealism or simply disappearing into positivism), which makes it very difficult to examine this human relationship in depth. Thus, the idealistic notions regarding friendship were eclipsed by a reductionist conception that saw friendship as simple camaraderie. This is how Pedro Laín Entralgo saw Hegel, Comte, Marx, or Schopenhauer. The 20th century continued to offer little regarding the theory of friendship. Heidegger takes an even more extreme view of camaraderie and, for this reason, misses the notion of a whole person, which is critical for understanding the human bond of friendship.[7] Nietzsche, who also has his own views on friendship, proclaimed in *Thus Spake Zarathustra*, "*There is comradeship: may there be friendship!*"[8] As an important reflection in recent philosophical thinking, we should mention Jacques Derrida and his work *The Politics of Friendship*,[9] in which the postmodern and deconstructionist thinker analyses the great ruminations on friendship from Aristotle to Bataille. According to Jacques Derrida, friendship would need to be understood outside the homo-fraternal and phallogocentric perspective. Only through freedom and equality would a just friendship be evidenced, but just beyond the bounds of the law, that is, *to the extent of its excesses*.

The psychoanalytic field is also lacking a thorough systematic theory about friendship, which is quite surprising given the important role of friendship relative to the psychodynamics of most subjects. We find that Freud himself did not spend much time theorizing on this topic even though his life was marked by intense, rich, and sometimes conflictive friendships. After Freud, the absence of reflections on this topic would continue in subsequent psychoanalytic literature. One must search profusely through psychoanalytic works to find the occasional reflection on friendship,[10] even though psychoanalytic sessions are often marked by reflections on a subject's experiences with friends. Perhaps here we find one of the blind spots with the field of psychoanalysis.

---

7. See Pedro Laín Entralgo, *Sobre la amistad* (Madrid: Revista de Occidente, 1972), 116–152, 338.

8. Friedrich Nietzsche, *Thus Spake Zarathustra* (Cambridge: Cambridge University Press, 2006), 42.

9. Jacques Derrida, *The Politics of Friendship* (London and New York: Verso, 2005), 92–95.

10. A few psychoanalytic references worth mentioning are Edmund Bergler, *Psychology of Friendship and Acquaintanceship: Selected Papers* 1933–191 (New York: Grume and Stratton, 1969). Masud Khan, *Le Soi caché* (Paris Gallimard: 1976); Luis Kancyper "Metapsychology and Clinical Aspects of Transference-Friendship," *The Psychoanalytic Quarterly* 87 (2018): 101–26; Luciano Lutereau, "La amistad en psicoanálisis. La función del interlocutor," *Affectio Societatis* 11 (2014): 32–42; R. Sharabany, "Continuities in the Development of Intimate Friendships: Object Relations, Interpersonal, and Attachment Perspectives." In Ralph Erber and Robin Gilmour, eds., *Theoretical Framework for Personal Relationships* (New Jersey: Lawrence Erlbaum Associates Publishers, 1994), 157–78.

Because, as we will later analyze, friendship is likely accompanied by human dimensions to which psychoanalysis is particularly and characteristically resistant. Friendship cannot be understood without articulating the relationship between desire and its ideal, of affective dynamics with certain values that go beyond what would otherwise be understood as emotions. In this way, friendship falls within the realm of ethics and, inevitably, needs to be subjected to what psychoanalysis has understood as a sublimation process. But we well know that, when we reach this place of sublimation, we encounter one of the most problematic enigmas within psychoanalytic theory, and when we try to go deeper we are immediately met by a series of challenging aporias.[11]

We could hardly hope to reach an understanding of the friendship phenomenon from a purely ethical standpoint in which only altruism or closeness was taken into account. Friendship is an essential element, with an affective component that must be understood through a psychodynamic lens. Within friendship, we find one of the great expressions of desire. But our understanding would be incomplete if we refused to see that friendship entails an ethical component, call it commitment, respect for the other, benevolent love, or otherwise. Thus, it is through both affection and commitment that we must begin our understanding of friendship and which we will consequently analyze in more depth.

THERE ARE NO MERCHANTS OF FRIENDS . . .

As we know, the term *friend* can mean many different things depending on the context. Some refer to any acquaintance as a friend, no matter how superficial the relationship may be, while others reserve the term for those whom they are close to and are greatly trusted. Friends, colleagues, comrades, and pals thus form a constellation of terms that share some traits, but where the differences can be significant.

The concept of friendship has been trivialized, which is likely yet another symptom of a decline seen in relationships in general. As we mentioned in chapter 3, the consumer mentality, the mindset that we so easily introjected from our current throwaway culture, also permeates the world of interpersonal relationships and particularly friendships. The term *cronyism* denotes that perversion of so-called friendships that are driven merely by self-interest. This may seem clear; however, we still need to distill what we truly mean by the term *friend*, that is, how we can better define the concept of friendship.

11. Donald Capps and Nathan Carlin, "Sigmund Freud and James Putnam: Friendship as a Form of Sublimation," *Pastoral Psychology* 59 (2010), 265–86. We will explore this topic further in the last chapter.

What would the basic requirements be to truly refer to friendship? What conditions would need to be present so that a friendship could come about and be sustained? Would it be mutual affection? Would it be honest sharing between two parties? Would it be selfless love? What is it really that specifically characterizes and defines the essence of this privileged relationship?[12]

As we will soon see, friendship may be defined by more than one quality, but there is one defining characteristic without which a friendship can never come about. Additionally, this prerequisite serves as a way to differentiate between friendships and other types of relationships, something that gives it its most peculiar and distinctive character. A friendship cannot be called thus if it is not based on individual freedom and if that same freedom (understood as the absence of external pressure rather than internal conditioning) does not continue to be an essential aspect of the relationship.[13]

Affection, benevolent love, intimacy, the sharing of common ideals, all these can give rise to friendship, but none of them are determiners for this type of relationship. Rather, it is exemplified by what is freely given. There is very intense affection in parent-child or couple relationships. And yet, these individuals may not be friends. There is also benevolent love in many altruistic relationships. But that selfless love does not always assure the emergence and friendship between those parties. There is a very high degree of intimate sharing in relationships with a psychotherapist or priest, for example, without friendship emerging (in fact, in the case of the psychoanalytic sessions, friendship can become a hindrance). There are also great collaborations in joint projects that imply a sharing of the same ideals and tasks to be carried out in common, but that does not translate to a friendship outside of the collaboration. Affection, selfless love, intimate sharing, collaboration, everything can and may have to be considered important to friendships, but none of these things shape relationships into friendships on their own. If that bond does not arise from the reciprocal freedom of those who come together, the friendship will not ensue.

Friendship is likely the only human relationship that is not regulated in the way that other relationships seem to be. However, any other modality of human bond is subjected to it. The relationship between lovers, which might initially seem the least likely to align itself with norms or laws, is, however, subject to regulation through matrimonial law, common-law partnerships, or by legal reckoning in the case of adultery or sexual harassment. Parent-child relationships are regulated and nations and states monitor their compliance. Labor relationships are regulated, as are relationships of a commercial nature,

12. Regarding the definition of friendship, see Barbara Caine, ed., *Friendship: A History* (New York: Routledge, 2014), 52–53,168–69, 223–24, 251–52; Daniel J. Hruschka, *Friendship: Development, Ecology, and Evolution of a Relationship* (Los Angeles: University of California Press, 2010).

13. Ray Pahl, *On Friendship* (Cambridge, UK: Polity Press, 2000).

as are the relationships between members of various associations (foundations, social clubs, sports clubs, NGOs, and so on). It is hard to think of any entity that claims jurisdiction over friendships, however, that penalizes any failings within it or that does not necessitate any additional type of obligation. Friendship is a relationship that is truly free and open and can only endure for as long as that freedom exists. We are under no obligation to be friends with anyone, and no human being in this world has a duty to be our friend. There are no demands or shadow of any need. Friendship is unnecessary, free, like art. You don't need friendship for survival; rather it is one of those things that adds value to existence. It is not an art form or the result of a technique as outlined in the popular book *How to Win Friends and Influence People* by Dale Carnegie. Nor can one make a friend by mere effort or interest if the other does not desire it. One can gain submissive flatterers or servile acolytes, but not true friendship. Therefore, there are *no merchants of friends*, as the fox says in *The Little Prince*.

For this purpose it is worth remembering Dietrich Bonhoeffer's beautiful reflections regarding friendship, which he penned in a letter during his time in prison:

> I am much impressed by your remarks about friendship in this connexion. As compared with marriage and the ties of kindred, friendship has not generally recognized rights and is therefore wholly dependent on its own inherent quality. It is by no means easy to classify friendship sociologically. Perhaps it is a subheading of culture and education. . . . But what of culture and education? I don't think they can be classified under labour, tempting though that may be from many points of view. They belong not to the sphere of obedience, but to that of freedom. . . . The man who is ignorant of this sphere of freedom can be a good father, citizen and worker, and even a Christian, but hardly a complete man. . . . Just because friendship belongs to this sphere from freedom, it must be confidently defended against all the disapproving frowns of moralism, thus without claiming for it the *necessitas* of a divine decree, but only the *necessitas* of freedom! I believe that within the sphere of this freedom friendship is by far the rarest and most priceless treasure. . . . It cannot be compared with the blessing of the decrees, for it is *sui generis*; its relation to them is that of the cornflower to the cornfield.[14]

IDENTIFICATION AND BENEVOLENT LOVE

While friendship requires freedom, the place where it germinates and flourishes will also need a particular seed and frequent watering to bring forth the

14. Dietrich Bonhoeffer, *Letters and Papers from Prison* (New York: MacMillan Company, 1966), January 23, 1944, 124–25.

desired fruit. We will later analyze that offshoot manifested as affection, desire, and attraction, which is the vital force driving this uniquely human bond.

Nor is there friendship without affection, without loving communication, without some type of expression of tenderness, of affection, of identifying with and showing interest in the other. In short, there is no friendship without some intervention from desire. A desire that, as a prime impulse that propels us, and that, as we have been reflecting on, aspires to diminish the separateness and the difference that is innate within us as *discrete beings*.

With varying hues and intensities, instinctual desire is that impetus that enables and energizes friendships, and in turn, finds within it one of the richest and most liberating vehicles for individuals and the social groups they inhabit.

The desire that drives friendship will be manifested according to the particular dynamics of each subject. Within these dynamics, the identification processes will always play an important role that harmonizes dynamically with the other—identifying with past commonalities, recognizing shared interests in the present, or looking forward to common future possibilities. Process of identification that will also have to be based on respect and reciprocity. Without this foundation of respect that facilitates bonding, it will not possible to establish this relationship in this unique expression known as friendship. Therefore, a friendship with parents, bosses, or superiors can only be established if they succeed in putting aside whatever prevents that identification, complicity, and reciprocity. And that is why it is also particularly difficult to establish those friendships when the differences outnumber the commonalities necessary to establish the necessary identifications. It is not unusual that on occasion, a friendship will fall apart when one of the parties is promoted to a higher place of authority, and therefore the feeling of equality is diminished. The mutual identification that sustained the relationship before dissipates.

This type of identification that occurs within friendship finds in each stage of life its own specific ways of manifesting. Children identify with each other in their games and shared fantasies, adolescents find in the other an image of what they want to be themselves, adults participate together in the projects, ideals, and worldviews that are common to them. The process of identification thus offers a foothold for friendship. But throughout the various stages of life, these processes of identification must give way to the manifestation of separateness and difference that is innate and particular to each of us. For this reason, the maturation of desire through these different stages will allow one to respect the uniqueness of the other.[15] In this way, friendship taps into an important dimension, which is the ethics of openness and commitment to

15. Adrian Furnham, "Friendship and Personal Development," in Roy Porter and Sylvana Tomaselli, eds., *The Dialectics of Friendship* (London: Routledge, 1990).

otherness. It requires the acceptance that we are *discrete beings*, and it requires us to tolerate our differences. With that acceptance, we can now move beyond seeing the other as an object of identification, but rather of love. What Freud conveyed to his friend Romain Rolland in 1931 is perhaps significant in this regard. He confessed that he had rarely experienced that *mysterious attraction* (*"die geheimnisvolle Anziehung"*) for another human being as he had with him, and that perhaps this was due to his awareness of their differences (unserer Verschiedenheiten).[16]

Without this other dimension in which a give and take can be articulated, where support can be offered and accepted, friendship becomes a farce. For this reason, conventional wisdom relates that true friendship can be verified by the ability to weather difficulties, where one can demonstrate a willingness to sacrifice for the other, to rise above the complacency and pleasures that the process of identification provides. We know that we have a friend when we trust that that other will be able to give, to risk, to lose something of himself for the other if necessary. And we know that only to the same extent that we are willing to reciprocate will we be able to be a true friend to another. Precisely because it is the freest relationship, the least forced, can it best exemplify by that ethical dimension that humans are capable of offering.

It is through this expression of desire combined with commitment where trust, another essential aspect of friendship, can arise. Being able to trust in the friend for help or company when needed. Trusting our friends with our most intimate feelings, to be able to have that reciprocal *loving communication* referred to by Entralgo. But not only trusting alongside the friend but *in* the friend. We believe in the friend's capacity to care and go out of his way for us, from the conviction (which implies risk) that he will not betray us. Without absolute certainty, without guarantees of any kind, we trust the friend.[17]

We are thus at a crossroads between the dynamics of desire and the world of values that shape it and, at the same time, outdo it. Any attempt then to understand friendship without this ethical component that transforms it and ripens it would be flawed. Likely, the psychoanalytic restraint in approaching axiology and difficulty in understanding the sublimation processes has failed to analyze this important ramification of desire.

The ethical and philosophical view has insisted (perhaps too fervently) on the ethical aspect of friendships. As Aristotle pointed out, although friendship is not a virtue, the degree of maturity within a friendship cannot be understood without virtue. For Saint Thomas Aquinas, friendship was characterized by benevolent love, while recognizing that such benevolence was not enough

16. Sigmund Freud, *Briefe 1873–1939* (Frankfurt: S. Fischer, 1980), 424.
17. As Francis Bacon affirmed, that trust that amplifies the joys and lessens the sorrows requires honesty with oneself before another.

to bring about a friendship. Kant insisted on respecting the other in such a way that the other is never a mere means but the object of love itself. And Voltaire knew how to express beautifully this essential articulation of desire and personal commitment when he defined friendship as "the marriage of the soul. . . . It is a tacit contract between two sensitive and virtuous persons."[18]

DEFINING THE CONCEPT OF FRIENDSHIP

Given all that has been said, it is evident that, in light of the aforementioned breakdown in the concept of friendship, it becomes something that can only arise and be sustained in certain conditions, and that it evolves only when certain requirements are met. Freedom is the first condition; it is what allows friendship to flourish and grow. If there is no freedom, there is no friendship, and if once established that freedom is constrained, that friendship becomes precarious.

It the field of freedom, it is desire that will allow the seed to, it will be that impulse toward a union that alleviates our lack of being, that creates a bridge with another person from our innate separation. That desire pushes the child to seek companionship with others in similar situations, energizes the adolescent to seek the company of peers, encourages the adult to search for interactions and loving communication with others. The identification with the other generates that particular attunement that allows for empathic listening, intimate communication, the expression of affection, and that also, as in any caring relationship, gives rise to sorrow due to the inherent separation, to suffering from frustration and conflict, to disappointment and the possibility of a fall-out, to the pain made possible by the loss of the beloved object, either because distrust grows or by the friend's departure.[19] In short, friendship manifests uniquely through the force of desire that drives every human being to seek bonds of affection and a line of communication based on what one is and aspires to be.

But if friendship has its basis in freedom, and if desire is the seed for growth, what will give the most fruitful results is ethical commitment. Only in this way can friendship be shaped into its full and mature form. The emotional attraction, identifying with the other, that loving bond, all of

---

18. Voltaire, *Voltaire's Philosophical Dictionary*, trans. H. I. Wolf (New York: Knopf, 1924), s.v. "Friendship." See also the previously cited work by Barbara Caine, *Friendship: A History*, 169.

19. The intense pain felt for the physical loss of a friend is best exemplified in Michel de Montaigne's writings on friendship due to the death of his friend La Boétie. See Carolyn James and Bill Kent, "Renaissance Friendships: Traditional Truths, New and Dissenting Voices," *Friendship: A History*, ed., Caine, 148–50. Among the Spanish poets, Miguel Hernández's elegy for his departed friend Ramón Sijé is a stirring tribute to the loss of a beloved friend.

these require a personal commitment that develops the capacity for delivery, contribution, and even, where appropriate, the possibility of sacrificing and renouncing for the other. Only in this way does it becomes possible not only to trust *alongside* the friend but also the trust *in* the friend, understanding that they are the ends for each other and not only means.[20]

Simultaneously, the ability to give is what demonstrates that the desire that birthed friendship has indeed evolved. Only when desire matures can selfish interests be isolated and the openness in which otherness is manifested be conquered. It is with great difficulty that a child renounces his pleasure for a playmate. Only when infantile omnipotence has been renounced, when one comprehends that we can never be anything for everyone nor will anyone be everything for us, does that encounter based on freedom and acceptance of differences translate to an enjoyment of the other through a caring exchange. It becomes true then that, "No one shows greater love than when he lays down his life for his friends" (Jn 15:13) and that in that act of giving one is fashioned and perfected.

Given what we have discussed and being mindful of the current reductionist idea of friendship, we could conclude that we can only speak authentically of this type of human relationship when it is open, when desire is limited to the role of attraction, closeness, communication, and reciprocal expression, and when that connection leads to a mutual commitment.

Pedro Laín Entralgo gives a similar definition when he says that friendship is "a relationship between human beings that, because these humans are what they are, there is benevolence, beneficence, and trust between them."[21] Elsewhere, the author defines friendship as "a loving communication between two people, in which, for their mutual good, and because of the uniqueness of each one, human nature is realized and perfected."[22]

These basic values of friendship are those that, in effect, are reflected in the different cultural conceptions of friendship. Friends can behave quite differently depending on the culture, but the relative values are surprisingly analogous in different societies.[23]

---

20. All the classic authors on friendship differentiated between those where the friend was a vehicle of utility or amusement and other more mature ones where the friend himself was the end goal. Aristotle differentiated friendships based on interest, pleasure, or virtue. Aelred of Rievaulx in his famous treatise on spiritual friendship distinguished between carnal, worldly, and spiritual friendship. Saint Thomas differentiated between useful, delightful, and honest friendships, and Kant distinguished between aesthetic and moral friendships. Refer to Laín, *Sobre la amistad*, 29–152 and Caine, ed., *Friendship: A History*.

21. Laín Entralgo, *Sobre la amistad*, 272.

22. Entralgo, 157.

23. See R. Adams and G. Allan, eds., *Placing Friendship in Context* (Cambridge, UK: Cambridge University Press, 1998).

And, yet, it is not always easy to differentiate between this type of human relationship and others in which desire is involved. Complexity is inherent in any relational experience; feelings and attitudes are easily intermingled that make it impossible to distinguish something pure from something contradictory. Therefore, the love felt in friendships is not always distinguishable from romantic love, altruistic love, companionship, camaraderie, or affection. A brief differential analysis between some of these various modes of relating could be quite elucidating.[24]

FRIENDS, COMRADES, OR LOVERS?

Fellowship or camaraderie can easily be confused with friendship because they share some commonalities. Laín Entralgo explains that etymologically speaking, a comrade is a roommate, one who shares a chamber with another—two individuals who eat and live together.[25] From there, he defines the one who shares another's fate and by extension, the friend. However, work and collaboration are characteristic of camaraderie (and fellowship) and are so central to it that we must reasonably see it as distinct from friendship. With the friend, there can be, and usually are, collaborations, but friendship is different in that projects are done out of affection and not because of any obligation, unlike how they might transpire with a comrade or a colleague. It is true that in the workplace and other collaborative scenarios friendships can easily emerge. But it is also true, as Pedro Laín Entralgo points out, that workplace friendships run up against three considerable obstacles—misery, rivalry, and labor polarization.[26]

The comrade or colleague usually relate to each other within an institutional setting or some kind of movement or collective (educational, military, political, or athletic, for example). At its heart lies a relationship marked by the pursuit of common objectives, where collaboration can lead to friendships based on solidarity. But the sharing of a common mission or ideals will not be enough for that trust and commitment so characteristic of friendship to flourish.

It is, however, the differentiation between friendships and the relationship of lovers that will be most beneficial in helping us to distill the true essence of friendship, within the array of affection-based relationships in which desire intervenes.

24. Kaarina Määttä and Satu Uusiautti, "Mission Impossible? A Scientific Comparison between the Overlapping and Diverging Phenomena of Friendship and Love," in *Many Faces of Love* (Rotterdam: Sense Publishers, 2013), 121–27.

25. The term originating in the Spanish language and used in military contexts was eventually passed to French as *camarade* and to English as *comrade*.

26. Laín Entralgo, *Sobre la amistad*, 309.

The phenomenon of falling in love occurs during a specified time and is usually an *all or nothing* scenario. There are no degrees of love; you are either in love or not. It is also a passion and because it is a passion it brings suffering. It's an ecstasy, but it's a torment too. Friendship, however, flees from suffering and, when it can, avoids it.[27] The lover, as Pedro Laín Entralgo affirms, is a needy and hyperbolic being because there is a need that is oriented toward the *all* and, from there, undergoes a self-absorbed and intense reality that seeks out a physical and spiritual communion with the beloved.[28] Additionally, the process of falling in love does not assure reciprocity, something that does not happen with friends. If the other does not want to be friends, our own desire vanishes. It is not worthwhile to try to be friends with those who do not wish to be friends with us.

But the most significant difference between the state of falling in love and that of friendship is the natural tendency to be possessive in the former. The lover, for example, wants to know everything about the loved one, their ideas and their feelings. The friend does not need so much. The friend welcomes what is offered with gratitude, but without insistence. The possessive tendency that the lover suffers from is absent. Freedom, which we have identified as a necessity for friendship, becomes questionable when falling in love. Therefore, the lover feels jealous. But friendship is spared from such feelings, and, if jealousy should arise, one would have to suspect that the relationship was concealing something else. The edges of friendship and romance can become blurred. This happens easily, as we know, in adolescent friendships.

The act of falling in love is impregnated with Eros and facilitates romantic expression. It seeks the union of bodies as a means of eradicating the separation and the difference that is innate within us. Friendship, however, aims to mend that gap differently—through the sharing of ideas, feelings, and common objectives. Through spoken word, gesture, and in knowing silence, communion arises. The friends no longer seek skin to skin but rather word to word. It will be a discreet closeness that avoids the exhibitionism that would weaken that trust. The friend, unlike the lover, is also understated in displays of affection. As Alberoni points out, friends do not say "what a great time we had together!" Lovers do that. Hence, as Alberoni also points out, a curious phenomenon often occurs between friends, where they can tell each other the most intimate secrets, but without being too forward about how they feel about each other.[29] There is no need to seek out that love fusion, that eroticism and sexuality that are inherent in romantic love. Therefore, although the

---

27. See Francesco Alberoni, *Friendship* (Leiden: Brill, 2016).

28. See "Teoría y realidad del otro," *Revista de Occidente*, Vol. II (1961): 208–19.

29. Alberoni, *La Amistad*, 116. See also James M. McMahon, "Intimacy among Friends and Lovers," in *Intimacy*, ed. Martin Fisher and George Stricker (Boston, MA: Springer, 1982).

friend enjoys and appreciates the presence of the other, there is no need to long for or reproach the other's absence.

And, yet, despite the obvious differences between the dynamics of falling in love and friendship, we cannot forget that both are nourished by the same force—by desire as an aspiration for a union that alleviates the inherent lack that defines us as separate beings. In that shared root of desire, psychoanalysis found that vibrant source that fuels friendships.

BACKGROUND DESIROUS URGES

Friendship was also an area that psychoanalytic theory shook up. Freud was correct in asserting that the purpose of psychoanalysis was to be controversial and therefore to irritate people. In his interpretation of friendship (understood as same-sex friendships) Freud linked it to one of the more controversial aspects of our affective world—homosexuality.

Friendship at that time was considered and still understood today in the psychoanalytic field as a type of sublimation or a derivation of the primitive instinctual desire that, being thwarted from its original erotic aim, instead finds a vehicle through the social construct of collegial encounter. Through this vehicle, the primitive erotic current is inhibited in its sexual intent, rising to another level where the participation of the psyche becomes more prominent. Freudian theory is very clear in this regard, "And we are thus led to the discovery that all the emotional relations of sympathy, friendship, trust, and the like, which can be turned to good account in our lives, are genetically linked with sexuality and have developed from purely sexual desires through a softening of their sexual aim, however pure and unsensual they may appear to our conscious self-perception."[30] Its common root, instinctual desire, spreads into a series of ramifications that always remain true to the spring that nourishes them. Self-love, in either its healthy or pathological form of narcissism, parent-child love, the general love for humanity, the conjugal affection, or the warmth between friends—these are all expressions of that background dynamism that energizes how human beings relate to other humans, ideas, or things.[31]

Where same-sex friendships are concerned, it is the homosexual aspect within us all that is redirected positively, benefiting society through the stable connections that are created. To this end Freud affirms in 1911, "After the

30. Sigmund Freud (1912b), "The Dynamics of Transference," in *Standard Edition*, 12: 105. See also (1925d), "An Autobiographical Study," in *Standard Edition*, 20: 38–39.

31. See Sigmund Freud (1921c), "Group Psychology and the Analysis of the Ego," in *Standard Edition*, 18: 90–91. Freud refers in these pages to the extension that psychoanalysis has operated in the traditional concept of sexuality.

stage of heterosexual object-choice has been reached, the homosexual tendencies are not, as might be supposed, done away with or brought to a stop; they are merely deflected from their sexual aim and applied to fresh uses. They now combine with portions of the ego-instincts and, as 'attached' components, help to constitute the social instincts, thus contributing an erotic factor to friendship and comradeship, to *esprit de corps* and to the love of mankind in general."[32]

The social and cultural dynamics thus become energized through these types of friendships. Instinctual desire never ceases to unite individuals. Furthermore, in its specifically sexual incarnation, it helps families to form and helps to perpetuate the species. Meanwhile, the inhibition of sexuality contributes to the creation of friendship, which because it is non-exclusive, contributes to creating a broader and often, more robust and long-lasting partnerships and networks.[33]

Where the opposite gender is concerned, the erotic aim is equally inhibited and redirected toward other socially valued interests, such as those of common participation in ideals, hobbies, or cooperative activities. In any case, establishing friendships with the opposite sex will always be challenging, to the extent that the primitive erotic attractions make themselves known, therefore transforming the friendship into something else.[34] It can also occur that a relationship starting out in the throws of passion gradually simmers down into a more affectionate, tender, and friendly one that provides stability and duration, something that the passionate relationship could not.[35]

Thus, we see the complexity of those relationships where the amicable feelings and romantic ones become intertwined. In some cases, the combination of feelings will eventually become incompatible, while in others, feelings of friendship will become amorous. More challenging and yet possible, relationships based on romantic love can transition to pure friendship, just as the coexistence of these feelings is often seen within the same relationship. There are friendships between people of a different sex (and also within homosexual friendships) where romantic feelings are absent, just as there are crushes without friendship. On other occasions, however, it will be friendship that is

32. Sigmund Freud (1911c), "Psycho-Analytic Notes on an Autobiographical Account of a Case of Paranoia," in *Standard Edition*, 12: 61. Cf. Christopher Lane, *The Burdens of Intimacy: Psychoanalysis and Victorian Masculinity* (Chicago, IL: Chicago University Press, 1999); Peter M. Nardi, ed., *Men's Friendships* (New York, NY: Sage Publications, 1992); Peter Redman, Debbie Epstei, Mary Jane Kehily, and Martin Mac An Ghaill, "Boys Bonding: Same-Sex Friendship: The Unconscious and Heterosexual Discourse, *Discourse* 23 (2002) 179–91; Timothy Barret, "Friendships between Men across Sexual Orientation: The Management of Sexual Difference through Humour," *Journal of Sociology* 52 (2016): 255–370.

33. See Freud (1930a), "Civilization and its Discontents," in *Standard Edition*, 21: 101–107.

34. See Barbara J. Risman and Pepper Schwartz, eds., *Gender in Intimate Relationships* (Belmont, CA: Wadsworth, 1991).

35. See Freud (1921c), "Group Psychology and the Analysis of the Ego," in *Standard Edition*, 18: 140.

the highest expression of romantic love. Because it is true that *philia*, as Laín Entralgo states, is what perfects the feeling of *eros*.[36] Francesco Alberoni, however, is more skeptical about the compatibility of romantic feelings with friendship. This author believes that friendship is unrelated to eroticism and that they are therefore difficult to reconcile. A relationship can go one way or another, and it is usually unidirectional. Eroticism does not generate friendship, but the author accepts that friendship is compatible with eroticism.[37] In short, we see once again that desire's various streams can become fused and confused with extreme ease.[38]

A person's history will always influence those particular dynamics of love or friendship. Those sympathies and antipathies experienced among people that create bonds, that give rise to identifications or disdain, are inextricably intertwined to the experiences of personal biography and, in particular, of childhood and family relationships. In this sense, Freud insisted again and again that "the individual's emotional attitudes to other people, which are of such extreme importance to his later behavior, are already established at an unexpectedly early age. . . . All of his later choices of friendship and love follow upon the basis of the memory-traces left behind by these first prototypes."[39]

Freud did not hesitate to ascribe his friendship choices later in life to his early childhood bonds. Both in his most earnest friendships and his deepest enmities with people around him were linked to his childhood experience with his nephew John, who was a year older than himself. This nephew dominated Freud, who had to learn to defend himself. The effects of this early relationship are described in *The Interpretation of Dreams*:

> How we were inseparable friends, and how, according to the testimony of our elders, we sometimes fought with each other and—made complaints to them about each other. All my friends have in a certain sense been re-incarnations of this first figure who "long since appeared before my troubled gaze" *[früh sich einst dem trüben Blick gezeigt]*: they have been *revenants*. . . . My emotional life has always insisted that I should have an intimate friend and a hated enemy. I have always been able to provide myself afresh with both, and it has not infrequently happened that the ideal situation of childhood has been so completely reproduced that friend and enemy have come together in a single individual.[40]

His intense and conflicting relations with Wilhelm Fliess and with Carl Jung indicated that his friendships were impregnated with both love and hate.[41]

---

36. Pedro Laín Entralgo, *Sobre la amistad*, 308.
37. See *La Amistad*, 119.
38. See Kaarina Määttä and Satu Uusiautti, *Many Faces of Love* (Sense Publishers, Rotterdam, 2013).
39. Freud (1914f), "Some Reflections on Schoolboy Psychology," in *Standard Edition*, 13: 243.
40. Sigmund Freud (1900a), *The Interpretation of Dreams*, in *Standard Edition*, 5: 483.
41. Linda Donn, *Freud and Jung: Years of Friendship, Years of Loss* (New York: Charles Scribners's Sons, 1988). Stefano Mariano Carta, "Friendship: Beyond Oedipus," in *Transformation: Jung's*

Through these intense relationships, he had the opportunity to observe, après coup, the homosexual current that circulated unconsciously. In a letter to Fliess dated May 7, 1900, he says, "But no one can replace for me the relationship with the friend which a special—possibly feminine—side demands."[42] And a year later on August 7, he also comments, "In my life, as you know, woman has never replaced the comrade, the friend."[43] There was also a letter he wrote to Sándor Ferenczi after a trip they took together to Italy in 1910. After the trip, his travel companion expressed disappointment in the lack of reciprocity to his openness and sharing of confidential information. To this, Freud replied, "Not only have you noticed that I no longer have any need for that full opening of my personality, but you have understood it and correctly returned to its traumatic cause. Why did you thus make a point if it? This need has been extinguished in me since Fliess's case, with the overcoming of which you just saw me occupied. A piece of homosexual investment has been withdrawn and utilized for the enlargement of my own Ego. I have succeeded where the paranoiac fails."[44] With this last thought, he alluded to his theory on the cause of paranoiac conflict—homosexuality.

After his traumatic relationships with Fliess and later with Jung, Freud was very reserved and cautious with his friends. Though he broadened his connections perhaps, he did so without going too deeply. His unique friendship with Pastor Oskar Pfister, however, deserves special mention. Though Freud felt deeply ambivalent about the Protestant pastor's religious ideals, he felt a fondness for him that other colleagues had trouble understanding.[45] His role as teacher with his various disciples and the openness to friendship with some women like Lou Andreas Salomé, Marie Bonaparte, or his sister-in-

---

Legacy and Clinical Work Today, ed. Lucinda Hawkins and Martha Stevens (London: Karnac, 2014).

42. Sigmund Freud, *The Complete Letters of Sigmund Freud to Wilhelm Fliess 1887–1904*, trans. Jeffrey Moussaieff Masson (Cambridge, MA: Harvard University Press, 1985), 412.

43. Freud, trans. Moussaieff, 447.

44. Letter dated October 6, 1910: Eva Brabant, Ernst Falzeder, and Patricia Giampieri-Detuch, *The Correspondence of Sigmund Freud and Sándor Ferenczi*, 1908–1914, Vol. 1 (Cambridge, MA: The Belknap Press of Harvard University Press, 1993) Vol. 1, 221. On the relationship of Freud and Ferenczi, cf. Benjamin Kilborne, "Human Foibles and Psychoanalytic Technique: Freud, Ferenczi, and Gizella Palos," *The American Journal of Psychoanalysis* 68 (2008): 1–23; Michael Schröter, "The Beginnings of a Troubled Friendship: Freud and Ferenczi 1908–1914," in *Behind the Scenes: Freud in Correspondence*, ed. Patrick Mahony, Carlo Bonomi, and Jan Stensson, 123–54 (Oslo: Skandinavian University Press, 1997).

45. I explored this relationship in "History of a Friendship," which was the first section of a work titled *Psicoanálisis y religión: diálogo interminable. Sigmund Freud y Oskar Pfister* (Madrid: Trotta 2000), 13–100. See also Isabelle Noth and Christoph Morgenthaler, "The Friendship between Sigmund Freud and Oskar Pfister as Seen in the Correspondence between the Jewish Atheist Founder of Psychoanalysis and the Swiss Pastor Who Pioneered Pastoral Psychology," *Pastoral Psychology* 63 (2014): 81–90; Herman Westerink, "On True Friendship and on the Anthropological Relevance of Freud's The Future of an Illusion," *Pastoral Psychology* 63 (2014): 97–100.

law Minna Bernays seems to have satiated his needs for friendship.[46] These are the examples of the complicated dynamics in Freud's friendships. Each individual also weaves his or her own particular way of relating to others in the areas of friendship, based on character and past history.

PSYCHODYNAMICS OF FRIENDSHIP

We recall Michel de Montaigne's explanation for the love toward his friend La Boétie through the sentiment that "he was he, and I was I."[47] Because the uniqueness of each individual makes these types of encounters possible, the friendships created are themselves also unique and special.

Spanish humanist Luis Vives explained that different temperaments lead to different ways of relating within friendship and love. The fiery temperaments are passionate and unpredictable; the author compared them to hay that burns quickly versus more temperate ones which burn slowly like firewood, exemplifying different ways of interrelating within friendships.[48] Also in Kant's work *The Observations on the Feeling of the Beautiful and the Sublime*, he arranges different types of friendship according to temperaments. Thus, for example, melancholic individuals are more suited to friendships based on morality because, according to the philosopher, their behavior is guided by principles. The sanguine individual, however, would likely veer toward a friendship based on aesthetics, in which the pleasure and joy of being with the friend prevails over the principals of respect and personal commitment. The choleric individual, Kant thought, was not fit for any kind of friendship, considering that those interactions would be based on pretense.[49]

As we pointed out earlier, from a more psychoanalytic lens we need to look at the identification processes as the key to how bonding is established. The harmony that is experienced with the friend is in fact the identification process one feels with the other's way of thinking, feeling, and projecting onto life. If friendship is one soul in two bodies, as Aristotle beautifully put it, it is because the process of identification is an important psychodynamic factor. In this sense, the *omoios* (ancient Greek for "the shared") can be seen in the bonds of friendship, both with the same sex and the opposite sex.

---

46. In this regard, see Bernard Bensidoun, "Sigmund, Josef, Wilhelm et les autres," *Enfances & Psy* 31 (2006): 119–24; Patrick Mahony, Carlo Bonomi, and Jan Stensson (Oslo, Norway: Scandinavian University Press, 1997.
47. Michel de Montaigne, *On Friendships* (New York: Penguin Books, 1991).
48. See Luis Vives, *Tratado del alma* (Espasa Calpe, Madrid 1957, 3ª), 151.
49. Immanuel Kant, *Observations on the Feeling of the Beautiful and Sublime* (Cambridge: Cambridge University Press, 2011).

That resonance will often be perceived clearly and consciously; on other occasions, however, as is also the case in love dynamics, perception will work at the unconscious level, also giving rise to that odd phenomenon where attraction and appreciation for another person occurs without an apparent reason. Throughout life, our desire leads us toward certain people (and moves us away from others) because our unconscious believes it can recognize certain possibilities or obstacles to producing encounters.

That identification process is also an affective current that will not always be able to clearly set those love boundaries, in which the *relating to* of the identification process turns into the *must have* of love. This is the case when the homosexual dimension, always present in same-sex friendships, does not succeed in containing and limiting its ultimate goals, and giving free rein to the ultimate inhibition, leads to those so-called "particular friendships" that must remain hidden. On the other end of the spectrum, it can also be the case that this homosexual dimension is so constrained and blocked that it prevents the normal expression of affection, hindering the possibility of friendship in its essential aspect of affective closeness. It is not possible to have that closeness, not even that normal body proximity that the friend offers, without experiencing it as a danger to that repressed homosexual part. Thus, Freud explains, "Even an affectionate devotee, even a friend or an admirer, desires the physical proximity and the sight of the person who is now loved only in the 'Pauline' sense."[50] In friendships with the opposite sex, the transition from identification to love, as we noted above, can be smoother.

Within friendships, somehow, we see ourselves in the other, we see our face reflected in the mirror of our friend. "What after all is the face of your friend?" Nietzsche asks himself. "It is your own face, in a rough and imperfect mirror."[51] In it, we perceive indeed our attempts to be, to think, and to feel, either through our actual reality or through our hopes and dreams. The narcissistic component is one of the most important sustainers within friendships.[52] Aristotle affirmed in his *Nicomachean Ethics* that the affection that friends have for each other, those feelings that define true friendships, originates in the idea that man has himself.[53] In other words, the friend is another *I*.

The identification, then, occurs from our real *Ego*, but also our own *Ego Ideal* projected onto the friend. The friend reflects our dreams, what we hope to manifest for ourselves, whether it is realistic or not. It supports us in all the ways in which we wish to be and act.

---

50. Freud, "Group Psychology and the Analysis of the Ego," in *Standard Edition*, 18: 139.

51. Nietzsche, *Thus Spake Zarathustra*, 41.

52. See Sharon M. Hymer, "Narcissistic Friendships," *The Psychoanalytic Review* 71 (1984): 423–39; Hruschka, *Friendship: Development, Ecology, and Evolution of a Relationship*, 156–60.

53. See Aristotle, *Nicomachean Ethics* (New York: Oxford University Press, 2009) IX, IV.

But the image that the friend reflects back to us can also show us our shadow side. This is the case with those who seek out "bad company" in order to live vicariously through that person, even at the level of fantasy, to experience what is forbidden for oneself. From childhood to adulthood, this kind of complicit friendship can play an important role in our relationship dynamics.

In any case, the identification process that is fundamental to forming emotional bonds in friendships requires some kind of reciprocity (whether real or imagined) and equality. *Philotes-isótes*, was an affirmation in the Greek world, which meant, *friendship-equality*. This is something all treaties regarding friendship insist upon. Because, while it is true that friendship is able to overcome many differences, if the differences were too great, it would be very difficult to establish those identification mechanisms that create the bonds that allow for the flourishing and maintenance of friendship. Thus, the friendships that can occur between parents and children, teachers and students, bosses and subordinates will always be limited, and will only arise to the extent that feelings of superiority are set aside. Aristotle remarked that friendships cannot endure the distance between gods and men.

This sharing that facilitates the identification process involves the transfer of previous, real, or imagined fraternal relationships. The friend takes on the internal brotherly representation, and through that friendship all of the intense positive and negative feelings that were previously felt with siblings are mobilized.[54]

But within these representations, there is another series of transferential aspects derived from previous object relationships that transpired during childhood. Friends, operating within the limits of reciprocity and a sense of fairness, take on roles, usually at the unconscious level, that are closely linked to the parental figures. Siblings also do this. In seemingly balanced friendships, in both childhood and adulthood, the motherly or fatherly role being played out may go undetected. Even among adults, such parental representations may be present, regardless of the age of the individuals, or even when the portrayed roles of parent and child are age-inverted.[55] The combination of personality traits and identifying tendencies become prominent, pushing reality away. Each one is complicit in playing out the role that helps to maintain the relationship.

But the bonds of friendship can waver; they correspond to the particular dynamics at play. Friendships can be stable, or they may require maintenance.

---

54. See Prophecy Coles, *The Importance of Sibling Relationships in Psychoanalysis* (London: Routledge, 2018).

55. Rebeca G. Adams and R. Bliesner, "Midlife Friendship Patterns," *A Lifetime of Relationships*, eds. Vanzetti and Duck (Pacific Grove, CA: Brooks/Cole, 1994), 336–63; Luis Kancyper, "Metapsychology and Clinical Aspects of Transference-Friendship," *The Psychoanalytic Quarterly* 87 (2018): 101–26.

They may evolve or decay or fade altogether. All these possibilities have a direct correlation to the individual's psychodynamic processes. A relationship established primarily in the parent-child transfer dynamic may have a crisis when one of the parties refuses to maintain the role he had played thus far, even when that role had once been relished. Just as a relationship based on a sibling transference that satisfies a need for competition and rivalry can be disrupted when that rivalry unleashes a level of aggression that cannot be maintained. The triggering of suppressed erotic tendencies can also alter the dynamics of the relationship, making it impossible to go on when one of the parties cannot or does not want to respond as the other now wishes.

EVOLUTION OF FRIENDSHIPS

There are few human relationships that are as present throughout the various stages of life as friendships are. Children, teenagers, adults, and the elderly have friends. Each stage has its specific peculiarities, it fulfills various functions, takes on different roles that can come and go. The idealized image of adult friendship should not, therefore, obscure the value of friendships throughout our lives. We should not view friendships in earlier stages as infantile steps toward the fullness of adulthood.

That tendency to eliminate the separation that is innate in us as individuals is apparent from birth, in that fascination that babies display when interacting with each other and in that seeking of closeness. Thus begins the potential for *friendly* encounters with others, with the fascinating and unexpected attractions and repulsions that emerge.[56] It has been observed, for example, that from one year on, babies prefer to spend time with those of the same age and only one-on-one. Only after turning three years old, when the consolidation of their social Ego begins, will they adopt a less self-centered attitude, with a greater awareness of others' emotions and a greater willingness to share. These early relationships also open up the subject for the first time to experiences beyond the limited family circle.

At around the age of six, children begin to have a capacity for dialogue, allowing for much greater ability to form friendships. Between eight and ten the first cliques appear, with a typical segregation between the sexes, as the processes of psychosexual identification are aided in this way. Friendship thus plays a very important role in the evolution of one's identity. Throughout later childhood, the friend becomes a fundamental support system in that

56. See Zick Rubin, *Children's Friendships* (Cambridge, MA: Harvard University Press, 1980); Selma Fraiberg, *Understanding and Handling the Problem of Early Childhood* (New York: Scribners, 1968).

wonderful, surprising, and sometimes also anguishing exploration of the mysteries of life. Perhaps because of this, these friendships are never forgotten and always evoke warm and profound emotions in us.

After puberty, the process of overcoming childhood dependency starts with a search for broader social integration. Thus, a process of expansion in interpersonal relationships begins by searching for friendships that can last from a few weeks to a lifetime. In any case, the relationship of camaraderie is giving way to the search for more selective and challenging relationships, not without a significant degree of idealization that often leads to frustration and consequently to feelings of disappointment. It is the moment when we hear teens declare: "True Friendships (with a capital F) do not exist!" The adolescent has not yet understood that this capital letter, which showcases the impossible totality to which desire aspires, will not be found anywhere.

During adolescence, the Ego does not yet have solid boundaries, and therefore lacks the ability to show affection to others who are equally vulnerable. Additionally, there is great insecurity in the handling of one's own feelings of loneliness, fear, and sadness. In that context, friendships are usually maintained with others of the same sex and with intense homosexual undercurrents that are (usually) ultimately inhibited. These teens confide with each other with clear exhibitionist nuances. The other sex is scrutinized and the first encounters are sought, preferably in the company of same-sex friends as auxiliary supports. These friendships also serve to attain greater autonomy from adults. Hence, these teenage friendships have that hopeful, fruitful, and often, aggressive character as well.

According to Erik Erikson, adulthood represents a fundamental challenge: to progress in one's ability to be intimate, both in friendship and in love.[57] In the twenties to thirties, the relationship with friends becomes very time-consuming. Later, there may be a conflict of interest between friendships and a significant other, as well as between professional and interpersonal relationships. But friendships generally become more selective, stable, and entrenched as well.[58]

Once the family is formed, friendships usually take a back seat to accommodate new life circumstances, at least for a certain period of time. Usually, friendships will be distilled so that the significant other can try to adapt to them. Friendship with other couples could, on the other hand, facilitate the role of becoming parents, just as adolescent friendships facilitated that initial sepa-

---

57. Erik Erikson, *The Life Cycle Completed: A Review* (New York: W.W. Norton & Company Inc., 1982).

58. See Joyce Edward, "Friends in Old Age," *Clinical Social Work Journal* 44 (1996): 198–203; Sarah Matthews, *Friendship Through the Life Course: Oral Biographies in Old Age* (Thousand Oaks, CA: SAGE 1986). In this work, he shares the testimony of sixty-three seniors who speak about the impact of their friendships from childhood to old age.

ration from parents. The ability to incorporate friendship in a romantic relationship demonstrates a wise attitude that will give balance to romance, while introducing sex to friendship could easily hinder and disrupt that friendship.

Finally, in old age, the awareness of death easily makes one appreciate those human bonds, assuming that the individual hasn't regressed or withdrawn inwardly due to bitter life experiences. Group relationships seem very beneficial at this stage, by providing community and facilitating the sharing of resources.

CRISIS, LOSSES, AND RUPTURES

Throughout all these phases of life, the living and dynamic process of friendship will also, just as with individuals themselves, go through moments of tension, stagnation, abundance, regression, loss, and death. We should consider the role that friendship plays in the crises that can occur, and the hope for surmounting these problems versus stagnating in them or seeing the friendship simply fall apart. There are certainly many factors that can come into play. Both those related to one's style of relationship or external circumstancer can trigger a crisis, as well as its subsequent evolution.

Having a friend who falls in love and marries can often cause a predicament, due to the resulting triangular relationship. It can also, however, lead to a strengthening of the bond, precisely by the introduction of the new element. As we know, unlike romantic relationships, friendships have no difficulty in including and incorporating new ties. However, friendships can become destabilized in cases where, for example, a couple splits up and a mutual friend feels let down through the shattering of that idealized fantasy of a successful union. Parental transfers, no doubt, become an important part of these triangular dynamics.

If triangular dynamics caused by an intersection of romantic relationships with friendships can lead to creons, so can similar situations arise between siblings. Sibling relationships, which often involve a degree of friendship, can also see an amplification of feelings of rivalry, or even superiority, when one succeeds in the areas of love and the other does not, leading to a breakdown of the relationship. French philosopher La Rochefoucauld lamented in the seventeenth century that one's own success was not enough since we strived to see our friends fail.

When one of the parties is overly dependent on the other, this can also result in the crises that arise within friendships. An excessive demand for favors, money, attention, affection, and so on rattles the very basis of the relationship as that essential freedom that is necessary for friendship to blossom.

On the other hand, sociocultural factors must also be taken into account in regard to the factors that inhibit or contribute to friendships. It is widely acknowledged that the types of friendship seem to conform to societal models and according to the times and conditions of each era. Today, the *single-use* consumerist mentality undoubtedly permeates our friendships, making them more accessible and numerous, but also increasingly fragile and superficial. The current internet chatting fever illustrates our current state of affairs. There has never been so much opportunity to choose with whom to communicate and to do so in such an impersonal and detached way.

The fact is that there are also, as with romantic relationships, broken friendships. Friendships that do not help an individual to evolve, but rather, become an obstacle and invite regressive or pathological dimensions of personality. There are friendly relationships that endure thanks to a strange complicity that allows the most problematic nuclei of the subjects to be activated. Like the relationship of lovers, all kinds of regressive and pathogenic dynamics are possible. From the infantilizing dependence that keeps an individual in a position of passivity, to the sadomasochistic relationship, in which both parties know how to nurture these tendencies with an astonishing unconscious ability. These are relationships in which autonomy and personal identity are threatened because of a dangerous association—they are like two drops of mercury that merge into one when in close proximity. With that fusion, however, we would only find a strange drop, an aberration resulting from the annihilation of these two autonomies.[59]

All these personal and sociocultural factors contribute to the idea that friendships do not aspire to an eternal state the way that love does. However, many friendships display great strength and capacity to overcome disappointments, frustrations, or fallouts, even becoming revitalized and more deeply bonded. It depends to a large extent on the initial expectations, on the capacity to deal with disappointments, on the ability to understand the other's actions, and on the strength of affection.

These crises will have to be resolved through clear communication and goodwill. But naked truth stripped of kindness is in fact an aggression that will put a friendship in jeopardy. But affection that covers over built-up frustrations increases the most regressive dimensions of the relationship and will create a strain that will, sooner or later, take its toll. It is time, then, for those "loving cruelties" that Spanish poet Gabriel Celaya spoke of. Friendships need to be based on the constructive confrontation of the inevitable limitations, failures, and frustrations inherent to every human relationship.

59. See Hazel Weinberg, "Clinical Aspects of Friendliness and Friendships," *Journal Contemporary Psychoanalysis* 25 (1989): 357–70.

But it is also a fact friendships do not always survive despite the depths reached and the attempts made to save it. And they end in all manner of ways. Letty Cottin Pogrebin, author and activist, synthesizes them into three main types: *baroque endings*, that is, exaggerated, bombastic and dramatic (hysterical, we might add), *classical endings*, which are carried out in a rational and serene way, and *romantic endings*, which occur through a gradual and progressive fading.[60] Friendship, as Kant reminded us, is a rare black swan, which, like all living things, is always threatening us with death and disease. And also like all living things (which may be a good thing to accept to have wholesome friendships) it never reaches its highest and desired level of fulfillment. Therefore, we can all proclaim that saying attributed to Aristotle—*Oh my friends, there is no friend!*

THE ALLIANCE BETWEEN DESIRE AND THE IDEAL

There is probably no other bond like friendship that embodies the melding of desire and ideal. Ethics and aesthetics thus merge in a unique and paradigmatic way.[61] Through a psychoanalytic lens, we might consider that no other human relationship offers, because of its nature, the potential of expression and the possibility of balance between the strength of the Id and the ideals of the Superego.

No wonder Francesco Alberoni affirms that friendship contains the ethical expression of Eros. Desire, as we have analyzed, is an early influence, but it doesn't take long, even in childhood friendships, to see a rising up of the important moral components of justice, fairness, and interpersonal commitment. When we notice these ethical components fading, it does not take long for desire to fall off and for the friendships to collapse. It does not have the additional support typically found in families or love relationships. In friendships, the Id needs to derive strength from the Superego ideal.

Desire and ideal are thus articulated in the relationship of friendship in a specific and unique way. The passion of love can do without justice, it can survive betrayal, and it can consent to all kinds of annoyances or lies. Desire, which is stronger than justice, overrides all else. On the other hand, the bond between benefactor and recipient can dispense with affection, warmth, or care in order to maintain this charitable relationship, regardless of what is emotionally craved in return.

---

60. Letty Cottin Pogrebin, *Among Friends: Who We Like, Why We Like Them, and What We Do with Them* (New York: McGraw-Hill, 1987), 110–25.

61. See Michael Mitias, *Friendship: A Central Moral Value* (Amsterdam and New York: Rodopi, 2012).

However, for friendships to last, fascination and desire, affection, and caring, must be tempered by commitment. We do not need the friend to be fair, honest, or loyal. We can be friends with a wicked person. But we need that relationship to be steered by that loyalty and justice that may be lacking with all other mortals. Otherwise, the other cannot call us a friend either.

Just as it is possible to be the center of attention, being lavished with nurturing and compassion, without the spark of friendship taking place. Pedro Laín Entralgo illustrates this dimension of friendship with a beautiful reference to the parable of the Good Samaritan. It may be that the Samaritan showed the full extent of his mercy with the poor wounded man he found on the side of the road. He took care of him, took him to the inn, cleaned and healed his wound, and was willing to pay for expenses involved. However, none of this merited the designation of friendship. For this to be friendship, they would have needed to confide in each other, to have a closeness, the exchange something personal. Only in this way could the "we-subject" of friendship spring forth. "My name is Daniel; what is your name?" These are the words that the Good Samaritan could have spoken to the wounded man. And only after the wounded man answered, "I am so-and-so," could friendship have arisen. This does not require the divulging of one's most intimate secrets, but rather, some sort of emotional bond established through simple but personal gestures, and with trust. As Laín Entralgo himself suggests, it would suffice to say *look* while observing a beautiful sunset, to prove one's willingness to connect. Friendship, in this way, perfects the charitable act, adds the human element to theological grace.[62] When referring to friendship, the Superego Ideal also needs to connect with the vitality of affection that has its origin in the dark forces of the Id.

Friendship is not a virtue, Aristotle reminded us; but friendship needs virtue.[63] As Voltaire explained it, friendships are tacit contracts made by two sensitive and virtuous peope, or perhaps more eloquently put, they are a marriage of the psyche between two virtuous human beings. But mere sympathies or commonalities are not enough; nor does virtue generate friendship on its own. Love and respect were the necessary elements described by Kant, those that feel somewhere between the ethical and the aesthetic.

It is a type of respect that represents an ethical attitude that does not constrain love and desire. That respect is the best expression of a desire that has matured and, therefore, is faithful to the separateness and the uniqueness that must be accepted in the encounter with the other. The other is not a morsel to bite off and used to satiate that feeling of lack. Nor is the other an object to dominate, control, and possess. But a free and unique being, who can please or frustrate, and whose freedom and autonomy should be accepted.

62. See Laín Entralgo, *Sobre la amistad*, 296–98.
63. Entralgo, *Sobre la amistad*, 259–62.

For this reason, the friend expects nothing in return; rather, the friend is thankful for whatever is freely given. Nor does he rush in head first to save the other, forgetting that maybe the other doesn't want to be "saved." This respect allows the other to take risks and make mistakes with all that that entails, not coming to his aid unless the friend, implicitly or explicitly, requests and desires it. Only then is he respecting his own lack and only thus respecting the freedom that springs from the lack of the other. The friend is not a crush, nor a nutritious mother, nor a protecting father. And knowing only this way, as a close and committed you, accompany the other from his solitude and feel accompanied by the common adventure of existing.

But when things transpire in this way, friendship is a bond that can significantly enhance one's growth and personal development. The ideal itself is catapulted and driven by the force of affection that, from a mutual identification, feeds and sustains the bond. Friendship, therefore, has an enormous capacity to transform and to propel the subjects forward.

The friend must be a longing for improvement. "For your friend you cannot groom yourself beautifully enough, for you should be his arrow and longing for the overman," exclaimed Nietzsche's Zarathustra.[64] The friend is not the landing strip but the launching pad. We also know that Freud was always in need of friends in order to navigate life and be productive. As he expressed to Fliess at the beginning of their friendship, and as is seen throughout their correspondence, their relationship gave him confidence and was an impetus for his work. "When I talked with you and saw that you thought well of me, I even used to think something of myself, and the picture of absolutely convincing energy that you offered was not without its effects on me."[65]

But if the friend is an arrow and a yearning for self-improvement, he must also be discerning and truthful: "In one's friend one shall have one's best enemy (*Man soll in seinem Freunde noch den Feind ehren*),[66] affirmed Nietzsche's Zarathustra, demanding a truth that could be painful and even cruel at times. It is a duty, also wrote Kant, that the friend reveals the other's faults, for he does it for his own good and it is therefore an act of love. We run into those "loving cruelties" again that may become necessary, not only to face potential crisis, but also as a necessary means for the friend to grow, or even be saved from a place of ignorance we inhabit.

Born of freedom, energized by the seed of Eros that brings together all living things, friendship can bear the fruit of personal commitment, respecting the separateness and uniqueness that is innate in all of us. It becomes true

64. Nietzsche, *Thus Spake Zarathustra*, 41.

65. Refers to an August 1, 1890, letter, see Freud, *The Complete Letters of Sigmund Freud to Wilhelm Fliess 1887–1904,* trans. Jeffrey Moussaieff Masson (Cambridge, MA: Harvard University Press, 1985), 27.

66. Freud, *The Complete Letters of Sigmund Freud to Wilhelm Fliess 1887–1904*, 67.

then that "Greater love has no one than this: to lay down one's life for one's friends" (Jn 15:13), and by giving of ourselves we transform and become more refined beings.

BIBLIOGRAPHY

Adams, Rebecca G., and R. Bliesner. "Midlife Friendship Patterns." In *A Lifetime of Relationships*, Nelly Vanzetti and Steve Duck eds., 336–63. Pacific Grove, CA: Brooks/Cole, 1994.

Adams, Rebecca G., and Allan Graham, eds. *Placing Friendship in Context*. Cambridge, UK: Cambridge University Press, 1998.

Alberoni, Francesco. *Friendship*. Leiden: Brill, 2016.

Aristotle. *Nicomachean Ethics.* New York: Oxford University Press, 2009.

Bacon, Francis. *Friendship.* Whitefish, MT: Kessinger Legacy Reprints, 2010.

Bensidoun, Bernard. "Sigmund, Josef, Wilhelm et les autres." *Enfances & Psy* 31 (2006): 119–24.

Bergler, Edmund. *Psychology of Friendship and Acquaintanceship: Selected Papers* 1933–191. New York: Grume and Stratton, 1969.

Bonhoeffer, Dietrich. *Letters and Papers from Prison.* New York: Macmillan Company, 1966.

Brabant, Eva, Ernst Falzeder, and Patricia Giampieri-Detuch, eds. *The Correspondence of Sigmund Freud and Sándor Ferenczi, 1908–1914*, Vol. 1. Cambridge, MA: The Belknap Press of Harvard University Press, 1993.

Brun, Danièle. "La pasión en la amistad." *Revista de psicoanálisis* 60 (2003): 1081–1090.

———. "A gramática amorosa da amizade." *Ágora: Estudos em Teoria Psicanalítica.* 10 (2007): 311–19.

Caine, Barbara, ed. *Friendship: A History*. London and New York: Routledge, 2014.

Capps, Donald, and Nathan Carlin. "Sigmund Freud and James Putnam: Friendship as a Form of Sublimation." *Pastoral Psychology* 59 (2010): 265–86.

Carta, Stefano Mariano. "Friendship: Beyond Oedipus." In *Transformation: Jung's Legacy and Clinical Work Today*, ed. Lucinda Hawkins and Martha Stevens. London: Karnac, 2014.

Ciceronis, M. Tullis. De Re Publica, De Legibus, Cato Maior de Senectute, Laelius de Amicitia. Oxford: Oxford University Press, 2006.

Derrida, Jacques. *The Politics of Friendship.* London and New York: Verso, 2005.

Domínguez-Morano, Carlos. *Psicoanálisis y religión: diálogo interminable. Sigmund Freud y Oskar Pfister.* Madrid: Trotta 2000.

Donn, Linda. *Freud and Jung: Years of Friendship, Years of Loss.* New York: Charles Scribner's Sons, 1988.

Edward, Joyce. "Friends in Old Age." *Clinical Social Work Journal* 44 (1996): 198–203.

Elredo de Rieval. *L'amitié spirituelle*. Bruges-Paris: Charles Beyaert, 1948.

Erikson, Erik. *The Life Cycle Completed: A Review.* New York: W.W. Norton & Company Inc., 1982.
Fher, Beverly. *Friendship Processes.* Sage: London, 1996.
Freud, Sigmund, and Ernst Freud. *The Letters of Sigmund Freud 1873–1939.* New York: Basic Books, 1960.
Freud, Sigmund (1900a). *The Interpretation of Dreams*. In *The Standard Edition of the Complete Psychological Works of Sigmund Freud*, edited and translated by James Strachey, 7. London: Hogarth, 1966.
——— (1911c). *Psycho-Analytic Notes on an Autobiographical Account of a Case of Paranoia*. In *Standard Edition*, 7: 9–82.
——— (1914f). "Some Reflections on Schoolboy Psychology." In *Standard Edition*, 7: 241–44.
——— (1921c). *Group Psychology and the Analysis of the Ego*. In *Standard Edition*, 7: 65–143.
——— (1925d). "An Autobiographical Study." In *Standard Edition*, 7: 7–70.
——— (1930a). *Civilization and Its Discontents*. In *Standard Edition*, 7: 5–145.
——— *The Complete Letters of Sigmund Freud to Wilhelm Fliess 1887–1904.* Translated by Jeffrey Moussaieff. Cambridge, MA: Harvard University Press, 1985.
Hruschka, Daniel J. *Friendship: Development, Ecology, and Evolution of a Relationship.* Los Angeles: University of California Press, 2010.
Hymer, Sharon M. "Narcissistic Friendships." *The Psychoanalytic Review* 71 (1984): 423–39.
Kancyper, Luis. "Metapsychology and Clinical Aspects of Transference-Friendship," *The Psychoanalytic Quarrtely* 87 (2018): 101–26.
Kant, Immanuel. *Groundwork for the Metaphysics of Morals.* Edited and translated by Allen W. Wood. New Haven and London: Yale University Press, 2002.
Laín Entralgo, Pedro. *Sobre la amistad*. Madrid: Revista de Occidente, 1972.
Lane, Christopher. *The Burdens of Intimacy: Psychoanalysis & Victorian Masculinity.* Chicago: Chicago University Press, 1999.
Lejarraga, Ana Lila. "A noção de amizade em Freud e Winnicott." *Natureza humana* 12 (2010): 1–20.
Lewis, Clive S. *The Four Loves.* New York: Harvest Books, 1960.
Lutereau, Luciano. "La amistad en psicoanálisis. La función del interlocutor." *Affectio Societatis* 11 (2014): 32–42.
Määttä, Kaarina, and Satu Uusiautti. *Many Faces of Love.* Rotterdam: Sense Publishers, 2013.
Mahony, Patrick, Carlo Bonomi, and Jan Stensson. *Behind the Scenes: Freud in Correspondence.* Oslo, Norway: Scandinavian University Press, 1997.
Matthews, Sarah. *Friendship through the Life Course: Oral Biographies in Old Age*. Thousand Oaks, CA: SAGE, 1986.
McMahon, James M. "Intimacy among Friends and Lovers." In *Intimacy*, edited by Martin Fischer and George Stricker. Boston, MA: Springer 1982.
Mitias, Michael H. *Friendship: A Central Moral Value*. Amsterdam and New York: Rodopi, 2012.
Montaigne, Michel. *On Friendships*. New York: Penguin Books, 1991.

Nardi, Peter, ed. *Men's Friendships*. New York: Sage Publications, 1992.

Nietzsche, Friedrich. *Thus Spake Zarathustra.* Cambridge: Cambridge University Press, 2006.

Noth, Isabelle, and Christoph Morgenthaler. "The Friendship between Sigmund Freud and Oskar Pfister as Seen in the Correspondence between the Jewish Atheist Founder of Psychoanalysis and the Swiss Pastor Who Pioneered Pastoral Psychology." *Pastoral Psychology* 63 (2014): 81–90.

Pahl, Ray E. *On Friendship.* Cambridge: Polity Press, 2000.

Parks, Malcolm R., and Kory Floyd. "Meanings for Closeness and Intimacy in Friendship." *Journal of Social and Personal Relationships* 13 (1996): 85–107.

Pogrebin, Letty Cottin. *Among Friends: Who We Like, Why We Like Them, and What We Do with Them*. New York: McGraw-Hill Companies.

Porter, Roy, and Sylvana Tomaselli, eds. *The Dialectics of Friendship.* London: Routledge, 1990.

Risman, Barbara J., and Pepper Schwartz, eds. *Gender in Intimate Relationships*. Belmont, CA: Wadsworth, 1991.

Rubin, Lillian B. *Just Friends: The Role of Friendships in Our Lives*. New York: Harper&Row, 1985.

———. "On Men and Friendships." *The Psychoanalytic Review* 73 (1986): 165–81.

Schneider, Monique. "Entre l'objet et le témoin, l'ami." *Revue Adolescence* 25 (2007): 529–39.

Sharabany, R. "Continuities in the Development of Intimate Friendships: Object Relations, Interpersonal, and Attachment Perspectives." In *Theoretical Framework for Personal Relationships*, edited by Ralph Erber and Robin Gilmour, 157–78. New Jersey: Lawrence Erlbaum Associates Publishers, 1994.

Weinberg, Hazel. "Clinical Aspects of Friendliness and Friendships." *Journal Contemporary Psychoanalysis* 25 (1989): 357–70.

Wilkinson, Jennifer. *The Public Life of Friendship: Work, Neighbourhood and Civil Society*. London and New York: Palgrave Macmillan, 2019.

[illegible] 1913.

Chapter Ten

Sublimation: Transformed Desire

It is the widest expression of desire. It spreads extensively through the myriad manifestations of human activity. It is that which sets us apart from the animal world and allows us to become cultured beings. What is referred to as *sublimation* in psychoanalysis can be understood as a dynamic type of desire that changes and is transformed to facilitate the integration of cultural values that, grafted onto the tree of instinctual desire, becomes energized and branches out into endless possibilities.

We saw how biological instinct, limited and singular in its aims, was transformed into a force through which instinctual desire aspires to something much greater than the mere reproduction and survival of the species.[1] An expansive force that, without clear biological definition, is essentially shaped by life circumstances and the power of social relationships. Instinctual desire seeks out and identifies objects of satisfaction and, at the same time, evolves by transcending those primitive objects to open up to new opportunities in wider arenas—those offered by society and culture. All this thanks to the complex processes of the psyche that Freud called *sublimation* and that perhaps could be more aptly referred to as symbolization.

AN INDISPENSABLE AND PROBLEMATIC CONCEPT

Freud, as well as most psychoanalysts that came after him, used the term *sublimation,* although even today it is unclear exactly what was being referred to. Even though Freud referred to this concept repeatedly throughout his writing, he never found a satisfactory explanation for the mechanisms involved. Ap-

1. See chapter 2, in the section titled "Biography Substitutes Biology."

parently, he set fire to an essay on the subject that he intended to include in his work *On Metapsychology.* The intrinsic relationship between sublimation and values, between sexuality and culture, between drive and ideal, made it difficult for him to make sense of the phenomenon. Especially when we consider that his previous positivist conceptions and an overly psychopathological lens certainly did not facilitate this task. The result, as Ricoeur rightly pointed out, was that Freud was puzzled by the idea of sublimation, a contradictory phenomenon that challenged his understanding of culture, in general, and religion in particular.[2] However, as Antoine Vergote reminds us, it was a key concept on which the theoretical structure of psychoanalysis hinged. The term appears 134 times in Freud's works.[3] In his early writings sublimation had a negative connotation, portrayed mainly as a defense mechanism. We see this, for example, in a letter to Wilhelm Fliess dated May 2, 1897.[4] But progressively the concept shifted from something pathological toward something cultural. In effect, Freud sees sublimation as a way to understand the intersection between the drives and culture because it is precisely sublimation that can resolve the conflict that arises between the individual's instinctual desires and the demands of civilization.

Without sublimation, Freud would have found himself without a means to understand a series of important aspects of human emotion. Somehow, unable to fully decipher those dynamics that set us apart from the animal world and that make it possible for us to participate in cultural expressions with so much passion, energy, and effort, as well deriving so much satisfaction, pleasure, and delight from them. From the enjoyment experienced by the child who plays, using imagination in a way that no other animal could, to the engineer's glee at seeing the first vehicle crossing the bridge that he has designed. From the sculptor as she shudders in ecstasy as she contemplates the lifelike form that she injected into a piece of marble, to the ecstatic experienced of the religious person who is overcome by a divine merging with God. All of these acts are pleasurable and full of passion. A lot of energy is also used in conquering these pleasures that, beyond any philosophical or theological judgments, imply somatic, emotional, affective components, which psychoanalysis tied to desire and its expressions, called sublimation.

But while the concept of sublimation has been indispensable in understanding much of human activity, it has been simultaneously resistant to revealing its inner workings. From Freud's time to the present, psychoanalysts have

2. See Paul Ricoeur, *De l'interpretation. Essais sur Freud* (Paris: Seuil, 1965), 467–75. Also, Ricoeur, *Freud and Philosophy: An Essay on Interpretation* (New Haven: Yale University Press, 1970).

3. See Antoine Vergote, *La psychanalyse à l'épreuve de la sublimation* (Paris: Cerf, 1977), 11–15.

4. Sigmund Freud, *The Complete Letters of Sigmund Freud to Wilhelm Fliess 1887–1904*, trans. Jeffrey Moussaieff Masson (Cambridge, MA: Harvard University Press, 1985), 238, 240.

struggled with this process, finding it both impossible to renounce, nor give it a suitable explanation. It is also likely that the concept of sublimation presents psychoanalysts with a series of frustrating theoretical quandaries. Rethinking this notion could cause a chain reaction where many other foundational concepts would also have to be reconceived. But regardless of these theoretical snags, the fact is that psychoanalysis has always struggled to understand that particular phenomenon by which Freud saw sublimation as a reorientation of the object and the drive's final objective.[5] The term was understood thereafter as a psychic process that, drawing its strength from libidinal energy, succeeds in moving toward socially valued ends and objects and, therefore, away from its primitive objects and purposes. All of this means that the set of forces within instinctual desire can be derived toward a set of new activities (literary, artistic, intellectual, or so on) that no longer speak to their most direct primitive objects. This is seen in Freud's most important text on sublimation, which is his 1910 "Leonardo da Vinci and a Memory of his Childhood."[6] This complex process of which Freud tried unsuccessfully to write a monographic text, is seen as one of the four fundamental vicissitudes of the instincts, alongside *reversal into the opposite*, *turning round upon the subject's own self*, and *repression*.[7]

Certain psychoanalysts like Melanie Klein, however, have revised the term *sublimation*. This way of looking at sublimation emphasizes the process that results from the ability to transcend the drive's most primitive objects by the symbolization that occurs as a person evolves (particularly from the *depressive position*) and that expands to different and broader meanings. Freud thought of sublimation as the symbolization process that can transform the loss of those early emotionally charged objects into something else. This Freudian terminology should not be understood in the material sense, as if the drive's transformation was a chemical process or a mysterious alchemy.

In fact, the one common aspect of these different approaches is the need to renounce the most primitive instinctual goals for the sublimation to take place. Without this renunciation, there can be no sublimation or symbolization. The transformation of libidinal drives into creative processes necessitates a mourning process for the early emotionally invested objects, with the hope of rediscovering them through interaction with others. Freud stated in 1907 that, "A progressive renunciation of constitutional instincts, whose

5. Freud (1910a), *Five Lectures on Psychoanalysis*, in *Standard Edition*, 11: 9–55. Cf. also the concept of "Sublimation" in Jean Laplanche and Jean-Baptiste Pontalis, *The Language of Psychanalysis* (London: Karnac, 2006); Elisabeth Roudinesco and Michel Plon, *Dictionnaire de la Psychanalyse* (Paris: Fayard, 1997); Burnes E. Moore and Bernard D. Fine, eds., *Psychoanalytic Terms and Concepts* (New Haven, CT: Yale University Press, 1990).

6. Freud (1910c), *Leonardo da Vinci and a Memory of his Childhood*, in *Standard Edition*, 11: 57–137.

7. Freud (1915c), "Instincts and Their Vicissitudes," in *Standard Edition*, 14: 105–34.

activation might afford the ego primary pleasure, appears to be one of the foundations of the development of human civilization."[8]

Only in the void created by renunciation, in the open space of lack, does symbolization emerge. And it is through symbolization that sublimation takes place. Only through the mourning process of biological parenthood can a sublimated form of maternity or paternity arise, only by renouncing the possibility of acting out sadistic impulses might there be a possibility to sublimate these tendencies into, for example, becoming a medical surgeon. Only by renouncing the need for some sexual exploit could one be *driven to know* (what Freud termed *Wisstrieb*). Only in the emptiness left behind by a desire to contemplate or show off could sublimation hope to give us the aesthetic pleasures of art, film, or music to share with others. In these and many other activities that we could mention, what stands out is perhaps not the *transformation* (*Umsetzung*) of the drive, but the allowing of new meanings to emerge, which is only made possible by overcoming instinctual drive's most primitive ambitions.[9]

From a different perspective, that of the Ego psychology, it has also been understood that only when the Ego has gained independence from the most instinctual forces, can symbolization and the capacity of sublimation make itself available to other human endeavors. In Heinz Hartmann's opinion, only when libido or aggression is neutralized and separated from its most instinctive tendencies can sublimation open up new paradigms of meaning.[10] This is in reality how Freud perceived it when he linked sublimation to the libido's process of desexualization through the Ego, making it possible to invest in new objects.[11]

THE FIELDS OF SUBLIMATION

Through sublimation the objects of desire can be transformed into other objects, diverging from those to which they were once naturally oriented. Art, scientific research, religious experience, careers, or hobbies are areas where new objects can make themselves available through the sublimation processes and which channel those primal instinctual desires.

However, psychoanalysts do not agree on how to categorize those "socially valued" objects that would enable the sublimation processes. We know that

8. Freud (1907b), "Obsessive Actions and Religious Practices," in *Standard Edition*, 9: 127.

9. See Pedro Fernández Villamarzo, *Frustración pulsional y cultura en Freud* (Salamanca: Universidad Pontificia de Salamanca, 1989), Vol. 1, 153.

10. See Heinz Hartmann, "Notes on the Theory of Sublimation," in *Essays on Ego Psychology* (New York: International Universities Press, 1960), 215–40.

11. Freud (1923b), "The Ego and the Id," in *Standard Edition*, 19: 45.

Freud always tended to consider scientific research (the *desire to know*, more broadly) and the lure of the aesthetic as the two most prototypical avenues by which the sublimation processes could occur. This is why Freud viewed Leonardo da Vinci as the perfect embodiment of the sublimation process. In effect, the Italian humanist seemed to have achieved a balance between the scientific and artistic realms with equal adeptness, thanks to the sublimation of a rather problematic sexual reality and due also to challenging life circumstances. Freud, like other commentators, sees a strong homosexual orientation in Leonardo that is skillfully channeled through his commitment and passion for learning and through his creativity via painting and drawing activities that enriched this famous Florentine Renaissance man and made him a balanced person. Leonardo's sexuality, instead of being inhibited, thus blocking his personal and intellectual development (as would happen via hysteria) or *libidinizing* his rational activity, permeating it with a pleasure linked to anguish and guilt (as occurs in obsessive neurosis) chose the sublimatory route. In this way, he channeled his libido and put himself at the service of intellectual and aesthetic pursuits. For Freud then, science and art become the two critical means by which Eros can be sublimated.

Freud felt differently about religion. Coming from a place of belligerent atheism, his negative view of faith was well established. He saw religion as a type of repression and, therefore, a neurosis. In his view, the religious experience could be understood in the context of neurosis—trauma, a latency period, and a resurfacing of repressed elements are typical steps that needed to be taken into account, both in the case of neurosis and with religious belief.[12] However, it was hard for him to deny that religious experience appeared to give people emotional strength. On more than one occasion, he also recognized the potential for sublimation that religion offered. There are texts by Freud (contrary to what Oliver Flournoy proposed)[13] where he refers to sublimation by way of religious experience. Thus, for example, in his 1914 work *On the History of the Psycho-Analytic Movement*,[14] he contrasts religious sublimation with the regression that takes place in sleep or neurosis. Another example can be found in his 1914 "On Narcissism,"[15] where, finding himself at odds with Jung, Freud differentiates between the overcoming of repression by religious sublimation versus falling into neurosis or psychosis.

Freud's eventual acceptance of faith as a form of sublimation was rather reluctant and seems to have been related to his long and beautiful friendship

---

12. The text that most clearly illustrates this idea is Sigmund Freud (1939a), *Moses and Monotheism*, in *Standard Edition*, 23: 72–79.

13. Olivier Flournoy, "La sublimation," *Revue Française de Psychanalyse* I (1967): 59–99.

14. See Freud (1914d), "On the History of the Psycho-Analytic Movement," in *Standard Edition*,14: 61.

15. See Freud (1914c), "On Narcissism: An Introduction," in *Standard Edition*, 14: 81.

with Oskar Pfister, which I analyze in one of my other works.[16] Throughout their friendship, the issue of religion as a vehicle for sublimation surfaced again and again as a topic for discussion. While Pfister took a keen interest in sublimation, Freud felt ambivalent. Oskar Pfister criticized Freud for underestimating the importance of sublimation, which he felt psychoanalysis could greatly benefit from. Their divergent views were very apparent here. Differing sensibilities made them come to different conclusions.

The concept of sublimation was always of keen interest to Pfister and informed his approach to psychoanalytic theory. This is apparent in the correspondence between Pfister and Freud from early on, as the topic generated much dialogue and reflection. For Pfister, it seems to open up a range of possibilities inside his particular field of work, whereas Freud saw his psychoanalytical work hampered by this concept. Freud seemed almost envious in this regard when he stated in 1918, "As for the possibility of sublimation to religion, therapeutically I can only envy you."[17] Elsewhere he says, "For us, this way of disposing of the matter does not exist. Our public, no matter of what racial origin, is irreligious, we are generally thoroughly irreligious ourselves and, as the other ways of sublimation which *we* substitute for religion are too difficult for most patients, our treatment generally results in the seeking out of satisfaction."[18] Thus, for Freud, sublimation was not a viable solution, or at the very least a challenging one, due to his own irreligious nature and that of his patients. Thus, we have the impression that what at a theoretical level seemed quite clear in Freud's eyes, that is, the impossibility of a beneficial sublimation by religious means, was challenged by the consideration of Oskar Pfister's views and life example, a Swiss pastor and wholesome believer.

The subsequent field of psychoanalysis, freer from the antireligious prejudices of its founder, has had little problem in recognizing the value of religion for society and its role as a facilitator for sublimation. This does not mean that all religious experience is channeled into a healthy sublimatory activity or that it will not lead to more detrimental expressions such as a repressive defense mechanism. We should recall the experiences of luminaires and pseudo-mystics who showed traces of repression and neurosis behind their ecstasies, stigmatas, or mystical outbursts. On some occasions, a mystical revelation or vision seemed to hint at a corrupted sexuality. What should we think, for example, of that 13th-century Austrian mystic, the "venerable" Agnes Blannbekin, who was obsessed throughout her life in finding Jesus's "holy

16. See Carlos Domínguez-Morano, *Psicoanálisis y religión: diálogo interminable* (Madrid: Trotta, 2000).

17. Heinrich Meng and Ernst L. Freud, eds., *Psychoanalysis and Faith, The Letters of Sigmund Freud and Oskar Pfister* (New York: Basic Books, 1963), 63.

18. Meng and Freud, eds., *Psychoanalysis and Faith, The Letters of Sigmund Freud and Oskar Pfister*, 63.

foreskin" and who finally found it in her mouth, experiencing in that moment a sweetness, unlike anything she had known before?[19] There are many similar cases throughout history, illustrating the veiled collusions that have so often existed between marginalized sexuality and explicit religiosity. Collusions that have not always been so obvious, but have operated in other perhaps more subtle ways, impervious to conscious thought and external observation.

Beyond the controversy surrounding the sublimation of religious experience, the vehicles that facilitate sublimation were never sufficiently clarified by psychoanalytic theory, in part because of what Freud deemed to be socially valuable or not. Art, science, and religion are indeed seen as prototypical methods for sublimation. Professional development is also seen as a powerful vehicle for sublimation.[20] But, if we thoroughly analyze this, if we consider that once we enter the realm of the symbolic we transcend the primary objectives of instinctual desire, we would have to conclude that all thought and language processes are already made possible by sublimation. The opening of the symbolic dimension (using Melanie Klein's terms) or the signifier (in Lacan's terms) is what lies at the root of sublimation.

SCIENCE, ART, AND RELIGION

The fields of science, art, and religion are certainly unique in their activation of sublimation. They deserve further exploration, and perhaps the best way to do so is to give some examples that illustrate how sublimation can adequately channel instinctual desire. Jacques Lacan, Daniel Barenboim, Saint John of the Cross, and Teresa of Ávila are good exemplars.

Jacques Lacan, the most emblematic figure of French psychoanalysis, expressed how sublimation translates to a type of joyful expression when one day, in one of his famous seminars he said, "for the moment, I am not fucking, I am talking to you. Well! I can have exactly the same satisfaction as if I were fucking."[21] It is probably not *the exact same* satisfaction, but, without a doubt, a possibly substantial, healthy, and beneficial satisfaction. Because sublimation always implies the possibility of expressing and channeling desire, of formulating it and releasing it into the realms of the symbolic and relational. Hence, sublimation is always a source, if not of hedonism, of pleasure and contentment that can sometimes even be felt on an emotional or physical level. Jacques Pohier, a well-known French priest, was attuned to Lacanian thought when he would tell his students on occasion during lectures, "what

---

19. Letter dated February 9, 1909. Ibid., 16.
20. See Antoine Vergote, *Dette et désir* (Paris: Seuil, 1978), 205–65.
21. J. Lacan, *Seminars, Book XI: The Four Fundamental Concepts of Psycho-Analysis* (London: Tavistock, 1977), 165–66.

does preaching mean other than to express joy and make others feel joy through a give-and-take of action and passivity, giving and receiving?"[22]

Another noteworthy example, this time in the music world, is Argentinian pianist and conductor Daniel Barenboim, who stated that when he played Chopin he felt a kind of purely physical pleasure. And it is that artistic expression in general, in its nearness to the sensorial and sensual aspects of personality, and due to its association with unconscious fantasies, that facilitates the sublimation of instinctual desire.[23]

In another area, that of religious experience, the sublimation of instinctual desire is evident in the experiences of Saint John of the Cross or Teresa of Ávila.[24] How else can one make sense of Saint John's poetic verses in his *Spiritual Canticle*? There we find some of the most explicit and beautiful descriptions of Eros's intentions, of affection, of the passion for the beloved, of its sensual repercussions. The descriptions are so ardent that one has to wonder if there hadn't been a real flesh and blood love experience in the past, a passion that was never entirely sublimated. And yet, when one delves into the psychodynamics of what could be a true mystical experience, we might conclude that it cannot occur without having failed to satiate a love for someone at some point, an experience that could then give rise to another expression, that of symbolization and sublimation, and ultimately the mystical experience.

The mystical experience, which reveals the role of instinctual desire, is a joyful embodied expression. "I feel great delight in the body," observed Santa Teresa without trepidation, "and great satisfaction in the soul."[25] The physical experience thus becomes a metaphor for the spiritual state. This does not mean, as the myopic medical view tried to argue, that the physical manifestations are flagrant proof of repression and neurosis. As Lacan pointed out, there is something profound about the mystical experience that many have ineptly tried to reduce to "a matter of pure fucking."[26]

---

22. I heard Pohier express this sentiment firsthand in various lectures.

23. Among the numerous publications on psychoanalysis and art, we can highlight Ernest Jones, *Psycho-Myth, Psycho-History: Essays in Applied Psychoanalysis* (New York: Hillstone 1974), vol. I and II; Ernst Kris, *Psychoanalytic Explorations in Art* (New York: International Universities Press, 1952); Ernst H. Gombrich, *The Story of* Art (New York: Phaidon, 2013); Hendrik M., Ruitenbeek, *Psychoanalysis and Literature* (New York: Dutton, 1964); Janet Sayers, *Freud's Art-Psychoanalysis Retold* (New York, NY: Routledge 2007); Kennet Wright, *Mirroring and Attunement: Self-Realization in Psychoanalysis and Art* (New York, NY: Routledge, 2009); Sandra Gosso, *Psychoanalysis and Art: Kleinian Perspectives* (London: Karnac, 2004); Maria Walsh, *Art and Psychoanalysis* (London: Tauris Publishers, 2012); E. Ann Kaplan, *Psychoanalysis and Cinema* (New York: Routledge, 1989); and Vicky Lebeau, *Psychoanalysis and Cinema* (New York: Columbia University Press, 2019).

24. See Carlos Domínguez-Morano, *Mística y psicoanálisis* (Madrid: Trotta, 2020).

25. Teresa de Ávila, *Camino de Perfección*, C 31, 3.

26. Jacques Lacan, *The Seminar, Book XX. Encore: On Feminine Sexuality, the Limits of Love and Knowledge* (New York: W.W. Norton & Co, 1998), 76.

These intellectual, artistic, and religious spheres reveal instinctual desire's role and in Freudian terms could be seen as *libidinized.* This does not mean that these intellectual, aesthetic, or mystical experiences are simply a camouflaged form of sexual formation, or a substitution, as the medical-psychiatric field have so often implied. This is only the case when they stem from some form of repression. If there is genuine sublimation, instinctual desire has been transformed, it has renounced its primitive objectives and opened itself to the field of the symbolic. There it finds further meaning, which stimulates and brings alive those other human dimensions that get grafted on and feed off of it.

FORMATION OF CHARACTER AND CULTURE

All this leads us to conclude that becoming human implies possessing the ability to sublimate instinctual desire into language, symbol, thought, and culture. It is not, then, as it is sometimes assumed, that some people are especially gifted in spiritual matters or other sublime undertakings. If all the functions of the Ego are nourished by desexualized energy, sublimation is a continuous process and not merely an issue of certain social achievements.

Society and culture provide a good medium for transmuting a good part of these energies that can overwhelm the individual's sense of control, offering something of value in return. Society is therefore enriched and the individual can integrate all these forces more easily, which would otherwise be overwhelming. To the extent that desexualized fields are created, conflict-free spheres so to speak, the individual will gain strength, adeptness, and self-control. The greater capacity for symbolization allows the individual to evolve and also offers more possibilities for operating internally and externally. As Freud pointed out in *Inhibition, Symptoms, and Anxiety*,[27] the Ego works with desexualized energy, thus neutralizing the libido and separating it from the most primitive instincts. In other words, the sublimation process is a fundamental factor in the formation of character and "the source of a number of our virtues."[28]

Culture is nourished; it receives considerable energetic capital for its own purposes. Art, science, intellectual striving, economics, the political game, and so on, all benefit from that infusion of passion and enthusiasm that makes them sustainable, creative, and innovative. Social ties are also reinforced thanks to the sublimation mechanisms that allow, for example, nonerotic emotional bonds. As we have seen, sublimation feeds the bonds of friend-

27. Freud (1926d), "Inhibitions, Symptoms and Anxiety," in *Standard Edition*, 20: 75–172.
28. Freud (1905d), "Three Essays on the Theory of Sexuality," in *Standard Edition*, 7: 239.

ship, as well as feelings of motherhood or fatherhood, professional interests, artistic creation, or hobbies, for example. In this way, sublimation works as a kind of high-grade fuel that super charges social interactions and cultural evolution. Society takes full advantage of this.

Thus, for example, in later childhood, from the age of about six or seven, a stage begins where sublimation mechanisms play a fundamental role. Girls and boys begin to see a world beyond their family, where their deepest emotional aspirations had previously been focused. Society seizes the opportunity and through schooling offers a variety of subjects where the little ones will be able to channel a good part of their instinctual energy, transforming it through sublimation. It is an auspicious time to learn, to deepen relational skills, to enjoy play and imagination, to absorb ideas in Sunday school, and so on. All these cultural institutions can thus benefit from all of that energy that is redirected from the family environment and that needs to find a suitable channel to avoid overflowing.[29]

Similarly, in the period of adolescence, there is another intense sexual affective rush, and society is ready to capitalize on this. It is the stage of strong convictions and great passions. Throughout time, political and religious institutions have been well aware of this, providing the appropriate mechanisms to capture this youthful idealistic energy. Institutional frameworks and groupings are created to channel these interests. The individual finds a way of tempering the excessive force of the sexual drives in certain stages of life and also sees the Ego defenses go up for fear of a total and direct discharge. Sublimation plays an important counterbalancing role against the extreme force of the sexual drive during this time.

The early years of professional life are also an important time for sublimation mechanisms. In this way, society benefits and, simultaneously, the individual finds a way to better integrate his sexual affective world and consolidate the strength of his Ego. Sublimation is also one of the most influential mechanisms in the formation and development of personality. Because through sublimation, societies are nourished while individuals grow and develop.

The ability, however, to redirect instinctual desire in a flexible way through culture, that is, through sublimation, varies according to the individual. To a large extent, it depends on the ability of each person to detach from the early objects to adhere to different ones, those that society prioritizes. The vehicle for sublimation will depend largely on one's particular narrative or constitution (though this is often hard to clearly ascertain). It will depend on the inertia inherited from one's parents, on instinctual desire's propensity to follow along or get stuck, or to the contrary, to its flexibility.

---

29. See Freud, "The Latency Period," in *Standard Edition*, 7: 177–78.

How far each subject can go to sublimate his libidinal energy is not a matter that can be easily ascertained. And it may very well be that an individual's real capacities cannot easily fall in line with the desires or ideals that the world presents. Sublimation, we cannot forget, is not a matter of mere will or idealistic resolutions. They are certainly needed, but they alone cannot trigger sublimation and bring it to a successful resolution. Put simply, you sublimate what you can, not what you want.

It is a personal dynamic that derives from the individual's natural dispositions, and above all, on how the Ego was configured according to the identifications and counteridentifications that were experienced (those "I want to be like" or "I don't want to be like" ideas that define us). These will facilitate or hinder the sublimation process and the degree to which one may renounce some aspect of their sexual and emotional life. It is important to remember that a mere determination to carry out the sublimation processes is not enough, and, as Freud reminded all of those who struggle to be nobler than what they were designed for, they will eventually succumb to neurosis.[30]

It is important to recognize that although having an ideal is not sufficient for sublimation to take place, an important dose of ideal, that is, Ego Ideal, *is* needed for the process to commence. It is through that particular pathway that the Ego's idealized proposals set forth that instinctual desire's enigmatic transformation can occur. On the other hand, sublimation cannot occur in a forced violent way from a rigid and tyrannical Superego. The ideals, rather than the rules, are what facilitate the sublimatory processes, since repressing desires with too much force becomes an obstacle.

One's upbringing is a factor in aiding or obstructing the sublimation processes. It is the Ego's ideals that, through the identifications made throughout life, will be able to attract part of the libidinal energy that is redirected toward new social objectives. Freud illustrates this in the *Wolf Man* case, where a patient's experiences with a military instructor transformed his earlier religion-based sublimations. The masochistic aspect of his early sublimation process was overtaken by a more sadistic type, more beneficial according to Freud, although the earlier religious sublimation had also been useful—"It put a restraint on his sexual impulsions by affording them a sublimation and a safe mooring; it lowered the importance of his family relationships, and thus protected him from the threat of isolation by giving him access to the great community of mankind. The untamed and fear-ridden child became social, well-behaved, and amenable to education."[31]

30. See Freud (1908d), "'Civilized' Sexual Morality and Modern Nervous Illness," in *Standard Edition,* 177–204.

31. Freud (1918b), "From the History of an Infantile Neurosis," in *Standard Edition,* 9: 114–15.

The identifications that were experienced growing up were powerful engines for either facilitating sublimation, or, on the other hand, perpetuating the most primitive desires. Thus, when the models of identification through which the Ego is molded and transformed result primarily in the direct and immediate realization of the instinctual desires, the opportunity for sublimation will be greatly diminished. When, on the other hand, these identifications allow for the values and ideals of society to come through, the capacity for sublimation will not be guaranteed, but it will become much more likely.

Imagine the identification models that a boy or a girl in slums outside of Rio de Janeiro might find, children who are exposed to a world of pure and hard sexuality, of promiscuity and erotic stimulation and contact. In all likelihood, what will result is an identity in which instinctual desire seeks immediate gratification. It could also be that, as a defensive mechanism, a youth seeks to avoid such behaviors, resorting to repression. But it would be unlikely that the individual would channel that affective-sexual energy to cultural values that were absent during his or her life. We could also contrast this with a child growing up in a traditional European or American home with parental figures who might have fulfilling work, or intellectual and artistic interests, or deeply spiritual and religious commitment, or are dedicated to a social cause through an NGO or other organization. Obviously, the potential for sublimation will be different. The dynamics will always be complex and, without a doubt, there are many variables at play that will not always be apparent. But it seems clear that a child's upbringing will always be intertwined with the sublimation processes. Since society's attempt to apply the same sexual norms to everyone can be misleading and even harmful, regardless of what Freud called the "libidinal economy" (how psychic energy is distributed within each individual),[32] perhaps we should also make social and cultural resources more accessible to everyone since these spheres are in such need of an infusion from the sublimation processes.

SUBLIMATION AND NARCISSISM

The relationship between sublimatory capacity and the ideals of the Ego leads us to consider the role of narcissism. Indeed, for the sublimation process to occur, a strong feeling must build up and take over the Ego and its idealistic aspects. As we have seen, without this passage through the Ego Ideal there is no sublimation. But we cannot forget that this Ego Ideal, as we discussed in chapter 8 concerning narcissism, is a personality structure linked to one's self-image, a beloved one, we should add.

---

32. See Freud (1930a), "Civilization and Its Discontents," in *Standard Edition,* 21: 84.

The Ego Ideal is the pretty picture, so to speak, that we all have of ourselves as a prototype or model of what we would like to become. Everyone builds his Ego Ideal according to the external identifications and models that we incorporate as ourselves. For some, the Ego Ideal will cause one to believe that he is quite intelligent, like a young Einstein. For others, their Ego Ideal will be based on how they see themselves, as friendly or socially successful, while others strive to be like their most idealized saint. Everyone is, in one way or another, taking those ideal references for the Ego to use. We need them as a growth engine and inspiration to uplift us above our everyday selves. The Ego Ideal, therefore, introduces a healthy tension between who we really are and what we would like to become. When the tension is extreme, however, we risk living in perpetual dissatisfaction with ourselves, being victims of what is commonly known as an *inferiority complex*. One can never live up to his standards because the Ego Ideal has been set too high.[33]

In any case, what is interesting to highlight thus far is that the Ego Ideal, as we have seen, is a personality structure linked to narcissism. In a way, it springs from the remains of childhood narcissism. In essence, this is what an individual was bound to contribute, which leads us to conclude that the sublimation process must have started with the narcissistic dimension of personality. It is an important fact that should not be overlooked because it brings along with it some potential problems that could affect the outcome of the sublimation processes.

When sublimatory processes begin, it is the Ego that, through its ideals, becomes charged with affection and passion. An enthusiasm that, in the early stages of a vocation or a professional project, is raised in relation to the idealized self, clearly reveals the narcissistic dimension that sublimation requires in its initial stages. Seeing oneself as an important figure within a given field, as a political or religious leader, a well-known personality in the arts or sciences, and so on, is sometimes essential for sublimation to take place in an individual.

That self-image, based on the ideals that were developed through previous identifications, polarizes instinctual desire and carries out the work of transforming that same desire. This is in effect how this mysterious desexualization of the libido occurs, which Freud began to describe with conviction in his work *The Ego and the Id*. In this text, he concluded that "If this displaceable energy is desexualized libido, it may also be described as sublimated energy, for it would still retain the main purpose of Eros."[34] Ricoeur also insisted on the importance of this moment in Freudian formulations on sublimation. He

33. See Freud (1921c), "Group Psychology and the Analysis of the Ego," in *Standard Edition*, 18: 131; Freud (1923b), *The Ego and the Id*, in *Standard Edition*, 19: 51.

34. See Freud, *The Ego and the Id*, 45.

explains that sublimation is no longer a perverse infantile component derived from the nonsexual, but an object investiture of the Oedipal era, internalized through desexualization and by pressure from the systems that dismantled the Oedipus complex.

In the chapter on narcissism, we saw the need to differentiate between a healthy narcissism and a pathological one, and now we can appreciate one of narcissism's important functions in the proper development of personality. Through sublimation, the self-image will have to be involved in the process of transforming instinctual desire. By going through the Ego, other symbolic meanings outside of the primitive instinctual aspirations will be able to form. In Freud's terms, the Ego serves as the springboard that allows desire to leap into new transformed objects and goals. But neither society nor the individual should have illusions about what kind of ideals or values instinctual desire should invest in. The process of sublimation has limits that must be respected.

NOT ALL DESIRE CAN BE SUBLIMATED, NOR IS ALL SUBLIMATION SUBLIME

In fact, sublimation can never be fully realized; we can never completely channel our instinctual desire. A significant portion will always remain, particularly in its more specifically erotic and sexual dimension, perpetuating its earliest aspirations and unable to transform and divert through alternate means. It remains in its original state, wanting to obtain direct sexual pleasure and with its most primitive and natural expression. For the vast majority, those needs will have to be met. Thus, Freud was right in asserting that the vast majority of people in society are not physiologically prepared for abstinence.[35]

Not all areas of our affective-sexual world have the same ability to transform and transcend through sublimation. Indeed, there is still disagreement about what kind of impulses are susceptible to sublimation in the current psychoanalytic literature. In particular, thinkers disagree about whether genitality is capable of being sublimated or not. Many do not believe that this is possible. Hein Hartmann and Otto Fenichel exemplify this rift. While the former believed in the possibility of sublimation for both pregenital and genital drives, Fenichel thought it to be impossible.[36] Meanwhile, Antoine Vergote believed that Freud saw sublimation as applicable to practically all

35. See Freud (1908d), "'Civilized' Sexual Morality and Modern Nervous Illness," in *Standard Edition*, 9: 194–201.

36. See Heinz Hartmann, "Notes on the Theory of Sublimation," in *The Psychoanalytic Study of the Child (New York: International Universities Press, 1955)*, 9–29; and Otto Fenichel, *The Psychoanalytic Theory of Neurosis* (New York: W.W. Norton Co., 1945), 141–42, 471.

modalities and components of sexual drive.[37] Even if this were the case, it is unlikely that sublimation would occur as easily as with the so-called pregenital impulses, in other words, with the oral or anal. It is as if nature wisely left us an ingrained reminder of our biological and instinctive roots. Blaise Pascal lucidly asserted that when we make the mistake of thinking that we are angels, we become beasts. There, then, is always that blurring without biological condition in its most primitive and instinctual sense, to remind us that despite the typically human process of sublimation, we are also rooted in the animal world. Therefore, our condition as primarily desirous beings at the biological and genital level will always remain with us somehow.

Besides, we shouldn't forget that while sublimation does not result in us becoming angels nor allow us to disregard our most instinctive parts, neither does it guarantee physical and mental well-being. Here we should stress that not all sublimation is *sublime*.

The term sublimation has generally been associated with the higher dimensions of the human being. Sublimation has often been likened to turning earthly tendencies into more spiritual ones. It dignifies lowly realities and makes them more valuable and respectable. From here the idea of "spiritualizing," which has contributed to the notion that sublimation is obviously beneficial and desirable and, above all, lifts us from the most terrestrial and mundane aspects of ourselves.

The origins of the term sublimation in the psychological sense was extracted from German romanticism, where it was used to define the aesthetic elevation common to all humans and of which some seem especially gifted. Something, as we can see, related to the ability to elevate the physical reality to the spiritual realm of beauty. Nietzsche, in particular, made frequent use of the term by applying it to both the sexual and aggressive instincts. "Good actions are sublimated evil ones,"[38] he said on occasion.

The reality is that it is quite easy to confuse the psychic process of sublimation with something that would be a natural response to a positive, desirable dynamic for human development. All sublimation would seem, by its very nature, to be good. Sometimes we have also tried to fit sublimation into a kind of *Deus ex machine*, used to justify positions that, in reality, were nothing but marginalized or denied sexuality. Of course, the understanding was that sexuality was somehow lowly and unseemly and that sublimation, therefore, was an excellent way to escape from that undesirable materiality. Sublimation has always been extolled in the name of questionable interests and equally problematic value judgments. For example, preferring the sublimation mechanism

37. See Antoine Vergote's already cited work, *La psychanalyse à l'épreuve de la sublimation*, 26.
38. Friedrich Nietzsche, *Human, All Too Human: A Book for Free Spirits* (Edinburgh: T. N. Foulis, 1910), 108.

over awareness of instinctual desire that in the context of religion has translated to esteeming religious celibacy over coupled life.

We must, however, recognize in all honesty that not all sublimation is by its very nature a positive thing. Perversion can also be sublimated. And in the sublimated form those contents remain, the original perverse character will linger. We know of sadistic and masochistic drives that get sublimated into certain ways of exercising authority and demanding obedience. Roger Fretigny uses Hitler as an example of those sexual energies that get transformed into social movements that are not to be lauded. And, as the author himself points out, it unclear why certain cultural values should automatically be superior to recognizing instinctual desire, nor why de-sexualizing life energies for the sake of the cult of the Virgin Mary, for example, or any other aspect of cultural experience, is preferable.[39]

We must, therefore, be wary of the cult of sublimation. Frequently, what is hidden is simply a powerful and very problematic defense strategy toward sexuality and the ghosts that trail behind it. We find this psychoanalytic term used in some spiritual discourses, which are but the remains of a naiveté that, in reality, have little to do with sublimation and are rather a distorted renunciation of instinctual desire. A renunciation that is idealized and does not address a fundamental question if one wants to talk seriously about sublimation—to find out whether or not that concession responds to the true emotional transformation, which is the only way through which we can truly be liberated. In short, as French psychoanalyst Janine Chasseguet-Smirgel affirms, the wool is usually being pulled over our eyes through the idealizations and lyricisms that usually accompany it, but in authentic sublimation, there is no deception involved.[40] Thus, *all that glitters is not gold*, nor can everything be sublimated, nor is sublimation everything that we think it is.

REPRESSION CAMOUFLAGED

Often, we are forced to distinguish between sublimation and repression. Indeed, these two psychic mechanisms were always opposite both in their way of operating and, above all, their outcomes. However, given the enormous complexity of the psyche, it is not always easy to decipher when one or the other is influencing the dynamics of an individual. The capacity we all possess to camouflage is immense. And the fact that unconscious mechanisms

39. Roger Fretigny, "Sublimation," in *Vocabulaire des Psychothérapies*, ed. André Virel (Paris: Fayard, 1977), 288–89.

40. Fretigny, "Sublimation," 125–26.

are almost always involved makes discrimination and diagnosis even more challenging.

The fact is that the term sublimation may be covering up a subtle, unconscious, and embellished avoidance of desire. In many discussions on the subject, whether in academic circles or informally, a type of defense mechanism seems to come up that rationalizes the repression of desire (using based an idea that is true, but with the underlying objective of suppressing another intolerable truth).[41]

The dissemination of psychoanalytic concepts has resulted in misinterpretations of some key concepts, repression being perhaps the most obvious one. Generally, it is understood as an individual's conscious attempt to avoid behavior that is desired deep down, but that clashes with certain aspirations, ideals, or life constraints. But repression has little to do with those scenarios. It has more to do with "renouncing the drives," which, in general, can be a healthy mechanism insofar as it is truly consciously controlled by the individual, because of the need to adjust to reality or by ethical motivations.[42] This differs greatly from real repression, which is a totally unconscious defense mechanism. Therefore, before desire can reach the subject's conscious mind, it is subjected to a process by which it tries to remain undetected. Through repression, the subject tries to either reject or retain certain representations related to the drives (thoughts, images, or memories) in the realm of the unconscious. This process occurs when the fulfillment of a drive could also cause displeasure in other areas.[43]

But a repressed desire is not a dead or annulled desire. It is a desire that is maintained elsewhere and that continues to operate. However, in this state, desire will intensify, and certainly, become more conflictive. The individual will experience certain forces—countercharges that will try to inhibit those forbidden desires. But the tendency of this repressed desire, however, will continue to become more conscious and to seek recognition and fulfillment. The struggle, then, becomes inevitable. Opposite forces are at play within the individual, and, sometimes seriously hinder one's daily life. All this results in a significant expenditure of energy. Energy that will have to be withdrawn from what would ideally be channeled toward love and work, which, as we saw in chapter 5, are the key ingredients for personal maturation.[44]

---

41. See Anna Freud, *Ego and the Mechanisms of Defense* (New York: International Universities Press, 1967).

42. These concepts are exhaustively compared in the Pedro Fernández Villamarzo's previously mentioned work titled *Frustración pulsional y cultura en Freud.*

43. See Sigmund Freud (1915d), "Repression," in *Standard Edition*, 14: 146–58; and (1911c), "Psycho-Analytic Notes on an Autobiographical Account of a Case of Paranoia," in *Standard Edition* 12: 67.

44. See the previously cited work of Jean Laplanche and Jean Baptiste Pontalis, *The Language of Psychoanalyse*, s.v. "repression."

However, according to everything we have seen, sublimation transforms desire; it does not annihilate it or dispel it from consciousness. It offers a way to transform the object and its objective. There is an inherent renunciation, but there is an undeniable satisfaction as well. Sublimation always implies the possibility of expressing and channeling desire, of formulating and releasing it. The sublimation of Eros must expand Eros. That is, a loving, nonregressive dynamic that brings life together, which is the fundamental objective of Eros. Otherwise, we would have to conclude that the idea of sublimation signifies a repression hidden to a greater or lesser degree.

In the state of repression, desire seeks satisfaction without changing its object or its objective. The original intent remains unchanged. But by not finding an adequate way for these intentions to rise to consciousness they get twisted and diverted. They are called *substitutive satisfactions*. Unconscious desire is cunning and will find a thousand ways to satisfy itself in that substitutive way, usually through undesirable means, since constructive ones are not available. But the object and desire's goal remains intact, however camouflaged they may be. This was illustrated in the aforementioned case of the pseudo-mystic Inés Blannbekin who was forever obsessed with her spiritual purpose of one day finding Jesus's foreskin. A perfect example of a distorted fulfillment of desire, of misdirection and neuroticism, a conflict in which the original desire persisted and only found the path of mystical camouflage to achieve its satisfaction. Sublimation works differently. It changes the object of desire by acquiescing and transforming its purpose into another type of satisfaction diffused from eroticism.

Tics (muscle spasms) and dance could also illustrate the differences between repression and sublimation. In both cases, the body moves. In both cases the body *speaks*, the body communicates something, it expresses an inner movement. But in the first case, this movement has all signs of being symptomatic of something else: it is repetitive, it is involuntary, it is not adaptive, it does not create anything, nor does it liberate in any way. It is just an aborted movement. It is an attempt to release something that cannot find expression. It is a waste of energy. It creates suffering. In dance, the body finds a liberating movement, it is the Ego that directs it at will, it adapts to the environment, is creative. It uses energy and also generates it. It offers enjoyment to self and others.

THE ADVENTURE OF THE CELIBATE ROUTE

To many, it is considered an odd phenomenon. It is met with wonder since the fact that certain men and women try to set aside a basic dimension of their bodily reality and inner being never ceases to surprise, that part of themselves with which they could hope to connect intimately with another. Men and women who are willing to give up one of the most central aspects of their being and that, as we all know, have such an influence over personality and a balanced psyche.

And yet, there are plenty of examples throughout history and through different religious manifestations that give us individuals who have abandoned this essential aspect of their instinctual desire to focus as much as possible on bonding with the sacred. Instinctual desire, and more specifically, sexuality, has always been closely aligned with the religious experience. It has either been an object of fascination or terror. Either it has provided an opening to the sacred or, to the contrary, it has been marginalized and excluded as God's most dangerous adversary.

In fact, desire has flowed within the religious spheres freely and, without a doubt, it has served as one of the most eloquent vehicles for human expression. Psychoanalysis, however, has not given it the attention it deserves. And as British psychoanalyst Wilfred Bion put it, "Psychoanalysts have been particularly blind to the topic of religion."[45] There it is, however, articulating different visions, instinctual desire finding a thousand ways of channeling and expressing itself, in different hues and with diverse analytical aspects as well.

For the sake of religion, many men and women have, in effect, renounced the chance to have a life companion with whom to share their innermost selves, without the possibility of experiencing an erotic encounter with another body and giving up the opportunity for parenthood as well. They have channeled their passion into the realm of the sacred and the utopian project therein. The risk will be to confuse that sacred reality with the impossible object to which instinctual desire seeks out. They should remember, as we spoke about earlier, that desire is caused by a missing object and not by the goal to which they are attracted, such as the divine. They will have to understand, then, when relating to God, it still holds true that desire has to die so that an encounter becomes possible. Because only in the recognition of absence, and of seeing the correlations between the aspiration of desire and God as Other that comes to the fore, does the possibility of an authentic relationship open up. Only in this way can we avoid confusing God with our longing and only in this way can God Himself also be understood as free and unique and not as mere sustenance to be devoured by a lack that refuses to be acknowledged and accepted.

When this is the case, the celibate route, made possible by untethering instinctual desire to the biological need for procreation, becomes a phenomenon that deserves to be looked at and analyzed as a particular and significant

45. Wilfred R. Bion, *Tavistock Seminars* (New York, Routledge, 2019).

expression of desire. According to certain views, it is a risky option, to say the least (on one end of the spectrum we have Wilhelm Reich who did not believe in sublimation and argued that sexual experience was a requirement for a healthy mind). Today, as we could analyze in chapter 3, we are in the midst of a sociocultural wave that has revolutionized how we approach and enjoy sex and that no longer puts much emphasis on purity or virginity as something to strive for at an individual or social level. The way of viewing sex has likewise changed within religious spheres. Certainly, this leads one to question why somebody would freely choose celibacy. In any case, celibacy continues to be a reality that calls forth men and women, Christian or not (there was a time when also in the Spanish political arena, for example, when the radical anarchists chose celibacy to help them fight for their cause) and it raises some interesting questions about the manifestations of desire.[46]

The truth is that both theoretically and based on observed data, the psychic process known as sublimation gives us celibacy as a viable option, which continues to be relevant to spiritual aspirants. It is a verifiable fact for those willing to look closely, that imbalanced and mature states are found in both married and celibate individuals, and clinical psychology has been unable to characterize a specific pathology for those choosing celibacy.[47] There have also been many men and women throughout history, and even in our time, who have succeeded in living a life of plentitude without the need for sex in its erotic aspects, and have shown a great ability to work creatively and to interact easily with others.

Even Freud himself recognized that there are people "who are able to put up with a deprivation of this kind without being injured."[48] Other psychoanalysts and clinical psychologists from different backgrounds also agree, they have a deep understanding regarding the complexity of human feeling and sexuality, and also of its admirable plasticity. Because of this, it can be channeled into very different expressions, according to the particular psychodynamics of each individual. Celibacy could undoubtedly be one of them. And it is easily verifiable that there are celibate people that display a wholesome personality, which is not only balanced and stable but also rich, motivating, and fruitful.

46. I explored this connect in-depth in these works: Carlos Domínguez-Morano, *La aventura del celibato evangélico* (Vitoria: Frontera, 2000), and *Amores y desamores en la vida consagrada* (Vitoria: Frontera 2014).

47. Donald B. Cozzens, *The Changing Face of the Priesthood: A Reflection of the Priest's Crisis of Soul* (Collegeville, MN: The Liturgical Press, 2000); and *Freeing Celibacy* (Collegeville, MN: Liturgical Press, 2006); Richard Sipe, *Celibacy in Crisis* (New York: Brunner-Routledge, 2003); Jean Dierkens, "Psychopathologie du celibate," in *Le célibat. L'homme sans compagne. La femme sans compagnon*, ed. Robert Gubbels (Bruxelles: Université de Bruxelles, 1974), 111–23.

48. Sigmund Freud (1916–1917), *Introductory Lectures on Psycho-Analysis*, in *Standard Edition*, 15: 345.

But also, if we put aside excessively theoretical approaches to the possible pathological aspects of celibacy (often ideologically biased in either case), we would have to agree, from a more modest and perhaps more realistic psychodynamic lens, that often, despite the initial trauma of renouncing coupled life, these individuals attain a degree of stability in life that would probably not have been possible otherwise.

Regarding balanced celibacy, Paul Chauchard rightly stated that there are more balanced imbalanced people than the so-called disturbed ones—those who are aware of their weakness and their imperfections and who suffer for them, who remain there but continue to seek, not always successfully, fall down and experience setbacks, yet slowly progress toward balance. On the other hand, we have the seemingly balanced ones, settled and apparently without problems, who are in fact neurotically blocked and only give the appearance of stability. This apparent strength is actually the repression of the individual's weakness.[49]

In many cases, we might need to accept that in an individual's life trajectory, the most important thing may be to find the situation in which one's inherent inner conflict finds the most suitable environment to recalibrate, and also be able to make the best of one's unique potential. It may not be a perfect balance, but perhaps a suitable one for that individual. Nothing more, but also nothing less. The idealization of maturity, equilibrium, or purity that can be seen in many treatises on this subject, may itself be an expression of a very narcissistic infantilism, which clothes itself in psychological terms or advanced spirituality. There is nothing like consecrated celibacy to capture the meaning of what Janine Chasseguet-Smirgel called the *illness of ideality*. There are many spiritual discourses with a scientific tone about virginity that reveals a morbid darkness, reminiscent of perverted and denied sexuality, rather than sublimated one. Probably an expression of troubled relationships that are oftentimes established between sexuality and religious institutions.[50]

The fact is that for many individuals, the consecrated celibacy project represents the path by which they achieve a satisfactory way to navigate through life, offering fertile ground for expansion for themselves and for those with whom they associate—although this lifestyle is not without its risks. In a way, it is quite like an adventure—an adventure, that is certainly unpredictable, and that is just as likely to end happily, as well as to end catastrophically. One always sets a high bar for an adventure, in celibacy too. Hence, the potential for risk is equally high. If the objective is not achieved, the outcome can be devastating—an experience that turns into a type of self-mutilation, a feeling

49. See Paul Chauchard, "Celibat et équilibre psychologique," in *Sacerdoce et celibate*, ed. Joseph Coppens (Leuven: Peeters Publishers, 1971), 499–518.

50. I delved into this topic in Carlos Domínguez-Morano, *Experiencia cristiana y psicoanálisis* (Santander: Sal Terrae, 2005), 131–48.

of conflict and a destructive tension, or narcissistic isolation where one is only interested and passionate about oneself. The goal, the real and perhaps best of all achievements would always be open to discovery, wonder and giving to others, to anyone, merely for being another.

In any case, the celibacy phenomenon should not fail to surprise us, given the essential role that the sexual-affective sphere has on personality as a whole. Celibacy demonstrates the peculiar human capacity for transcending the biological determinations of the drive, and the potential therefore of becoming a being of culture.

Instinctual desire, as we have seen in these pages, expresses itself in many ways. These expressions have their own unique potential as well as concrete risks. But none of them will give us that elusive object that generates that never-ending and tireless search in the first place. Because, as Luis Cernuda reminded us, "desire is a question without an answer, a leaf without a branch, a world without a sky."[51] Hence it is also an endless process, an energy that branches out in many directions, transformed through the realm of the symbolic, bringing us face to face with the great mystery.

BIBLIOGRAPHY

Bergler, Edmund. "On a Five-Layer Structure in Sublimation." *Psychoanalytic Quarterly* 14 (1945): 76–97.

Carlin, Nathan, and Donald Capps. *The Gift of Sublimation: A Psychoanalytic Study of Multiple Masculinities*. Eugene, OR: Cascade Books, 2015.

Cozzens, Donald B. *The Changing Face of the Priesthood: A Reflection of the Priest's Crisis of Soul*. Collegeville, MN: The Liturgical Press, 2000.

———. *Freeing Celibacy*. Collegeville, MN: The Liturgical Press, 2006.

Deri, Frances. "On Sublimation." *Psychoanalytical Quarterly* 8 (1939): 325–34.

Domínguez-Morano, Carlos. *Psicoanálisis y religión: Diálogo interminable. Sigmund Freud y Oskar Pfister*. Madrid: Trotta, 2000.

———. *La aventura del celibato evangélico*. Vitoria: Frontera, 2000.

———. *Amores y desamores en la vida consagrada* (Vitoria: Frontera 2014).

———. *Mística y psicoanálisis*. Madrid: Trotta, 2020.

Fenichel, Otto. *The Psychoanalytic Theory of Neurosis*. New York: W.W. Norton Co., 1945.

Fernández Villamarzo, Pedro. *Frustración pulsional y cultura en Freud.* Salamanca: Universidad Pontificia de Salamanca, 1989.

Flournoy, Olivier. "La sublimation," *Revue Française de Psychanalyse* 1 (1967): 59–99.

Freud, Anna. *Ego and the Mechanisms of Defense*. New York: International Universities Press. Revised edition: 1967.

51. From Luis Cernuda's poem "No decia palabras" [He didn't speak in words].

Freud, Sigmund (1905d). *Three Essays on the Theory of Sexuality*. In *The Standard Edition of the Complete Psychological Works of Sigmund Freud*, edited and translated by James Strachey, 7: 125–245. London: Hogarth, 1966.

——— (1908d). "'Civilized' Sexual Morality and Modern Nervous Illness." In *Standard Edition*, 9: 177–204.

——— (1910a). *Five Lectures on Psychoanalysis*. In *Standard Edition*, 11: 9–55.

——— (1910c). "Leonardo da Vinci and a Memory of His Childhood." In *Standard Edition*, 11: 57–137.

——— (1915c). "Instincts and Their Vicissitudes." In *Standard Edition*, 11: 105–34.

——— (1916–1917). *Introductory Lectures on Psycho-Analysis*. In *Standard Edition*, 15.

——— (1918b). *From the History of an Infantile Neurosis*. In *Standard Edition*, 17: 7–122.

——— (1923b). *The Ego and the Id*. In *Standard Edition*, 19, 1–66.

——— (1930a). *Civilization and Its Discontents*. In *Standard Edition*, 21: 59–145.

Gay, Volney P. *Freud on Sublimation: Reconsiderations*. New York: State of New York University Press, 1992.

Glover, Edward. "Sublimation, Substitution, and Social Anxiety." *Internationl Journal of Psychology* 12 (1931): 263–97.

Gombrich, Ernst H. *The Story of Art*. New York: Phaidon, 2013.

Gosso, Sandra. *Psychoanalysis and Art: Kleinian Perspectives*. London: Karnac, 2004.

Hartmann, Heinz. "Notes on the Theory of Sublimation." In *Essays on Ego Psychology,* 215–40. New York: International Universities Press, 1960.

Jones, Ernest. *Psycho-Myth, Psycho-History: Essays in Applied Psychoanalysis*, Vol. 1 and 2. New York: Hillstone 1974.

Kris, Ernst. *Psychoanalytic Explorations in Art*. New York: International Universities Press, 1952.

Kubie, Lawrence S. "The Fallacious Misuse of the Concept of Sublimation." *The Psychoanalytic Quarterly*, 31 (1962): 73–79.

Lacan, Jacques. *The Seminar of Jacques Lacan: On Feminine Sexuality, the Limits of Love and Knowledge, Volume 20, Encore Edition*. New York: W.W. Norton & Co., 1998.

Lagache, Daniel. *De la fantaisie à la sublimation*: *Oeuvres V*. Paris: PUF, 1984.

Laplanche, Jean. *Problématiques,* III. *La sublimation*. Paris: PUF, 1980.

Loewald, Hans W. *Sublimation: Inquiries into Theoretical Psychoanalysis*. New Haven, CT: Yale University Press, 1988.

Odier, Charles. "Essay on Sublimation." In *Drives, Affects, Behavior,* edited by R. M. Loewenstein. New York: International Universities Press, 1953.

Ricoeur, Paul, *Freud and Philosophy: An Essay on Interpretation*. New Haven: Yale University Press, 1970.

Roheim, Geza. "Sublimation." *The Psychoanalytic Quarterly* 12 (1943): 338–52.

Ruitenbeek, Hendrik. *Psychoanalysis and Literature*. New York: Dutton, 1964.

Sayers, Janet. *Freud's Art: Psychoanalysis Retold*. New York: Routledge, 2007.

Sipe, Richard, *Celibacy in Crisis*. New York: Brunner-Routledge, 2003.

Vergote, Antoine. *Dette et désir*. Paris: Seuil, 1978.
———. *La psychanalyse à l'épreuve de la sublimation.* Paris: Cerf, 1977.
Volney, Gay P. *Freud on Sublimation*. New York: State University of New York, 1992.
Walsh, Maria. *Art and Psychoanalysis*. London: Tauris Publishers, 2012.
Wright, Kennet. *Mirroring and Attunement: Self-Realization in Psychoanalysis and Art.* New York: Routledge, 2009.

Index

About the Author

Carlos Domínguez-Morano (Huelva, Spain, 1946) has doctorates in theology and the sciences of education and is a licensed psychologist. His psychoanalytic formation took place in both Paris and Madrid. At present, he is a psychology of religion professor within the School of Theology at the University of Granada (Spain) and a vice-director of the master's program in transcultural spirituality offered at Loyola University Andalusia. He is the director of the University Center Francisco Suárez of Granada, and he works as a psychotherapist. Since the 1980s, he has been carrying out educational analytical psychotherapy workshops with mental health professionals. He has been president of A.I.E.M.P.R. (International Association of Medical-Psychological and Religious Studies). He is a Catholic priest and a member of the Society of Jesus.

Carlos Domínguez has been a visiting professor in several Spanish and Latin American universities, such as Universidad Iberoamericana of Mexico, Universidad Católica of Buenos Aires, Universidad Católica of El Salvador, Universidad Complutense of Madrid, and Universidad Ramón Llu'll of Barcelona.

His book *Creer después de Freud* has been published five times in Spain and was also published in Argentina in 2010, with three Portuguese editions thus far (*Crer depois de Freud*, 2014). In 2018, it was translated into English with the title *Belief after Freud*.

A selection of his publications: *El psicoanálisis freudiano de la religión* [Freudian Psychoanalysis of Religion] (1991); *Creer después de Freud* [Belief after Freud] (1992); *Psicoanálisis y Religión: diálogo interminable* [*Psychoanalysis and Religion: Endless Dialogue*] (2000); *Experiencia mística y psicoanálisis* [*Mystical Experience and Psychoanalysis*] (2003); *La aventura del celibato evangélico* [The Adventure of Evangelical Celibacy] (2000);

Psicodinámica de los Ejercicios Ignacianos [Psychodynamics of Ignatian Spiritual Exercises] (2003); *Experiencia Cristiana y psicoanálisis* (2006) [Christian Experience and Psychoanalysis]; *Orar después de Freud* [Prayer after Freud] (2010); *Amores y desamores en la vida consagrada* [Love and Heartbreak in Consecrated Life] (2014); and *Mística y psicoanálisis* [Mysticism and Psychoanalysis] (2020).

www.ingramcontent.com/pod-product-compliance
Ingram Content Group UK Ltd.
Pitfield, Milton Keynes, MK11 3LW, UK
UKHW041842031026
15587UKWH00002B/946

9 781793 605764